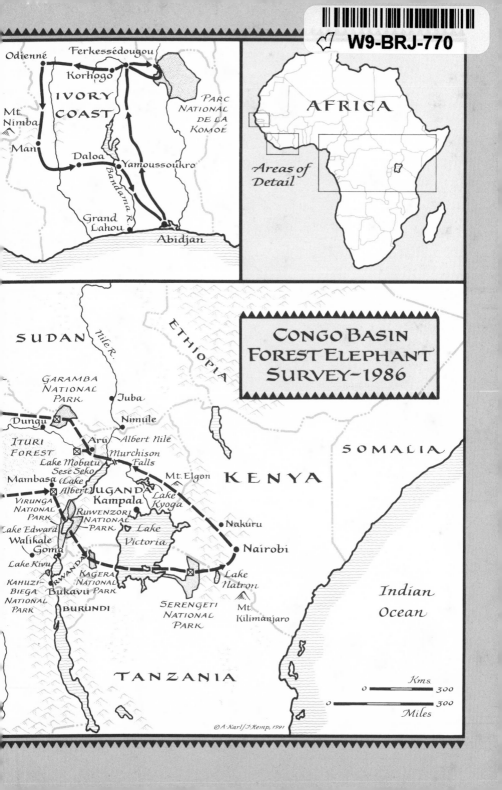

Fiction

Race Rock
Partisans
Raditzer
At Play in the Fields of the Lord
Far Tortuga
On the River Styx (and
Other Stories)
Killing Mister Watson

Nonfiction

Wildlife in America
The Cloud Forest
Under the Mountain Wall
Sal Si Puedes
The Wind Birds
Blue Meridian
The Tree Where Man Was Born
The Snow Leopard
Sand Rivers
In the Spirit of Crazy Horse
Indian Country
Nine-Headed Dragon River
Men's Lives

AFRICAN
SILENCES

AFRICAN SILENCES

PETER MATTHIESSEN

RANDOM HOUSE
NEW YORK

All rights reserved under
International and Pan-American Copyright Conventions. Published in the
United States by Random House, Inc., New York
and simultaneously in Canada by Random House
of Canada Limited, Toronto.

Portions of this work were originally published in
Audubon and *Outdoor* magazines.
"Pygmies and Pygmy Elephants: The Congo Basin"
was originally published in *Antaeus* as
"Congo Basin: The Search for the Forest Elephants,"
parts I and II.

Library of Congress Cataloging-in-Publication Data
Matthiessen, Peter.
African silences / Peter Matthiessen.
p.   cm.
ISBN 0-679-40021-4
1. Africa—Description and travel—1977– . 2. Matthiessen, Peter—
Journeys—Africa.   3. Natural history—Africa.   4. Naturalists—
United States—Biography.   5. Authors, American—20th century—
Biography.   I. Title.
DT12.25.M39   1991
91604′328—dc20   90-52893

Manufactured in the United States of America

Book design by Oksana Kushnir

*For George Schaller, Jonah Western,
Iain Douglas-Hamilton, Alec Forbes-Watson,
Peter Enderlein, Brian Nicholson, and
other mentors and companions of immemorial
long days on foot in Africa.*

ACKNOWLEDGMENTS

In addition to Drs. Gilbert Boese and David Western, I am grateful for help and hospitality, instruction, and good company, to almost all those people, black and white, who are mentioned in the book. Dr. Richard Carroll and also Drs. William Conway and William Weber of the New York Zoological Society provided helpful information and support. Finally, my thanks to Mr. William Shawn of *The New Yorker*, which paid my share of the considerable expenses of the forest elephant survey made in 1986.

CONTENTS

AFRICAN
SILENCES

Prologue

 On African journeys that began with an overland trip from Egypt to Tanganyika in 1961, I traveled widely in East and southern Africa (Botswana), the last great redoubt of large wild creatures left on earth. Not until the winter of 1978 did I reach West Africa—specifically Senegal-Gambia and Ivory Coast—accompanying a primatologist, Dr. Gilbert Boese, on an informal survey of what was left of West Africa wildlife, from the Sahel region, south of the Sahara, to the Guinea forest of the coasts, then continuing eastward to Zaire, hoping to join an expedition in search of the rare Congo peacock, and enjoying two meetings with gorillas along the way.

These journeys comprise the first two sections of this book. In 1980, I joined a safari into remote regions of the Selous Game Reserve, in Tanzania, and in the winter of 1986 I returned to Central Africa, accompanying ecologist David Western, director of the New York Zoological Society's Wildlife Conservation International, on the expedition described in the main section of the book. We planned a survey of the Congo Basin—Central African Republic, Gabon, Zaire—with the primary aim of determining the status of the small forest elephant, whose ivory was beginning to replace the larger ivory of the bush or savanna elephant in the world markets; we also hoped to shed some light on the elusive and mysterious "pygmy elephant," which had been reported from these central forests for nearly a century. In Haut-Zaïre, we would have a look at the last small group of northern white rhinoceros that have survived the wars and poaching in their native range (all other white rhinos not in zoos have been introduced in other countries, from Kenya to South Africa). On our return, we hoped to join an okapi research project in Zaire's Ituri Forest, home of the Mbuti Pygmies, perhaps the last large group of hunter-gatherers left on earth . . .

AFRICAN SILENCES: SENEGAL, GAMBIA, IVORY COAST
(1978)

 Seen from the air west of Cape Verde, at the westernmost point of Africa, in Senegal, the ocean sunrise, clear red-blue, turns an ominous yellow, and the sun itself is shrouded, ghostly, in this dust of the northeast trade wind of the dry season, known as the *harmattan,* that blows across the great Sahara desert. White birds and wave crests fleck a gray-blue sea, and the lean black pirogues of fishermen are very small off the rocky islets called Les Iles de la Madeleine. On the bare ground of the high cliffs stand the white mosques at Yoff, and beyond, low hills of Africa rise like shadows in hot winds that tilt the ragged wings of kites and scatter the dead paper of the world across Dakar.

Arriving in Dakar on a Sunday morning after a long night of no sleep, we are unable to find any office open, or anyone willing to rent us a vehicle that is up to the rough tracks of the interior; it is not until midday, after several hours of haggling in the great heat, that we come to terms with Mr. Baba Sow, a tall and august Muslim of the Ouolof tribe, who is putting himself and his small Peugeot at our disposal. We depart in the heat of afternoon, proceeding south and east through the litter of small factories in the red-earth wastes of Dakar's suburbs, along fringes of the thin eucalyptus trees that have been introduced all over Africa to replace cleared forests and combat the vast erosion that threatens to blow this whole continent away. On this silent Sunday afternoon, kites, pied crows, goats, and vultures rule the dusty streets, as dark figures in Muslim dress cross from one shade to another.

Even in late afternoon, the heat is terrific; the land shimmers in the hot breath of the *harmattan.* Senegal is the western borderland between the desert and the Guinea forests, and this region between desert and savanna, called the Sahel, is an arid country of poor soils, hundreds of miles wide, that stretches all the way east to the Sudan, and its parched thornbush of baobab and scrub acacia, red termite hills, starlings and hornbills, is very similar in aspect to the *nyika* of East Africa; when a ring-necked dove crosses the road, I know I am in Africa again. As the road moves south and east, this thornbush rapidly gives way to an open woodland and long-grass savanna, known to ecologists as the West Sudan or Sudanian Zone, that separates the Sahel and the equatorial forest for four thousand miles, all the way east across Africa to the Nile. In the savanna, small villages of thatched huts, the thatched huts clustered in green islands of banyan, tamarind, and mango, take refuge from the heat and the bright wind.

This journey is a preliminary inquiry into what remains of the wildlife of West Africa, undertaken by Dr. Gilbert Boese of Chicago's Brookfield Zoo; Dr. Boese, who based his doctoral thesis on the Guinea baboons of Senegal, has invited me along as an observer. I have never been to West Africa before and am eager to see how its people, wildlife, and landscapes differ from those in East Africa and South. Our first destination, some 350 miles inland, is Niokolo

Koba, in the southeast corner of the country near the borders with Mali and Guinea-Bissau, the first national park ever established in West Africa (1954) and the logical place to begin our survey.

Mr. Baba Sow says that Niokolo Koba, which he claims to have visited last year, is no more than three hours from Dakar, but apparently he is a dreadful judge of distance; when three hours have passed, we are not far beyond Kaolack, at least six hours from our destination, with some two hundred kilometers of rough red track between here and the next large town at Tambacounda. Baba Sow seeks to minimize this discrepancy with a speed excessive for this rough *piste,* so that we see little of the countryside besides red dust and blue sky. He is a good driver, with a keen eye for bumps and potholes, but his skill is repaid with a traffic ticket issued by two foot police who flag him down as he bores through an Ouolof village like a conqueror, scattering man and beast in all directions.

Though the ceremonial expostulation on both sides adds a half hour to our journey, it provides an opportunity to inspect these compact villages of square huts, mostly daub and wattle with looped thatching bound into a topknot at the center of the roof, each family cluster separated from the others by a fencing of upright split logs that support walls of raffia-palm matting. The Ouolof here grow cabbages and melons, maize and a few tomatoes, as well as the main crop of Senegal-Gambia and the foundation of its economy, the groundnut or common peanut, imported from South America in the sixteenth century by the Portuguese, who arrived in Senegal in about 1450—the first European contact with any part of Africa south of the Sahara. Near the road in every village stands an archaic red machine that separates groundnuts from their vine debris. The debris provides good fodder for the stock in this season of drought, when the high, pale, stalky grass is being burned and the earth is black. Goats, sheep, donkeys, long-horned cattle, and even a few horses must be fed, for here as elsewhere throughout Africa, ownership is the foundation of prestige. The donkeys and horses serve mainly to draw the colorful small two-wheeled carts that junket everywhere throughout the villages, which are also provided with wayside benches painted in bright reds and yellows.

By late afternoon the trees in the savanna country include such familiar East African forms as *Terminalia,* the white-trunked *Sterculia,* and the dark, majestic winterthorn acacia. Even so, the landscape is a strange one. The variety of vegetation, not only in the savanna country but in what is left of the dry woodland, seems much greater than in East Africa, and many more species remain green in the dry season; that gray fierce aspect of the bush is missing. On the other hand, there is no sign of animals—a striped ground squirrel is the only mammal seen. Though bird species are few, the huge Abyssinian ground hornbill is abundant, which suggests an absence of large predators, as well as veneration by the tribesmen, for one is struck by the abundance of human beings. Even after dark, two hundred miles inland, where the square huts of the Ouolof are replaced by round huts of Malinke and Fulani, there are few trees between one small village and another.

At nine in the evening we reach Tambacounda, one thousand feet above sea level on the vast plateau of Africa; from here, in *wagons-lit* of the Chemin de Fer de Senegal, which had a certain elegance in other times, one traveled east as far as Bamako, in that part of French West Africa now known as Mali, and from there by one means or another to Timbuktu and Niamey, on the Upper Niger.

From Tambacounda, early in the morning, we head south to the Parc National de Niokolo Koba, which at the time of its establishment, after centuries of remorseless slaughter in the region, had scarcely any wild animals left. In 1920, the last damalisk (the western topi) in Senegal had disappeared, and both giraffe and elephant were near extinction. A solitary elephant killed in 1917 was the last one in the Cape Verde region, and since there are no recent records for Mauritania, the elephants in Niokolo Koba are probably the last in northwest Africa. With protection, they showed good signs of recovery, and their number may now exceed three hundred, but in recent years the plague of poaching that has done such damage to East Africa's parks has set in here, with special attention to elephant and crocodile, and so despite the efforts of two-hundred-odd askaris who patrol on foot, bicycle, and by pirogue, the elephants are declining once again. Meanwhile, in the 1960s, the giraffe became extinct, and an effort to reintroduce it from Nigeria came to naught when a cargo of groundnut waste intended to feed the captive group was sent back by mistake, so that the creatures perished in their cages.

Niokolo Koba—which presently includes more than eight hundred thousand hectares—is the last stronghold of large animals in Senegal. The relict creatures of the region were spared by the park's remote location in the southeast corner of the country, in unsettled tsetse woods well south of the main trade routes. Watered by the upper reaches of the Gambia River, Niokolo Koba includes typical Sudanian savanna as well as the high forest typical of Guinea, which lies just over its south border. Therefore it can claim the only population of wild chimpanzees in Senegal. It also gives shelter to several hundred Derby eland, largest of all African antelopes, as well as the statuesque roan antelope for which the park is named: Niokolo Koba means "Place of the Roan Antelope." Otherwise, its large mammalian fauna is—or was—quite typical of the Sudanian region, all across West Africa: buffalo, hippopotamus, warthog and bush pig, and such antelope as the western kob, the large western hartebeest, Defassa waterbuck, bushbuck or "harnessed antelope," Bohor reedbuck, oribi, and a few species of duiker. Officially, at least, all the large predators are here (although the status of the cheetah is obscure). For many of its species, if not most, Niokolo Koba can claim the most northerly as well as westerly populations on the African continent.

In outlying areas accessible to poachers, Niokolo Koba's animals are few; one sees instead the round clay cylinders of the dead villages whose lands were taken as the park enlarged its boundaries. Then troops of *Papio papio* appear—the thickset, reddish nominate race called the "Guinea baboon." (Because European scientists came here early, many of the original descriptions of African fauna and flora derive from Senegal; hence the prevalence of the specific name *Senegalensis* for such widespread creatures as the Senegal cuckoo, which I first saw in Botswana, thousands of miles to the southeast, and renewed acquaintance with this morning in the dump behind the Estekebe Hotel in Tambacounda. And since most of the early naturalists were French, the common names are mostly French, as well; the hartebeest is *le bubale,* the buffalo *le buffle,* and the kob is called *kob de Buffon,* after the eminent taxonomist of the eighteenth century. We see a white-tailed mongoose, a patas monkey, vervets, then the red-flanked duiker, stamping black feet and flicking its tail straight up and down as it regards us: like all duikers, it has short horns and short forelegs and holds its head low to the ground—adaptive characters for quick escape in the dense bush or forest that duikers prefer. This colorful species is common here and very tame—indeed, the tamest of these shy, small, woodland antelopes I have ever come across.

In the rainy season, from May through October, Mare Sita N'di, a shallow lake or pan in the north part of the park, will overflow its banks as the greater part of Niokolo Koba becomes flooded, but in mid-March it is nearly dry and sparsely covered in a haze of green that attracts large groups of animals and a mixed company of birds. Beyond the Mare Sita N'di, and loosely named for it, is the Sementi Lodge, near the park headquarters, which overlooks a lovely stretch of the upper Gambia. The slow river of the dry season is clear and green, reflecting the soaring fan palms or borassus; this high dark gallery forest by the river is a riverine extension of the Guinea forests to the south. Here in the heat of midafternoon the elephants come down to water, and hippos may be seen not far upriver. The shy, small forest *buffles* have been here, too, to judge from the bovine dung along the way.

In the dead heat that persists into the dusk, the kob and waterbuck lie down on the dry mud of Sita N'di (the western kob seems to ignore the hottest sun) but the bushbuck and warthog have retreated to the shade of the hot dry woodland all around. Here and there, the woodland floor is white with silk-cotton from the *Ceiba* pods, which are eaten by baboons as well as vervets and thereby scattered in the time of seeding. Bamboo the brown color of burning white paper sprouts from a crust of lateritic stone, and the common *Pterocarpus* tree is coming into pretty yellow blossom, as if in anticipation of the rains, but over the white woods hangs a ghostly stillness, intensified by hot wafts of the *harmattan* in the dry fans of raffia and borassus.

In a grove of fig trees, by a dark creek of stagnant water green with algae, a company of beasts has gathered in the heavy shade. A big roan buck leads a band of hartebeest out of the woods to join a rabble of baboons and vervets, a pair of bushbuck, and a pair of reedbuck, pale and delicate. Not far away is a red-flanked duiker and two oribi, the color of brown grass. In East Africa, the oribi are reddish, and thus these brown ones seem to be an exception to a general tendency toward erythrism (prevalence of red pigmentation) that characterizes a number of West African forms. At Niokolo Koba, for example, the bush pig, bushbuck, buffalo, and baboon are all markedly more red than their counterparts in East and South Africa, and so is the pygmy hippopotamus of the river forests of Liberia and Ivory Coast. Why this should be so is quite mysterious; the con-

spicuous color would seem to be an evolutionary disadvantage. One theory holds that because, in early times, the
forests were much more extensive than they are today, most
or all of these "red" animals inhabited the forest, where
animal colors tend to be brighter than on the savanna,
perhaps for purposes of communication and display in a
dim light.

Farther south, another roan crosses the track, then a
long-tailed parakeet, bright emerald in color; as with many
birds of the savanna, its range extends across the continent
into northern Kenya, but as it happens, I have never seen
it. The parakeet flickers rapidly through the dry air, alight-
ing at last among white flowers of a *Vernonia* bush, at the
edge of marshes. Not far away, by the wet sump of a dry
pan, an extraordinary conference of birds has gathered, as
if reconciled by drought to their great differences—speckled pigeons, laughing and vinaceous doves, the red-billed
wood dove, black magpies and gray hornbills, the long-
tailed and the purple glossy starlings, cattle egrets, squacco
herons, and, on reed stalks, the Abyssinian and blue-bellied
rollers. All of these birds or their close congeners may be
found somewhere in East Africa; it is the makeup of the
group that seems extraordinary.

Although this is the tourist season, the Sementi Lodge
at evening is all but empty, and its gracious *patron,* Monsieur Patrice, supposes aloud that Americans "do not like
West Africa." One problem, of course, is the French language, and anyway, West Africa is less well known and does
not advertise, whereas East Africa is now an industry. Many
visitors have told Monsieur Patrice that they prefer West
African parks because the animals here are less predictable,
they cannot be taken for granted, things are more *sportif; ici,
Monsieur, il y a toujours plus des animaux que des touristes!* One
hears this a good deal in West Africa. Alas, the animals are
far fewer than in East Africa, not only in species but in
numbers. Even the "common" species are elusive. To see

chimpanzees or giant eland on a brief visit would be too much to expect, and as to predators, we had to be satisfied with some big lion pug marks on the road, but *buffles* are not supposed to be so shy. Of the twenty-five hundred *buffles* that are said to be here, we saw neither hide nor hair of even one, only *buffle* manure in great abundance.

From the Tambacounda road, we follow a narrow track across the back country toward Gouloumbo, in order to strike the main dirt road south and west to Velingara; our destination is the Parc National de Casamance, in the Guinea forest at the coast. The track wanders through small villages, in a fresh open countryside of light and silence, grassland and gigantic figs, rollers and helmet shrikes, long-tailed parakeets and speckled pigeons. This is a country of the Tukulor Fulani, who are agriculturalists as well as herders. As early as A.D. 700, the Tukulor maintained a powerful state that extended north through the Senegal Valley into present-day Mauritania, which had not yet been overtaken by the desert. In the fourteenth century they retreated south before the Berbers, who were fleeing in their turn before the Arabs. Apparently the Tukulor were the first people of this region to accept Islam, which they helped to spread among the Ouolof people on the coast. Meanwhile, nomad Berber groups pressed southward, occupying the drier tracts of the savanna and forming an economic liaison with this tribe, until gradually the two peoples intermingled. In this farming country, the Tukulor are Negroid in appearance, whereas the pastoral "Berber" populations, the Peulh or Fula or Fulani who followed the savanna eastward all the way to Cameroon, are much paler and more narrow in the face—hence the curious name "Tukulor," which is thought to be of recent derivation, from the English "Two Colors," or the French *"tout-couleur,"* or even "Tacurol," an old name for the country. The Tukulor maintained a separate state almost continuously until the middle of the nineteenth century, when the

▼▼

French subdued them on the way to the establishment of French West Africa.

This land is not nearly so dry as the Niokolo Koba country to the east, and yet the air is parched for lack of rain. Man's thirstless goats, which have helped to spread the deserts of North Africa, pay heat no mind, but the thin sheep press themselves to the clay walls, seeking thin shadow, and the cattle must be brought each day to the village wells. Pumped by draft animals walked in a circle, the well is the center of activity in each village, which here in the backland is no more than a cluster of daub huts.

In these settlements southwest of Missira, we are struck by the utter friendliness of everyone we see. Even a group of newly circumcised young boys who are living now outside their village, dressed in a uniform of ceremonial sacking, rush to greet us, smiling and waving, eager to be of help. Because the rough and narrow track has frequent forks—and because when giving directions for Gouloumbo, the tribesman, knowing nothing of vehicles, is apt to point eagerly to a fork that later narrows to a footpath—we stop and backtrack many times, and invariably our return is welcomed with glad smiles that whites don't see much anymore in Africa, smiles that make one happy and also a bit sad, like the last sight of a rare, vanishing bird. While the men laugh, consulting on directions, young children seated in the shade clean silver barbels from a lake not far away; women pause to lean on their big pestles, and girls wave prettily from the well, the water sparkling on round brown breasts.

These simple places far from the din of modern times reflect an order and well-being that seem missing in the villages by the main road, where noisy vehicles and the hard winds of change stir up the country folk and make them restless. The log mortar and big pestle like a hollowed stump, the three-stone hearth, a few bales of fresh raffia thatching, a few gourds drying on the roof—there is no excess and no waste, no debris or litter of any kind. The yards look swept. Outside each village, the people have piled the few metal containers that have found their way into these hinterlands, and the pile is neat. A sense of order underlies the harmonious tone of the whole countryside. Perhaps order is quite natural to rural Africans, perhaps the littered habitations of most African towns is a sad symptom of the loss of the old rhythms, of the overcrowding, poverty, and low morale that has come about through enforced exposure to the white man's way.

It is midday, very hot. We head west on the red dusty road to Velingara, in a landscape desiccated by the desert winds.

At Kolda, near the Guinea-Bissau border, the road enters a green tropic of banana groves, oil-palm plantations, and rice paddies like bright green glades among the huge boles of the gallery forest. Here the villages are prospering and the road is surfaced, and Baba Sow is driving hard again, one hand perched upon the horn. Repeatedly we ask him to slow down; there are too many goats and cattle on the road to drive so fast. But very soon he regains his speed, turning his head incessantly to address his passengers, and eventually a steer jumps out in front of him. Gil Boese yells a warning, and he swerves, brakes shrieking—BOOM!—a hateful jolt of metal upon flesh, a sprinkling of breaking glass as the heavy carcass looms, cracking the windshield, then spins, still kicking, into the ditch, its head wide-eyed on the road shoulder.

The car stops and its door creaks loudly as Baba Sow gets out; he inspects his car, ignoring the dying steer. A startled man in yellow rags—is he the herder?—had dropped his handful of long pods and now, without a glance at Baba Sow, far less the steer, he stoops over straight-legged to pick them slowly one by one off the hot pavement, continuing this for minute after minute in the dead silence as if unwilling to raise his eyes to the kicking animal, to us, to the silent folk hurrying this way from the nearby village.

Baba Sow in his green woolen cap is glaring at his shattered headlight, dented fender, the manure streaks down the side of his white car. *"Ils sont fous, ces bêtes! Et ces gens"*—he indicates the people—*"Ils sont comme leurs bêtes! Ils sont stupides!"* Baba Sow is very upset, but he does not bother to upbraid the herder, saving his energy for the owner of the steer or the village headman. For want of a better way to help, Boese and I are kicking glass shards off the road. We eye the approaching villagers, feeling white as milk; incredibly, a slow tom-tom has started up behind the trees.

By the time the villagers arrive, the steer is still. A stern old man yanks the steer's head up, lets it fall. Now he straightens, glares at Baba Sow; he looks at the whites not even once in the whole episode. The people steal glances but do not giggle or comment; for an African crowd, they seem ominously silent.

Baba Sow's nerves give way first; he mutters something. I expect an angry retort from the old man, but his answer is quiet. I do not know what dialect is spoken, but the sense is apparent even to the whites: Baba Sow is told that he drives his car too fast, that he must pay, and Baba Sow answers that peasants should learn to keep their animals off the highway. Both are correct: drivers in the new Africa go too fast, and life in the old Africa moves too slowly. A paved road has no place in medieval landscapes.

There is nothing to be done. Both sides wait politely in the glowing dusk, ceremonious, unhappy. The discussion is finished but abrupt parting would be rude. The village has lost a fine young steer, Baba Sow's new car has sustained grievous bodily harm, damage that in this inflated economy may cost much more than the steer is worth.

There is only silence as we get back into the car and drive away without good-byes to Ziguinchor.

▼▼▼

In the morning we cross a tidal river on the ferry and drive mile upon mile to the south and west across the salt marshes of Casamance. In the Palearctic, it is nearly spring, and the African marshes are peppered with migrating shorebirds bound for Europe—mostly ruffs and whimbrel, marsh sandpipers and stints.

Nearing the coast, the road enters a romantic region of old oil-palm plantations and high forest, old weathered gates of colonial times and old stone walls. Small Diola settlements crouch at the edge of jungle. Diola houses are larger than the huts seen inland, rectangular with high-peaked pyramidal roofs and a space that permits air circulation between wall and the low-hanging eave, but this improvement on the hut of his own Ouolof tribe does not impress our lordly Baba Sow, who jerks his chin impatiently at these *paysans,* these *animistes.* He discourses at length on the *slowness* of these forest people, these "people of the south," so markedly in contrast to the mental agility of northerners—*"le Ouolof, par exemple."* He shrugs his shoulders. *"Sont des vrais Africains, ceux-la,"* Baba Sow concludes, and not in praise. Since they are *animistes,* not Muslims, the Diola happily eat pork, and pigs are common here; perhaps these pigs came with the Portuguese, or perhaps, here at the jungle edge, they are relics of the old pig cultures uprooted by Islam all across North Africa.

Near the Guinea-Bissau frontier, a track turns off toward the sea and the Parc National de Casamance, a coastal rain forest dominated by big dark *Kaya* trees and figs and palms. Gratefully we walk about on foot, leaving Baba Sow to take his ease in his small, hot machine. Though the day is warm, the sea forest remains cool, its deep shade thinly filtered by the sun. We find the print of a small antelope, hear the telltale puff of what might be a nervous *buffle* back in the forest, but here as at Niokolo Koba, the *buffle* eludes us. The only mammals seen, in fact, are squirrels and monkeys—green vervets and the guenon or mona monkey, that handsome red-and-black relation of the blue monkeys of Central and East Africa. The rare western red colobus remains hidden—this is the species I most wish to see. The paths are strewn with *tamba,* the small brown monkey-apple, which is relished in these parts by every anthropoid, from these small circopithecines to *Homo sapiens.*

Where the forest subsides into red mangrove estuaries behind the coast, an observer with more time than ourselves might see a clawless otter or the swamp antelope called sitatunga. Here palm-nut vultures have convened in the most seaward of the trees—striking white birds that have mostly abandoned the vulturine habits of their kin and subsist largely on nuts of the oil palm, in the vicinity of which they are usually encountered. Therefore I am surprised, a little later, to see one alight on mud along the estuary and waddle about among the mangrove stilts in pursuit of fiddler crabs and perhaps mudskippers, both of which abound on the tidal rivers. Perhaps this is a well-known habit of this species, but I shall record it here in case it's not.

▼▼▼

At Ziguinchor is an "artisan's market" where a few old masks and carvings may be found amidst the heaps of that shiny, mass-produced *art folklorique* that finds its way into unsuspecting homes around the world. The artisans' traditional bird-head adzes, with their sets of hand-forged blades for finer work, are far superior in style and manufacture to their "art," and though these carvers were distressed at first that these rough implements and not their wares were what we wanted, they soon got used to the idea, and old adzes came at us from all directions—*"le vrai hâche de mon grand-père!"* one fellow shouted, an inspired lie that was taken up instantly by all the others. But we were satisfied with just one each, and so innumerable "true grandfather's adzes" remained behind in Ziguinchor—the nucleus, I fear, of a whole new industry.

Outside the market, workers stacked enormous sacks of peanuts on a truck. Two men on the ground would heave the heavy sack onto the truck bed, where two more would seize it up to waist level, then slam it down again, stooping quickly as they did so to make the most of an infinitesimal bounce, then hiking it high above their shoulders, where it was plucked from their outstretched arms by yet two more atop the cargo. The feat was funny and exciting, and the workers were merry in the pride of strength and timing, strutting a little for the girls and tossing stray peanuts to admiring young kids. Every little while, the kids were scattered by a scrawny Muslim clerk in a blue *djellabah,* but the clerk did not dare to admonish the workers, and the kids would soon drift in again to snatch wild peanuts from the air. On a warm mountain of unsacked peanuts, a yellow wagtail walked about, as if seeking a way to adjust millennia of insectivorous habit to such plenty.

At dusk, small bats replaced the swallows that dip in the blue water of the hotel *piscine,* and from the darkness of the town came the sound of tom-toms. We followed the pounding noise a mile or more through the soft night, arriving at last in unlit streets at the edge of town. In an open yard beneath a giant fig, tom-toms were struck in a blur of speed by three musicians, and within a circle of several hundred Africans, under dim light, a kind of tournament was taking place in which a young dancer, spry as a cockerel, would leap and rail at someone in the crowd to come out dancing; those who accepted were fierce dancers, too, and the shouts of the crowd were the best clue to which had won. Dancers came and went, the townsfolk milled in

▼▼▼

pleasure and excitement, and meanwhile the three tom-tom
players never faltered, filling the night with the beat of their
swift hands. Standing there half-hypnotized, content, I re-
called a group of young Senegalese drummers and dancers
who played years ago at a small Parisian *boîte* called La
Vieille Rose Rouge. At first their faces had been wild and
wary, but as the months passed, cigarettes appeared,
and modish trousers protruded from beneath their *kikois,*
and the fierce tom-toms were reduced to backup rhythms
for bad fire-eating acts and self-conscious recitations of the
poetry of Léopold Senghor, now president of Senegal.

Sang noir . . . sang d'Afrique . . .

In this crowd of several hundred, there were no white
people, not even one. Instinctively we kept moving, staying
back a bit, out of the light, never remaining in one spot long
enough to gather attention. Yet there arose an accumulat-
ing awareness of our presence, a kind of murmur, more
curious than hostile: who are these whites, how did they get
here? And after a while, we withdrew into the pitch darkness of the unlit streets and returned toward the hotel, as
the fading drums gave way to the growing shrill of tree
frogs in the big trees all around.

The people of Senegal—near the coast, at least—were
given a kind of civil status as early as 1848, and their feel-
ings toward France were so equable that for a time they
resisted the idea of independence. Even in the larger towns
of Senegal, there seems to be little of the brooding touchi-
ness and half-repressed hostility that one meets in the cities
of East Africa. I wondered if following music down long
dark African streets was something I would do these days
in Arusha or Nairobi; I think not.

▼▼▼

Early next day we cross the Casamance River by small ferry and, on a rough road across the airy coastal plain, drive north into Gambia, which lies enclosed by Senegal, like a narrow throat coming inland from the sea. Just beyond the border is the village of Seleti, where Gil Boese began his baboon studies in 1971, and, seeing baboons crossing the road, he sits forward in excitement, directing Baba Sow into a cow path. We continue on foot along a tongue of gallery forest that follows a dry streambed across the fields to a shaded place of boulders and damp sand—a rainy-season pool where animals can still dig down for water—and have scarcely arrived when a troop of western red colobus bursts forth in reckless aerial display from the high treetops, scolding and barking, hurling themselves down from re- bounding limbs and swinging and crashing into the dry bushes as if intent on tearing down the forest. Boese is delighted that the red colobus are still here, despite the forest clearing on all sides that has confined them to this narrow tongue of trees; and I am delighted that my first sight of this spectacular species—they are black above, rich chestnut-red below—should occur in the African country- side. Even in East Africa there are few places anymore where one may see such animals outside the parks.

The red colobus will not be there very long. Less than a mile beyond Seleti, the people are burning down the forest; a huge crackling flame riding the wind roars through a copse of high trees near the road. The fire is attended by European kestrels, Abyssinian rollers, cattle egrets: the egrets stalk about in the flame's path, intent upon the spear- ing of small fugitives, while the rollers and pale orange falcons hover and dart like spirits through the smoke, the harsh racket of the rollers lost in the violent crackling of the blaze.

One does not travel many miles in Gambia before one sees that too much forest has been burned—even more so, it appears, than in Senegal—and that the inevitable and fatal end to the destruction of the land is now in sight. "The Gambia," as it is known here, was formerly a British colony, and its dense population is a fatal consequence of that sensible administration on which the British pride themselves, whether or not it made sense for "the native." At any rate, its English-speaking citizens have no wish to join with Senegal, where they would become an unpopular minority. "The Gambia" is little more than a narrow enclave in that country, a strip of territory on both sides of the river, some two hundred miles long and in places no more than thirteen miles in width.

Gambia is a huge thorn in the side of Senegal, separating all Casamance from the rest of the country, and controlling a natural trade route—navigable by ocean vessels for 150 miles inland—that could serve eastern Senegal and even Mali. Because it is overpopulated, even by the standards of West Africa, such wildlife as remains in Gambia is largely confined to three small reserves and a southward extension of an international park that is to be shared with Senegal.

The credit for Gambia's reserves must be given to a dedicated British forester named Edward Brewer, who was mentor and friend to Dr. Boese in his days among baboons and who welcomes us to the Abuko Nature Reserve at Yumdum, not far south of the capital at Banjul. Though only 180 acres, this relict tract of gallery forest was the first of Gambia's reserves and remains the most significant, at least in terms of public education.

Set aside in 1916 as the Abuko Water Catchment Area, it was later fenced to keep out hunters and domestic stock as well as would-be farmers. But local people made holes under the fencing to introduce their pigs for random foraging, and hunters managed to get in, as well, and both groups were indignant when, in the 1960s, a leopard took up residence in the small forest, making too free with the pigs as well as frightening the hunters. Brewer, asked to shoot the leopard, became enchanted instead by the potential of Abuko, which at his behest was set aside as a nature reserve in 1968. Two years later, the leopard departed from Abuko, perhaps disconsolate over the expulsion of the pigs, but other native animals have been introduced, joining the few small mammals already in residence. In the 1.5-mile footpath through the forest, one may encounter a variety of birds, several duikers and the bushbuck, the serval cat, civet and genets, mongooses and porcupines, four species of monkeys, crocodiles, and pythons, as well as cobras, puff adders, and mambas.

"We're on our way here now, with any sort of luck," says Eddie Brewer, who is sunburned, husky, and unassuming, with fierce beetling brows and a gentle smile. He is delighted that Gambia's president has issued a "Banjul Declaration" in support of wildlife; that a high government official noticed a loophole in the game-protection laws and moved to close it; that children who once killed anything that moved are now bringing small animals into Abuko. As in Kenya, where the Wildlife Clubs have set an example for the rest of Africa, the education of this new generation is the only hope for the wild creatures.

On the coast, we find accommodations at a Swedish inn, and I revel in my first swim in West African surf. Feverish local rumor has it that the Swedes come here for sexual safaris, like the Germans on the Malindi coast in Kenya, and perhaps it is moral disapproval of Gambian Christians that makes our haughty Muslim Baba Sow question the hospitality offered him by the reception clerk; these English-speakers, his sour look implies, might make a stranger sit up all night in a chair. Though he complains to me in French, the clerk intuits what he says, and responds with considerable dignity to Baba Sow, who understands more English than he will acknowledge. "I am not rich," says the clerk. "I am black, like you. But if I offer you a bed, I do not mean that you shall sit up in a chair. And if you do not like my home, you may go elsewhere." To Baba Sow's credit, he confesses next day that he passed a restful night among the infidels.

At daybreak, we skirt an enormous processing plant for the groundnut, on which Gambia, like Senegal, has based its economy. Beyond this monument to the congenial peanut lies Banjul, formerly Bathurst, where we shall embark on yet another ferry, crossing the Gambia River and continuing northward into Senegal.

At the waterfront, in a cool dawn, the patient blacks, the fish smell, chicken baskets, fruit and sheep, the carrion birds and blowing trash, sweet smells, sweet voices, urine tang, and over the silent broad brown flood the white Caspian terns in from the sea are all familiar; how often in life, without ever having come to Gambia, I have arrived at this old river.

Over the passenger gate is a fair warning:

CARGO AND DECK LIVESTOCK RECEIVED HANDED [sic]
STOWED CARRIED KEPT AND DISCHARGED AT SHIPPERS
RISK AND THE GOVERNMENT SHALL NOT BE LIABLE
FOR LOSS THEREOF OR DAMAGE THERETO EVEN
THOUGH RESULTING FROM UNSEA-WORTHINESS OF THE
CRAFT OR FROM THE NEGLIGENCE OF THE
GOVERNMENT OR ITS SERVANTS.

The ferry to Kung is crowded with vehicles and folk of all descriptions, so tightly packed that a beautiful big woman cannot pass her majestic rump between Baba Sow's front fender and the car adjoining. Though one speaks in a sort of English and the other in French, the big woman and Baba Sow rail, hoot, and banter over this joyous natural phenomenon. Baba Sow, all dressed up in his white *kanzu,* with three boxes of bonbons to present to his children upon arrival in Dakar, is very disapproving of this ancient ferry that accepts chickens as passengers and depends on a narrow ramp at Kung, on the farther side. *"C'est mal organisé, tout ça,"* he frets, annoyed at the delay. *"Tout ça, c'est vieux, ce n'est pas bon!"* And, detecting a clear space, he quits the ferry and heads north with a dangerous turn of speed, so anxious is he to put Gambia behind him.

Crossing the Senegal frontier, the road passes along the Parc National de Delta du Saloum—the international park to be shared with Gambia, not yet fully opened to the public—which shelters the manatees and river dolphins of the Saloum River as well as the most northerly tract of mangrove left on the West African coast. Once again we have entered the dry woods of the savanna, but soon this vegetation changes to the acacia thornbush that marks the near-desert of the Sahel. At Kaolack, the Saloum is crossed, we strike the bitumened road again, Dakar is no more than two hours away.

▼▼▼

André Dupuy, the director of Senegal's national parks, to whom we went for some advice that afternoon, is a short, florid man with a big voice, much given to oratorical declarations. His self-confidence is quite remarkable, and his energy and enthusiasm most impressive. He dismissed the Parc de Waza (our proposed destination in north Cameroon) as a "lesson in what not to do," since it tries, says he, to combine too many different habitats. As an ecological unit, it was not to be compared with the six estimable parks of Senegal. Even the tiny Parc des Iles de la Madeleine—the group of islets off Dakar where the beautiful red-billed tropic bird comes to nest—was a precious ecosystem of coastal rocks, the only such in all West Africa! "These are *our* cathedrals, M'sieu Booze," he bellows, refusing to get Dr. Bo-zee's name right. It was not as in other lands of Africa, where parks were mostly tsetse wastelands for which man could find no better use; in Senegal, the parks were areas selected to preserve representative habitats, *"un ré-*

▼▼▼

seau des parcs complémentaires!" Besides, Cameroon was part
of Central Africa. As for the remainder of West Africa, the
chances were that any choice would be the wrong one. Mali,
of course, had a wild reserve near the Senegal border that
might be thought of as a *parc complémentaire* to Niokolo
Koba, and then there were the so-called "Parcs du W" in
Benin, Upper Volta, Niger. But access to such "parks" was
very difficult, travel inside of them impossible, so how could
one say what might be left in the way of animals? Dupuy's
shrug suggested that M'sieu Booze would be well advised
to take a closer look at Senegal. Failing that, the next best
thing was the Parc de la Komoé in Ivory Coast, since that
was where Dupuy's own former *adjutant* was warden. For
want of better information, we took Monsieur Dupuy's advice and arranged to leave next day for Ivory Coast.

▼▼▼

On the flight next day to Ivory Coast, the carry-on baggage
of one Senegalese lady consisted of three large and springy
fish; the tails of these whoppers refused to fold down neatly,
and kept flipping up the wings of their cardboard carton.
For lunch we were served "bush meat"—in this case, small
and cold dead birds with gloomy sizzled heads, smeared
with what we dearly hoped was pâté. Otherwise the flight
southeast over the Guinea forests was uneventful until, circling wide over the sea on the approach to Abidjan, there
came into view the reddish beach and long, unbroken line
of surf that spared this "Windward Coast" (now Liberia and
Ivory Coast, which lay to windward of the slave ports of the
Gold Coast—modern Ghana) from the worst depredations
of the slavers. In the 1770s there was heavy slaving activity
at the mouth of the Bandama River, in the region to the
west at Grand Lahou, but the absence of a port (and therefore of a European shore station) made the commerce er-
ratic, and until the race for colonies occurred, in the late

nineteenth century, few white men cared what lay behind the thick green jungle walls of this "Bad People's Coast," later renamed for the precious ivory of its elephants. Before 1950, when a channel through the barrier beach was stabilized, and a harbor constructed in the vast Ebrie Lagoon, Ivory Coast was no rival to Senegal in trade and benefits from Europe; now oil has been discovered here to augment a prosperous lumber industry and coffee, rubber, and oil-palm plantations, and Abidjan is a boom town of new buildings and new cars. Like Senegal, this country has maintained strong trade relations with the Western World, and today the two are far more prosperous than all other states of former French West Africa combined.

Because prosperity has come too fast, Abidjan is a European city that on this fetid, humid coast retains all the dirt, smells, and decrepitude of the old slave ports. Incompetence is masked with sullenness and the price of sullen service is exorbitant—not an unusual combination on this continent, yet more acceptable in those parts of Africa that are still "African." Except for a remarkably rude customs, all offices were closed *pour le weekend;* there was no way of obtaining information about travel north to the Parc de la Komoé. Our reservation at the Tiama Hotel, where huge fruit bats flop back and forth in the high trees, was the first of many in this land that were not honored; instead we were banished to Hôtel Ivoire, a huge, sterile, glaring "International Hotel" on its own bluff across the bay, a self-contained complex of expensive services and shops where the isolated guest, fearing the piratical cab fares to the city, is separated remorselessly from all his money. The high and shiny International Hotel in Nairobi is a snug family inn by comparison to its sister ship in Abidjan, which features bowling alleys, four bad restaurants and an awful "snack-arama," a wrap-around swimming pool so vast that part of its acreage has been set aside for boats, and the only ice-skating rink on the whole continent. The Hôtel Ivoire is almost everything that one had hoped would never come to Africa.

In foreign parts, so it is said, the pampered guts of Americans, then Scandinavians, are those most easily undone by the local germs, due to the fanatical hygiene in our countries. Regretfully, I add our names to the doleful list. Having survived without ill effect the casual back-country cookery of Senegal, we scarcely expected tumultuous stomachs on the *haute cuisine* of the Hôtel Ivoire; yet by Monday both of us were sick, although we had eaten nowhere else. Also, Gil Boese was going broke. We were frantic to leave Abidjan, but there was no space to be had all week on any flight north to Korhogo. We therefore arranged with the state-owned tour company for *wagon-lit* berths on the evening train for Ouagadougou (Wagga-doogoo) in Upper Volta, which would let us off just after daybreak at Ferkessédougou, in north Ivory Coast.

At six that evening, we were waiting at the railroad station for this train supposed to leave at seven, accompanied by a bright young Ivoirien named Jacob Adjemon who had been assigned to us by the tour office as a guide. Jacob turned out to be a fount of knowledge, not always easy to believe, far less turn off, and the first information that he offered was the evil news that the tour office had not bothered to secure our reservations in the *wagon-lit,* despite its breezy guarantees at nine that morning: we would have to take our chances when the train appeared.

People—not all of them going anywhere—were camped all over the railroad platforms, and peddlers hawked bread, fruit, and water, as well as "notions" of all kinds. One man specialized in socks and purses, another in fezzes and prayer mats, for in the north part of this country, as in Niger and Upper Volta, near the desert, the sway of Islam remains strong. Near where we stood in the dying heat that followed the sudden sinking of the sun was a group of black-garbed women with narrow, elegant brown faces—these are Peulh-de-Niger, says Jacob Adjemon, a nomad people who have drifted southward with their herds of zebu cattle since the great drought years of 1973–1976. "Peulh" is one of many names of the Fulani, whom we first saw as sedentary agriculturalists in Senegal. But while the Tukulor Fulani were Negroid in appearance, these people are distinctly "northern" in the caste of face, betraying much more of the ancestral Berber whose pastoral way of life they have retained; it is because of this "Ethiopian" appearance that the Fulani are thought to have come originally from the northeast. Bartering their animal products for food grown by the farmers, they have attached themselves to local tribes across the whole of the West Sudanian savanna, over two thousand miles from Senegal to Cameroon.

A scarred and drunken tribesman from Upper Volta was attempting to sell us "China Balm" in a green box decorated with bright dragons; the inscrutable packaging reminded me of "Foul Mesdames," the brand name of the cans of Chinese beans that may still be found in the back-country shops of Tanzania. Teased by a colleague who was seeking to tempt us with a bad sort of meat pie, China Balm's man threw a punch and nearly fell, having described a complete circle in the process. He was shouting angrily, and Jacob, translating, began to laugh: "Here I am talking to Big Man, *White* Man, and you come around here with your dirty food trying to spoil my business!" But even China Balm could not have soothed us in the series of mishaps that continued to befall us throughout our sojourn in the former Bad People's Coast. When the train appeared, it was quite clear that the *wagons-lit* were full, beyond all hope of argument or bribe, and the first-class seats to which we were entitled had been sadly overbooked; only quick action secured us stiff chairs in the dining car, which we would defend for the next fourteen hours.

The train moved fitfully toward the north into the heavy equatorial darkness. To blur the night ahead, we drank, and the early evening passed in a pleasant manner. A decent supper came and went as warm, sweet jungle air poured through the window, and afterward, staring outward at the forest, deep black against that other black of the night sky, I saw under the stars and moon an enormous burning tree of the doomed African forest.

Later on the air grew cold, and as we stopped at station after station—Dimbokro, Bouaké, Katiola—the dining car grew very crowded, until desperate travelers began to enter through the windows. Two of these were cadaverous young Frenchmen kitted out with rucksacks and guitars, who established themselves at a table of Africans and began to inveigh against the tourists who were starting to spoil this former land of French West Africa. The Ivoiriens, nonplussed, listened politely, but after a while, one man said quietly, *"Et vous, Messieurs? Vous êtes quelle sorte de touriste?"* Clutching his guitar, one youth said lamely, *"Nous sommes des touristes de la musique!"* No one laughed, and a merciful silence followed until dawn.

Daybreak came early to a broken country of low savanna woodlands, sudden hills. I had not slept, and my headache and increasing fever were intensified by transistor radios, a howling baby, and the exertions of a hungry man who was hammering coconuts on the car floor. In search of a breakfast chair for a rich old Muslim, the steward, put off by my grim expression, singled out the most defenseless among those who had filled the seats during the night, a confused peasant with young wife and infant who looked as if he might not know his rights. In the confusion, the infant urinated on the floor, in a sad puddle that rolled across the aisle as the train swayed; the mother rose, bent over forward, and laid the baby on her back, which it clasped unaided like a tree frog, its little seat supported by her own protruding rump, until she had bound it tight in her *katanga.* In my feverish state, it seemed to me that I had hit upon an explanation for the development of the African posterior, where the infant rides as an appendage of the mother: in early days when *katangas* were unavailable and a child was affixed precariously with a frond, this sturdy shelf on which it rode while its mother walked or worked her field would surely have been an evolutionary advantage.

▼▼▼

At Ferkessédougou, where the Chemin-de-Fer-Abidjan-Niger arrived four hours late, we were met by a very small red auto. Originally our plan had been to drive ourselves, dispensing with a guide; but though the car had been leased to us by the tour agent in Korhogo, its driver turned out to be its owner and would not be left behind, being determined to keep an eye on his possession. And so, in the great heart of midmorning, our band of four set out rather cross and crowded on the fifty-mile trip east over rough dirt roads to the Parc de la Komoé, which lies in the northeast corner of the country. By this time I was so feverish that I scarcely noticed the Malinke villages, nor minded much when, after noon, the car limped to a halt with a flat tire; I stood like a victim of cataclysm on the dusty road edge. By the time we reached the park the spare had gone flat, too, forcing us to hire the lodge vehicle to pursue our research. The two tires were repaired that evening by the park's mechanic, but the other two were flat next day at dawn.

Today I remember little of the Parc de la Komoé, a tract of more than two million eight hundred thousand acres set aside in 1958 as the Bouna Game Reserve and made a national park in 1968, eight years after independence. I was near-blinded by sick headache, and took small pleasure in the dozen kob and *bubales,* an oribi, a warthog, and three distant hippo in the Komoé River, which flows all the way south to Abidjan. Of elephants or buffalo, or even

their manure, there was no sign. The urbane manager of
the tour company had warned us about the lions of Komoé,
one of which had mauled a careless client, and a lepidopterist whom we met later in the Parc Marahoué, to the south,
claimed to have seen a lion and a leopard at Komoé, as well
as the obligatory *buffles* and *bubales* (or perhaps it was Buffon
kobs and *bubales*, for here, too, the crafty *buffles* eluded us)
and no doubt we failed to give proper attention to this park
which, excepting the chimpanzee and giant eland, is said to
contain most of the larger mammals that are found at Niokolo Koba. Yet by the standards of that park (which would
be thought meager in East Africa or Botswana) Komoé is
thinly populated indeed, by birds as well as by large mammals, tourists included.

In view of the alarming decline of wildlife throughout
Ivory Coast, a commendable law against shooting of any
kind was passed in 1974, but laws are ignored by the Lobi
hunters whose villages surround this north part of the park.
The Lobi, who have successfully resisted Islam and Chris-
tendom alike, bring their families into the park during the
rainy season when the tracks are too muddy to be patrolled;
they build their square huts, plant yams and millet, and
hunt very much as they have always done. Originally a wild
people from Upper Volta, they take it much amiss when
their old ways are interfered with, and only a few years ago,
Jacob has learned, the warden at Komoé felt so threatened
that he prophesied to several friends—correctly, alas—that
these Lobi would take his life. Understandably the present
warden, erstwhile *adjutant* to M. André Dupuy of Senegal,
has made no better progress against poaching, if these lone
sentinels of the vanished herds that could be supported in
this huge, well-watered park are any sign. The warden lives
outside the park, at Bouna, as we discovered when we
sought to interview him. Not that the warden would have
given us much hope about the prospects of the Parc de la
Komoé, or of any other park in all West Africa.

Zoologists assume that the wild ungulates of western Africa were always less common than in the east and south, not only in numbers but in species. The black rhinoceros, if it ever occurred here, vanished long ago, as did the wildebeest and zebra; for reasons not well understood, West Africa lacks the astonishing variety of antelope that is found south and east of the Nile. Edaphic poverty is sometimes blamed, but the weakness of tropical lateritic soils is fairly consistent almost everywhere throughout this fragile continent, including the game plains in the east that support the greatest biomass of animals, and perhaps the imbalance is better explained by a simpler reason, one that suffices easily all by itself: south of the deserts, in land inhabitable by man, West Africa is far more populous than East, and human beings have been here for a great deal longer, hunting and trapping, burning and cultivating, competing for the pasturage and water, and eroding and exhausting the poor soils. There are many fewer animals in West Africa today than there were fifty years ago, when the white man's tools and weapons became widespread, but the decline had begun many centuries earlier.

It is now assumed that the great West African states of early times were not in the equatorial rain forest but on the river plains of the savanna such as that region between the middle Senegal River and the Niger Bend where (it is thought) both pearl millet and sorghum were developed; and that the savanna all the way east to Lake Chad has been occupied by large and successful populations of cultivator-fishermen for at least two thousand years. Since these riverine margins, gallery forest, and savannas were also the optimum habitat for wildlife, it is not surprising that the wildlife is now gone.

Under the pressure of Islam and the Arab slave trade, the savanna peoples took refuge in the forests, putting to use the same tropical crops that the Bantu-speakers of Niger and Cameroon had used for their southeastward penetration of the Congo Basin—not manioc, maize, and sweet potato, which were brought from the Americas in the sixteenth century by Portuguese slavers, but the yam, taro, and banana introduced from Southeast Asia to the East African coast perhaps as early as the first century B.C. The deserted savanna was soon occupied by others—the pastoral Fulani, for example, and the Malinke, and the great Voltaic tribes of the Niger River, driven ever southward by the remorseless spread of the Sahara.

This open grassland of small, scattered trees that resist annual drought as well as fire is all but monotypic from Senegal east to the northern plain of the Republic of the Congo; the fauna (and flora) are essentially the same, not only in Niokolo Koba and the Parc de la Komoé but in the Mole Reserve in northern Ghana, a complementary cluster of wild parks—l'Arly, Pendjari, and the "Parcs du W," near the common borders of Upper Volta, Niger, and Benin— and several parks in Cameroon, in Central Africa. Since most of this region has been man's domain for thousands of years, and the rest will become so as tsetse is brought under control, there isn't much hope that the status of wild animals in any of the West African parks would differ much from the status here in Komoé, and the few reports would indicate that it does not, despite the establishment of "reserves" and even some token restocking programs (as in Nigeria). As early as 1934, in a book on his travels in West Africa, one observer remarked, "But I should have been surprised if I had been told that I should travel about seven thousand miles without seeing any live wild animal larger than an antelope."* Unlike Kenya and Tanzania, where the ambivalent attitude toward wildlife is quite similar but where the economic impetus of tourism is clear, these countries see small reason to protect what is left of their wildlife, far less restore what is now gone.

*Geoffrey Gorer, *African Dances* (1934).

Except in regard to Senegal, good data on the status of wildlife in West Africa is rather scant—a reflection in itself of official attitudes—but a comprehensive survey made in Nigeria in 1962 confirms most of one's worst fears about this region. Excepting the vast and empty lands of the south Sahara—Mauritania, Mali, and Niger—Nigeria is by far the largest of the West African states, and because it adjoins the states of Central Africa, such as Cameroon, where human beings and their weapons are less common, and where a reservoir of wildlife still exists, it might be expected to be better off than the smaller countries to the west. But according to this report, the last black rhinos in Nigeria were exterminated in either 1935 or 1945—no one really knows—the giant eland and several other antelopes have vanished, and almost all of the remaining larger mammals, even the jackals, are threatened with extinction, together with the larger reptiles and large birds. Of the thirty-two hoofed species, all but nine are extinct, threatened with immediate extinction, or "seriously depleted"; the exceptions are the bushbuck and a few species of duiker. Outside its only game reserve, Yankari, a tract of about eight hundred square miles northwest of the Benue River where it is claimed the fauna is increasing, it is unusual for the visitor to Nigeria to see *any* live wild animals other than, just possibly, a few primates; in five thousand miles of driving, the author of the 1962 report noted a dozen baboons, three patas monkeys, and two monkeys of unidentified species. Birds are scarce, too. Although Nigeria has the only ornithological society in West Africa, its national bird, the beautiful crowned crane, is at least as scarce as our bald eagle. "One is continually being reminded by Nigerians that theirs is the most densely populated nation in Africa and that perhaps, therefore, there is no place for wildlife."*

*Advisory Report on Wildlife and National Parks in Nigeria, 1962; G. A. Petrides.

In East Africa, the loss of habitat through intensive settlement, land use, and overgrazing has been the main threat to wildlife; but in West African countries such as Nigeria, which tolerates year-round hunting (often at night, and often in gangs) of every species, regardless of scarcity, sex, or age, together with epidemic use of steel traps, snares, and encircling fires, the outright destruction of the animals themselves may be more damaging. Out of seventeen animals in a collection made in recent years by a Monsieur Brandt, sixteen had been previously wounded by crude pellets from one of the estimated four million or more muzzle-loaders used in the back country for hunting "bush meat." In these populous, poor countrysides, wild game has always formed a high percentage of the meager protein diet; thus, *nama,* the local Hausa word for "animal," also means "meat" (apparently this word survived the southeastern migrations of the Bantu-speakers out of Nigeria and Cameroon and on into East Africa, where *nyama* is the Swahili word for "game").

Similarly, in Ghana, there are wildlife preservation laws that date back to 1901, but as late as 1953, game preservation was administered by the Tsetse Control Department, which was dedicated to "eradication of the tsetse flies through game shooting and habitat clearing along river and stream courses."* Since independence, in 1957, there has been a growing concern about wild creatures that older Ghanaians can still remember as part of their cultural and spiritual heritage; this is offset by a widespread belief that the wildlife is doomed and could never be restored to the abundance that might attract tourists. The only game reserve of significance at present is at Mole, across the frontier from the Parc de la Komoé. In 1967, a Department of Game and Wildlife was created, but as in Nigeria, there remains an almost total lack of public education and en-

*1970 *IUCN Report,*

forcement of wildlife legislation, which will be ignored in any case until the people's protein needs are otherwise taken care of. In Ghana, almost anything that moves is esteemed highly as a source of nourishment, even those creatures formerly protected by traditional taboos. Warthog, baboon, and the small antelopes are still the most common source of bush meat in the back country, but a great many other creatures, including puff adders and civet cats, are also consumed wherever they are found. The "grass cutter" or cane rat and the giant rat lead the list of wild creatures on the bill of fare at Accra, the capital city.

West of Ivory Coast, the situation is no better. As of 1970, when a survey of wildlife conservation in West Africa was made by the IUCN, neither Liberia nor Sierra Leone had a single national park or wildlife refuge. Sierra Leone had lost all but four percent of the primary rain forests that once covered the whole land (its Gola Forest is the last hope for conservation) yet it still permits almost unlimited hunting, even by foreigners. Liberia retains a lot more of its forest (twenty-one percent), but here, too, the destruction of animals is epidemic, and there is no limit whatsoever on the elephant, which is in danger of extermination. No export permits are required for ivory, hides, skins, and assorted animal parts, and export permits for live animals—mostly young chimpanzees, whose mothers are invariably killed—may be had for twenty-five cents. Formerly, trapping permits were required, but for some reason these have been dispensed with, either because nobody bothered with them or because there was so little left to trap.

All along the coast, the lumbering and burning of the rain forests have largely depleted the wild creatures, but those countries whose territories extend north into the Sahel have retained small populations of the more common savanna species, and Benin can claim two important national parks. The Parcs du W protect about two hundred

square miles of savanna, and the Parc Pendjari, about half
that size, includes savannas, combretum woods, and gallery
forest; there are also three game reserves adjoining these
parks where some effort is made to control illegal hunting.
Three other parks have been established across the border
to the north, one in Niger and two in Upper Volta.
Theoretically the savannas of Nigeria (see endpaper map)
could be replenished by the animal populations that are
protected by Benin and Cameroon. Although Nigeria was
a signatory to the African Convention for the Conservation
of Nature and Natural Resources (Algiers, 1968), and has
passed commendable wildlife legislation, it has not proceeded with the education of the public, which has an un-
derstandable contempt for laws that are not enforced. But
this prosperous country that has left no place for wildlife
has a reputation—among black Africans as well as whites—
as one of the "angriest" and most confused of the new
nations, and one must wonder if these two circumstances
are not related.

▼▼▼

After four flat tires, we had lost faith in our car, and, having
missed the early game viewing for want of a vehicle, Dr.
Boese decided to leave the Parc de la Komoé as soon as
possible. With tires repaired, we headed west again across
the Bandama River, which flows down to the coast at Grand
Lahou. In the empty country beyond Ferkessédougou came
the fifth flat tire in twenty-four hours, and this time, in
attempting to repair it, Sauri the driver stripped the lug
threads, making it impossible to remove the wheel. A vehicle bound for Korhogo, twenty miles away, took Sauri in,
and when, two hours later, he had failed to reappear, Jacob
Adjemon caught a ride in the same direction, returning an
hour later in a taxi. We proceeded straight to the tour agent
in Korhogo, to have words about the caliber of the car, but
this Malinke gentleman, M. Toure Basamanno, blamed ev-

erything on poor Sauri, and swore roundly that Sauri would pay; far from expressing regret at our inconvenience, Basamanno saw himself as the real victim. He had another driver, Mamadou, whose car was in such superb condition that Basamanno's great regret—and here he belched—was that he could not accompany us himself. This weary and cynical fellow had just lunched, and now he lay across his desk in postprandial repose; his shifting eye did not inspire confidence, and his questing mouth contained an outsized kola nut, bright orange in hue, that rolled into view like a hanged man's tongue each time he spoke. Later we were told by Mamadou that this *sacré* Basamanno had yet to pay him for four days' work performed last January.

Korhogo is a great center of Senoufou culture, and before leaving we visited its markets, where masks and statues, brown-and-black paintings on raw linen weavings, anklets and bracelets of old brass, carved ivory, wooden boxes, beads, and exotic knickknacks of all kinds are hawked by the network of Senegalese who control most of the antiquities trade in Ivory Coast. While some of the wood carvings were old, most were quite new, and in another street, we watched the carvers hard at work with "*les vrais hâches de leurs grandpères*." The growing tourist trade has taken precedence over tradition, and most of the stuff, hacked out with an eye for quantity rather than quality, is rather bad; the wax job that gives it a high shine only points up the facile decadence of style.

The Senoufou, like the Lobi, are a Voltaic people from the north; they call themselves Sienamana. Like many other peoples of West Africa, they were driven south toward the forest edge by Arab slavers, and have remained here due to the spread of the Sahara. Senoufou Land was formerly much larger, extending from Odienné to Kong and Katiola, but it was pressed in from east and west by invasions of the Malinke (or North Mande or "Mandingo"), a Niger River people who were also driven south by Arab encroachment.

As early as the seventeenth century some Malinke were converted to Islam, and in the nineteenth century, led by a famous despot named Samory, they scourged and ruled almost all of the interior—Mali, Niger, Upper Volta, the northern Ivory Coast, Sierra Leone—until French troops from Senegal captured Samory and assigned his enormous empires to themselves. Like the Peulh, the Malinke are widely scattered in West Africa, north to Timbuktu and all the way west to Casamance, in Senegal. In the country east of Ferkessédougou (which was founded in the nineteenth century by Senoufou driven north and west by the king of Kong) they are called "Dioula" or "Traders," having turned their warrior instincts toward commerce. The insistent pressures of the Malinke have forced the Senoufou to congregate in the large communities that are probably the source of their advanced culture, instead of littering the landscape in the usual pattern of savanna villages, and in the open countryside a few birds may still be seen—stone partridge, francolins, laughing doves, a hawk.

This is the season of feast and celebration, before the plowing that starts with the first rains, and unlike most *spectacles folkloriques,* in which the dancers are taken from planting or harvest for the titillation of the tourists and sometimes bribed to perform ritual dances that only initiates should see, the Senoufou dances staged here by the nearby villagers were performed joyfully, with a spontaneity I saw nowhere else.

The N'Goron dance took place in a garden square beneath a huge silk-cotton tree, around a bonfire that attracted quick, small bats. The troupe from the village of N'Dara included six young girls, none more than fifteen, in the first period of their initiation, and also a group of musicians led by the *caparia* or whip man (who later did a whip dance and walked barefoot across the fire); the group included a flutist, three tom-tom players, and three players of the balafon, a kind of xylophone with hardwood strips laid across the mouths of opened gourds. The tom-toms, set off by the weird balafons and flute, filled the night with their wild sound; the flute was melodious and wistful, high, unceasing, like the whisper of unseen water in the forest or music for a dance of forest ghosts. Alas, there was no oliphant, or elephant-tusk horn; one can only surmise how balafons and oliphants might sound in concert.

Hair whisks shimmering in each hand, on each back a shivering bird's-tail tassel of straw plumes, the children danced forward and back, forward and back, like scratching fowl, yet quick and light, leaping and pantomiming in bird courtship, pausing to strut, flutter, and display, then skipping on again. The dance was a beautiful and stirring ceremony that summoned the deep mystery of earth. Before vanishing out of the firelight into the dark, the little girls dipped forward, touching each guest on both shoulders with their whisks, teasing, tantalizing, yet impersonal, expressionless.

▼▼▼

While in Senoufou Land, we stopped at back-country savanna villages, very clean and quiet by comparison to the large towns. At Ouazamon, the small stone hearths, gourd calabashes of a shining bronze color, long wood ladles and log mortar and pestle seemed laid out, like ancient art objects, on the swept earth. Old women culled groundnuts, a vat of maize was being prepared, young women lifted a mortar, let it fall. An infant boy with fly-filled eyes slumbered in a wooden trough; a black hunting dog with rattan hoops about its neck, to protect it against cornered animals, moved silently away. The village people were not friendly or unfriendly; they avoided looking at us, they waited for us to go.

The thatched houses with their walls of straw and clay were mostly rectangular, with round maize cribs on clay legs off to the side. Fetish houses were located in a nearby grove of trees. If an unauthorized person should enter a fetish house, said Jacob, he or she would certainly be killed, if not by fetishes then by outraged tribal action; even the groves—high islands of silk-cotton trees that soar from the low woodland—are out of place in the savanna, therefore full of power, therefore sacred.

In a small shed behind the village, a blacksmith forges heavy blades for tools; a child perched like a troll under the peak cranks a crude bellows that fans the coals. On the ground outside the forge sits an ancient *awale* game (called *bau* in East Africa). The smith has made small, hand-faceted iron balls for the wood board, yet is quite indifferent to the most beautiful artifact I have seen in Ivory Coast; he says he would sell it happily, but it is the property of his brother, who has gone off to Korhogo. Jacob Adjemon is indifferent to it, too, indeed he is faintly contemptuous of our interest in these old-time things, the death fetishes, the dusty masks. Before all, this young man is the new African, admiring and envious of Western artifacts, frowning in unslakable discontent.

▾▾▾

West of Ouazamon, the red road enters a new land broken by huge black boulders, the granite outcroppings of Africa's old mantle. We pass an ancient hunter with his muzzle-loader, an old woman of Niger selling medicines, a solitary patas monkey near the road. The hundreds of miles of rough dirt track that we would travel in this land was not once crossed by a baboon; nor did we see the Abyssinian ground hornbill that was so common in back-country Senegal. This turkey-size hornbill is venerated by the Senoufou as a primordial animal, and is a common subject of the carvings, but even this privileged status has not spared it.

Odienné is a Malinke stronghold, a high and open town with a white mosque, set in low hills in the northwest corner of the country, near the Guinea and Mali borders.

Of the native woodland, there is little left. At noon, the dust is bright, and the hot wind of the *harmattan* blows unimpeded through the naked branches of the flame trees. From Odienné a track goes north to Bamako, on the Niger, while the main road back to Abidjan turns south, among citrus groves, guava, and cashew trees. From hilly terrains of thickening vegetation flow thick streams, and farther south the savanna gives way to tropic forest. In the distance, tall pale boles of teak appear at the edge of the green wall, and at the forest edge are birds—big, dark forest hornbills, red-eyed doves, the gray-headed and pygmy kingfishers, elegant shikras and a Gabar goshawk, cattle egrets in multitudes, a tawny eagle. But no animal is seen or heard, only a band of twenty hunters armed with ancient guns, marching empty-handed home along the road. Behind them rises the dark smoke of a fire, for in the absence of public education, local hunters cling to the belief that wildlife is inexhaustible until it disappears entirely, and rarely make the connection between wildlife and habitat that might keep them from using fire as an aid to hunting.

▼▼▼

Not far from Gouessesso is the Dan village of Biankouma, perched on a series of natural steps that rise into hillside forest, and scattered with small groves of banana and papaya, kola nut and coffee. (It was near Biankouma, in 1898, that the Mandingo leader Samory was captured by the French.) Unlike those of the savanna tribes, the houses of this forest people are round, built solidly with sturdy walls and sapling roofs that are lifted onto the hut cylinder in a single piece; the chief's house, in this village, at least, has a roof of tin. All houses are decorated with a broad white band of kaolin on which red drawings and designs have been inscribed. The designs are made by young initiates to the tribe, and mostly portray the hunting and fishing that is swiftly disappearing from their lives. In addition, there

are three fetish houses scattered wide apart in the big village, and readily distinguished by a half-circle of palmettos
and a flat stone altar near the entrance. Outside one sits an
old man whom everyone ignores; the silence all around is
very strange. Indeed, he is like a sacred mask, for according
to Jacob, nobody is supposed to see him enter or leave the
fetish house; children playing anywhere near are called
away. Nor is anyone permitted to take photographs. Ex-
plaining all this, Jacob keeps glancing at the fetish house,
and before long he is accosted by a man who is offended by
Gil Boese's camera and demands to know why strangers
lurk about; hurriedly we apologize and move away. It is the
power of the fetish houses, Jacob says, that keeps these Dan
from obeying official orders and moving over to New Biankouma, a treeless, muddy, and depressing litter of hard
government housing that adjoins the village; such develop-
ments, built with customary bureaucratic disregard for the
traditions of the people who must live in them, are all too
reminiscent of the "efficient" government housing on Indian reservations in the United States. They are a common
sight these days in Ivory Coast, and most of them—deser-
vedly—are empty.

At the next village south, a dancing march is under
way, led by a figure in a headdress mask who is hoisting a
high pole; a number of costumed figures follow, leading a
crowd of stamping, singing villagers. Many of these Dan
wear Muslim dress, and it is true that the Malinke have
made converts among these people, as they have among the
Senoufou, farther north. But Muslim dress is a fashion
here, and no proof of religion; where fetish houses and
masks occur, the people are still animists, including many
who have formally adopted Islam or Christianity. Our Jacob
Adjemon is "Christian" but his Beté tribe—of the Kru peoples, who came originally from the Windward Coast—remains in touch with the old ways, and Jacob himself believes
that his own brother died by sorcery. Jacob kindly invited

us to visit his mother's house on the way back to Abidjan; he says his room is still kept in waiting for his return. But Jacob has lost the family sense that is so powerful in Africa; by jitney bus, his village is not far from Abidjan, yet it has been eight years since he went home.

Jacob is generous and intelligent, but he is also arrogant and angry. Being a guide to the white tourists gives him a feeling of superiority, and so he resents very much that both of us have been to Africa many times before and might even know more than he does about wildlife, which like many young urban Africans, he fears and despises. His solution is to dispense information in a very loud, abrasive voice whether we want it or not, as if to say, This is my duty, and I mean to do it. Two days ago, he took offense when we declined a side trip out of Boundiali to view some hippopotami in a distant lake; everyone else he had ever guided had been to see those hippos, and although he granted the possibility that we had seen hippos rather often, while they, perhaps, had not, he could not reconcile himself to our defection.

Because his voucher entitles him to do so, and because he conceives of it as duty, Jacob insists on joining us for every meal. Having appeared, he slumps disconsolately in his chair, eats with his fingers village-style, and declaims against European food; almost invariably, an expensive dinner is left virtually untouched upon the table. In its place, he orders a Coca-Cola in which he marinates a large hard roll until it softens, whereupon he eats it out of the glass, using a fork. He is peremptory with waiters, then becomes furious when they ignore him and deal instead with us. He feels superior to Mamadou, who does not eat with us and is not entitled to a room in these hotels; as for Mamadou, who is quiet and gentle, he is even more exasperated by our haughty guide than we are. Jacob speaks German and English as well as French and expects to be hired shortly by Lufthansa; we'd like to warn him that his manners may

▼▼▼

count against him, but he is too touchy and volatile to
accept this counsel in the way that it is meant. He has a color
problem that is common in the new Africa: he envies and
imitates the whites and is ashamed of this, and therefore is
aggressive in his blackness, which makes him angry at both
blacks and whites.

And so, though we like him, he has gotten on our
nerves. Driving along, he will turn up Mamadou's radio to
full volume and join in very loudly and untunefully in the
latest love songs. He is an authority on love, and speaks for
Africa on this subject as on all others. "In Africa," says
Jacob Adjemon, "we say that first love is the best . . ."

▼▼▼

Even more than the Senoufou, the Wobe and the
"Yacouba" or Dan of the Man region, are famous for their
masks, which have a serene and classical expression as well
as a shell-like delicacy and lightness that has made them the
favorite of Western amateurs of West African art. It is not
strange that the Senoufou and the Dan have produced the
most sophisticated art (as well as the most striking dances)
in the Ivory Coast, since both derive from ancient and intense traditions; as in the great art of Benin, the Dan culture
was already advanced before the first white man appeared
on the Windward Coast.

The masks are in no way ornamental, nor is beauty
sought; they are consecreated manifestations of the spirits,
given human likeness so that they may be perceived by man.
There are "small masks" that serve only the maker, and
"Great Masks" that serve and protect the whole society in
such ways as seeking out sorcerers, dispensing justice, and
granting fertility and harmony. In these tasks and others,
the masks are abetted by powerful secret societies with
animal totems, notably the Gor or Leopard, which impose
respect for the masks as well as punishment for those who
disturb the public harmony; since this punishment may take

the form of a fatal dose of crocodile bile, administered by a shaman who can make himself invisible, or even transform himself into the leopard, the secret societies, and Gor especially, are much respected—all the more so, perhaps, now that real leopards have disappeared.

The names "Wobe" and "Yacouba" are distortions of the confused responses from outsiders that met the early inquiries of the white explorers; in the great tradition of colonial impatience, words that mean nothing to the tribes became their names. Thus "man," which in the Dan tongue signifies "I don't know," became the name for the great town of this region, the center of the trade in kola nuts to Mali and Senegal, and a depot for Mali cattle on their way south into what is now Liberia. It is still the great trade center of west Ivory Coast, with a vast and tumultuous African market that overflows a great two-story shed, spreading its rich smells and bright colors into the mud streets all around. The town itself is set into a mythic countryside of towering green forest walls and flowering trees surrounded by eighteen conical hills up to four thousand feet in height; the most stirring of these hills is the sacred guardian called the Tooth, which is crowned by a sheer monumental block of granite, and comes and goes mysteriously in the mist. The cloud forest is a phantasmagoric setting for the masks and dances, for Gor the Leopard, for the waterfalls and spidery bridges across the mountain torrents, made of miles of liana that climb to the highest and most delicate branches of the trees, strung magically in a single night, tradition says, and able to carry a weight of fifty tons. But the totem animals of these jungles, from which so much of the power of the old ways derives, are almost gone.

▼▼▼

From these hilltops on the rare clear days, one can see as far west as Mount Nimba, which forms a common corner of three countries (Ivory Coast, Liberia, and Guinea) and at

▼▼

6,069 feet is the highest mountain in West Africa. Using "bush taxis"—small jitney buses with such names as "Tahiti" and "Bob Dylan"—I had hoped to go straight across from Man to the slopes of Mount Nimba, in Liberia, to join friends on an ornithological safari, but the tour people in Abidjan, as well as the authorities in Man, assured me that this journey was not possible; there was no passable road beyond Danané, which was separated from the frontier by dangerous rivers and impenetrable forest, nor was there any road on the far side. No, no, they said, I would have to return all the way east and south again to Abidjan, take an international flight west to Monrovia, on the Liberian coast, then make my way as best I could inland to Nimba; in other words, travel a thousand miles to reach a point less than a hundred miles from where I stood. I would later discover, as a fitting end to my sojourn in Bad People's Coast, that three months previously a new road had been put through that connected Mount Nimba to the main road to Man; instead of wasting six whole days and failing to arrive in time (which is what happened), I could have reached my destination in three hours.

And so from Man, we headed south again, on our way to the Parc Marahoué; this is the region of the Gagou, small forest folk who are sometimes described as being covered in reddish hair. (Both the Dan tribes and the Kru from farther south attest that they displaced these little hairy aborigines when they first came to these forests from the west; to the Lobi, in the far northwest, they are known as the Koutowa.) Western authorities have classified the Gagou as "small Negroes," not true Pygmies—a contradiction, since "Pygmies" are also regarded as small Negroes, despite marked morphological differences which may include yellowish skin color and thick body hair—and even suggest that the small size of Bushmen and Pygmies is quite recent, an adaptation to the marginal environments into which both groups were forced by stronger peoples.

There is a possibility, at least, that "little people" not described by science still exist. The eminent animal collector, Charles Cordier (whose work is much respected by no less an authority than Dr. George Schaller), was so impressed by field evidence of unknown bipedal anthropoids in the upper Congo that he published a paper on the subject. Earlier (1947) a Professor A. LeDoux, at that time head of the Zoological Department in the Adiopodoume Institute, outside Abidjan, testified to several persuasive recent reports of small, manlike creatures with reddish body hair, including one that was shot at that same year in the great forest between the Cavally and Sassandra rivers by a celebrated elephant hunter, Monsieur Dunckel. In fact, *agogwe*—which the Africans regard as a small man-ape— have been reported from many forest regions all across tropical Africa, from Ivory Coast to Tanzania, and a Belgian zoologist makes a bold suggestion: "Although these 'little hairy men' agree with nothing known to the zoologist or anthropologist, their description could not agree better with a creature well known to paleontologists by the name of *Australopithecus,* which was still living in South Africa not more than five hundred thousand years ago, at a time when all existing African species were already formed."*

▼▼▼

The Ivoiriens assure us that unbroken jungle is all that may be seen at Marahoué, but a large part of this two-hundred-fifty-thousand-acre park is comprised of grassland and small hills set about with woods. In the deep forest, we observe magnificent butterflies of several genera and a white-collared mangabey (*Cercocebus torquatus*) an angular gray monkey with a reddish crown, sitting sprawl-legged in a tree crotch on the farther side of a green meadow by the forest wall, keeping company with smaller relatives, the

*B. Heuvelmans, *Two Unknown Bipedal Anthropoids,* Rome: Genus, 1963.

mona monkeys. Atop a hill overlooking open country, we
came upon a lepidopterist, caught in an illicit act of lepi-
doptery, who testified nervously that hartebeest and buffalo
had been in view only this morning, but though we poked
about the tracks until late afternoon, we saw no sign of
bouffle nor *bubale,* nor even one dropping of the elephants
that are supposed to frequent Marahoué, as well. The best
that can be said for all too many of these "forest reserves"
in the West African countries is that one cannot absolutely
deny the presence of large animals, any more than one can
prove a negative proposition; how can one say they are not
there, since one cannot see them?

That night we stopped at Yamoussoukro, until recent
years the small home village of the country's president,
Félix Houphouët-Boigny, who owns a coffee plantation and
a factory there as well as a colossal modern palace that
overlooks a manmade "Lake of the Sacred Crocodiles."
(We detected no sign of crocodiles, sacred or otherwise.)
The village itself has been buried by grandiose housing
projects, for the most part empty, as well as a number of
pretentious, rather lonely modern buildings and an ornate
hotel with a *piscine* that all but rivals the lagoon at the Hôtel
Ivoire, all linked together by millions of dollars' worth of
broad triumphal avenues that soon die out in a worn countryside of red termite hills and scrubby bush. In Ivory
Coast, as in many other countries of the new Africa, a privi-
leged few have acquired enormous wealth, but for the rest
things are much the same as they were in the colonial times
from which their leaders saved them.

On Easter Sunday, we returned to Abidjan on the
"Grande Route," which is memorable chiefly for the number of dreadful wrecks along the way. A head-on collision
of the night before was still being unraveled, and a little
farther on was a truck-and-trailer, upside down, that had
rocketed deep into the jungle. As in Senegal, the new two-
lane roads are too narrow for the novice drivers, most of

them young and inexperienced like Mamadou, whose total lack of anticipation in combination with slow reaction time and love of speed makes his driving a grave business indeed. We passed a sunny Easter morning on the brink of dire emergency, veering southward among rich plantations of coffee, oil palms, rubber trees, and pineapple, disputing the road with the great timber trucks that are bearing away the downed giants of the forest. At Ajamé, the whole landscape is a patchwork quilt of Sunday laundry, which is done for the prosperous Ivoiriens by poor people from Upper Volta fleeing south in a desperate search for work; at Banco we pass a forest reserve that according to Jacob no longer contains a single animal of any kind.

Jacob Adjemon is the born tourist in our group. For his homecoming, he is attired in a new *kanzu* bought at Man, and among the many souvenirs he has acquired on our journey is one of the mass-produced antelope lamps knocked out and shined up in the art factory at Daloa. In his opinion, old masks and carvings and *awale* games from the back country are of no use to the new African, and obviously he feels about them much the same uneasiness and disrespect that he feels for wildlife. Mamadou, on the other hand, bought an imaginative traditional bird-toy of wood covered in dried skin that comes originally from the Niger, and had hung it from his mirror as a charm; within the day, he had lost interest in this pretty thing, and when it fell, had flung it sullenly aside, perhaps in envy of all Jacob's shiny purchases, or perhaps because Jacob had spent all of the money that he was supposed to give to Mamadou for his return journey. This injustice came to light after Jacob had been dropped off with his pile of packets near the beach, where he had persuaded us, wrongly as usual, that there was plenty of space in the hotels; his primary aim, it now appeared, had been to lure us somewhere close to his own lodgings. But Mamadou had not betrayed him, and even now, when we offered to advance Mamadou

money, he refused our help until we promised that we
would not get the perfidious Jacob into trouble with his
employers. Thus was Jacob Adjemon repaid with kindness
for his own selfish and unscrupulous behavior.

Poor Mamadou, poor Jacob—doomed to return to
Hôtel Ivoire, we felt depressed. It seemed to strike us all at
once that in hundreds of miles of travel overland in Ivory
Coast, the only animal we ever saw outside the parks was
that lone monkey on the westward road from Boundiali,
and that the greatest concentration of wild mammals we
had seen in the whole country were the fruit bats in the city
park here in Abidjan. Nor did anything that we could learn
of other countries in West Africa promise much better.

Earlier today, passing the road that leads toward
Grand Lahou, Jacob had said, "In Abidjan, when we wish
to regard elephants, we simply fly in an airplane to Grand
Lahou, and there look down upon them." Mamadou, at first
impressed but now fed up with the grand airs of his compa-
triot, had stared at me to see if I believed this arrant nonsense. But perhaps Jacob had sensed that we were
saddened by the disappearance of wild animals from Ivory
Coast, as well as by the many signs that for all the "reserves" that have been set aside, for all the governments'
proclamations of intention, the fatal destruction of West
African wildlife still continues. The arrays of steel gin traps
in the Man market, the gangs of hunters on the roads, the
hunting dog with the rattan hoops, the "bush meat" offered
in back-country restaurants, the unobstructed poaching
that, for lack of serious intervention, will soon destroy the
remnant creatures, and thereby aggravate the protein lack
in all these overpopulated countries—this obliteration of
the native fauna is a crucial loss throughout West Africa, for
reasons that go very much deeper than that "conservation
of a priceless heritage" that white well-wishers like to prate
about, having practiced it too late in their own lands. The
animals are the traditional totems and protectors of the

clans, the messengers of the One God that most Ivoiriens still perceive in all creation, the links with the world of the unseen, with the cosmic balance. Now the animals are gone, or at least so scarce that they have no reality in daily life. And perhaps even an urban boy like Jacob Adjemon, who has not bothered to go home to his Beté people in the last eight years, who is proud of the Hôtel Ivoire and disdainful of "the bush," now grows uneasy. And so he says in a bored voice, "In Abidjan, when we wish to regard elephants, we simply fly in an airplane to Grand Lahou, and there look down upon them."

OF PEACOCKS AND GORILLAS: ZAIRE
(1978)

 In 1913 the young ornithologist James Chapin of the American Museum of Natural History, doing fieldwork in what was then the Belgian Congo, discovered the rufous wing quill of an unknown bird in an African's headdress. He kept that feather for many years without finding anyone, white or black, who could identify the bird. In 1934, in the African museum at Tervueren, near Brussels, he matched the feather to the hen of an old pair of stuffed fowls that were thought to be juvenile domestic peacocks. The cockbird was dark blue and green, with a russet neck patch, while the hen was green above, russet beneath. The hen had peafowl-like eyes on the green feathers, and both sexes had peafowl-like crests; and while not true peafowls (*Pavo*), they turned out to be the only known African representatives of the great pheasant tribe, Phasianidae, separated by thousands of miles of desert and mountain from their nearest relatives in Asia. Subsequently, in 1949, the animal collector Charles Cordier obtained a small number of these birds trapped by local people near the lowland village of Utu, in the Congo basin, though he himself never saw the species in the wild. These seven "Congo peacocks" (*Afropavo congensis*) were exhibited at the Bronx Zoo in the 1950s, and subsequently a small captive flock was established at the Antwerp Zoo.

In the spring of 1978 *Audubon* magazine sent a small expedition in search of *Afropavo congensis*. Its leader was the British ornithologist Alec Forbes-Watson, who had known James Chapin and still regards him as "the best ornithologist who ever worked in Africa"; according to Forbes-Watson, Chapin was the only known non-African who had ever seen the Congo peacock in the wild. Alec was to be assisted by his friends George Plimpton and George's sister Sarah, who had been keen birdwatchers as children and have taken it up again in recent years; while in Africa they would also search for the three other "most desirable" birds on this huge continent—not "little brown birds," as Forbes-Watson describes them, but species that are spectacular as well as rare. "The peacock is first, indubitably," Alec had told me in Nairobi in 1977. "Then comes the shoebill stork, the lyre-tailed honeyguide, and the bare-headed rock fowl. On the fifth bird, no two ornithologists would agree; you'd get an argument whichever one you chose. The Pel's fishing owl, perhaps, or the yellow-crested helmet shrike, or the wattled crane." He discounted as unrealistic any search for the Prigogine's owl, or Congo bay owl, a nocturnal forest relative of the barn owls with a masklike face; *Phodilus prigoginei*, known from a single specimen found dead in 1951 at Muusi in the Bukavu highlands, has never been observed alive. Unlike *Afropavo*, it belongs to the same genus and resembles the Asian form, *P. badius*, and therefore its voice might be similar as well (for those who might wish to listen for it, the call of the Asian owl has been described as a high, whistling *ülee-uu üwee üwee üwee üwee*.) Alec himself had already seen the lyre-tailed honeyguide and the rock fowl, both of which occur on Mount

Nimba in Liberia; as far as was known, the Congo peacock (if it still existed) was confined to the lowland forests of Zaire. For the shoebill, the most accessible location seemed to be the Bangweulu swamp in Zambia.

My hope was to join Forbes-Watson and the Plimptons at Mount Nimba in late March 1978 in time to see the rock fowl and the honeyguide, then accompany them on the search for *Afropavo* in Zaire. On Friday, March 24, I was at Man in western Ivory Coast, where I was assisting in a wildlife survey; Mount Nimba was less than a hundred miles away. But local informants assured me the journey was not possible, and by the time I'd made my way back to the coast and got a flight to Roberts Field, Monrovia, it was already Monday afternoon, when my friends would be preparing to depart Mount Nimba. Frustrated, I remained at the airport hotel.

Plimpton turned up early on Tuesday, between plumages. He was heeled over in the hot and humid sun by random baggage that included a stray tripod without telescope, and he wore a trim street hat, hot woolen blazer, soiled bush shirt, and checked Bermuda shorts. His face was flushed with sunburn and the heat, and his very long pale legs were livid from attacks by jungle insects—here was a birdman, tried and true! We spent an agreeable morning at the bar celebrating his tenth wedding anniversary and making plans for a rendezvous a fortnight later in Zaire. At Mount Nimba, he said, all three of them had seen the rock fowl (which, like *Afropavo* and Prigogine's owl, may derive from an invasion of Asian fauna in the far past, and is separated from its closest relatives by thousands of years as well as miles), and Alec and Sarah had every hope of catching up with the lyre-tailed honeyguide this very day. He had heard there was a track across the Liberian frontier that joined the road to Man, and he regretted that I had not found it.

Having wasted three days in airports and hotels, I

hoped Plimpton was mistaken, but Forbes-Watson, arriving
the next morning, assured me he was not; a new road across
the border to Mount Nimba had been put through about
three months before, he said, ordering a beer and sitting
back to enjoy my expression. Had I used it, he continued,
I would certainly have seen both the rock fowl and the
honeyguide, which he and Sarah had observed in its extraordinary courtship flights the day before. (It was James
Chapin who had first linked the lyre-tailed honeyguide to
the weird "song" it makes at courtship time with the odd
curving feathers of its tail.) Alec happened to know that I
had already seen the shoebill stork in the great marsh called
the Sudd, in the south Sudan, and he regretted my bad luck
even as he took delight in my chagrin: "You know, of
course, that had you been with us yesterday, you would now
be the only living ornithologist to have seen three of our
four birds." Because our plane had broken down in Dakar
and would not arrive here until next daybreak, eighteen
hours late, I spent yet another day of airport life digesting
this exasperating news and taking such comfort as I could
in the lovely pratincoles that coursed at dusk along the
jungle walls of the St. Paul River. To console me Alec
pointed out my first white-throated blue swallow, which sat
dejectedly on the pilings of the hotel dock.

▼▼▼

While still in London Forbes-Watson had tried to make
connecting reservations that would take us on from Kinshasa, east of Zaire's Atlantic coast, to Bukavu, in the center
of the continent, but Air Zaire had not once answered its
phone. Arriving in Kinshasa on Thursday morning, March
30, we were informed that there was not room on any flight
to Bukavu until the following Tuesday. After a number of
dispiriting encounters with lesser officials, we boldly sought
out the *chef de base,* in charge of the whole airport, who
promptly called in the Air Zaire man and ordered him to

put us on the next day's flight to Goma, whether there was
room or not. In Goma we would surely find a means of
reaching Bukavu, eighty miles off to the south. Anything
was better that staying in Kinshasa, where the rains had
arrived in flood just two days before and where we would
certainly go broke in very short order. Zaire has been stag-
gered by inflation since the drastic fall in the world price of
copper ore in 1974, and its transportation difficulties, always serious in a land so vast ("Without a railroad, the
Congo isn't worth one red cent!" declared Henry Morton
Stanley), have been severely compounded by the escalating
price of fuel; advertisements in the Kinshasa paper offer
new cars ordered from Europe for which the owners have
not bothered to turn up.

The city on the Zaire River (formerly the Congo)
seems haunted by the corruption and brutality of its days
as Léopoldville, seat of power of the cruel and terrible King
of the Belgians, whose "Congo Free State," with its mur-
derous abuse of conscripted labor (the Zairois estimate that
ten million people died in the period between 1880 and
1910) continued the depopulation of this shadowed country that the terrible days of slaving had begun. The Belgian
Congo colonial administration, though less brutal, continued the exploitation of the country while doing nothing
to educate the people for the transition that was already
inevitable, and when independence came at last, in 1960,
there was no bureaucratic structure to maintain order. The
consequence was anarchy and chaos, including the murder
of the legitimate prime minister, Patrice Lumumba, the
only leader with a national following, followed by installa-
tion of a puppet colonel who would dutifully endorse the
further exploitation of the country's resources.

The saying *"Plus ça change, plus c'est la même chose"* is
bitterly true in the former Belgian Congo. Some privileged
blacks now share the booty with the whites (in 1972, Zaire
imported more Mercedes automobiles that any country in

the world), but as in the colonial days the land is being
ransacked by foreign investors, and whole forests will fall
for the enrichment of a few, with no thought whatever for
the people or the future. To a degree unusual even in
modern Africa, graft and corruption are a way of life, and
their chief proponent is President-for-Life Mobutu Sese
Seko, who was imposed on a war-weary land by American
and European interests. (In September of 1960 this Colonel Mobutu, thrust forward by the United States, seized
control of the central government from the legitimate
prime minister Lumumba. In 1965, he consolidated his
military dictatorship, and he has ruled the country ever
since. As in the case of Houphouët-Boigny, Idi Amin, Jean-
Bedel Bokassa of the Central African Republic, and many
other African despots, Mobutu is assumed to have acquired
an immense personal fortune at the expense of his precarious new nation.) Even as this sick old capital of King Léopold sags and collapses, Mobutu spends millions on his
play city at his home village Gbadolite, south of the Ubangi,
complete with unused international airport, two presidential palaces, a Swiss dairy farm, and elaborate plans for a
private Disneyland. With a personal fortune of four billion
dollars, skimmed from his patrons' exploitation of Zaire's
immense natural resources in copper, industrial diamonds,
gold, cobalt, timber, and water, Mobutu can afford it. In this
huge, famine-haunted country where next to nothing is
undertaken for the public welfare, our man in Zaire is the
richest ruler in all Africa and perhaps the world.

The scattered vehicles that pass in the night streets are
mostly old taxis or expensive cars belonging to the prospering Europeans or to favored Zairois in the good graces of
the president. As if oblivious of human life, the automobiles
speed through the hordes of Africans who wander the dark
and dingy streets in quest of some means of survival, and
the hordes close again behind them. The rotting old colonial mansions use spiked fences and watchdogs and armed

guards to ward off refugees from the starving countryside, whose tin huts and shantytowns and half-finished or burned-out cement-block shelters crowd right up to their barbed-wire walls and spread like a crusting mold along each potholed boulevard and muddy byway. To forestall starvation, the refugees grow vegetables in the gaps in the cracked concrete of the broken city. In the utter breakdown of municipal systems, there is no way to control Kinshasa's population, which is thought to be close to four million, and this in a city that entirely lacks the most rudimentary sanitation system. Litter and sewage have become a part of the human habitat. At N'dola airport, where the refugees overflow the ramshackle hangars and abandoned service buildings, human excrement is all over the runways.

The Zairois seem proud of their one city, which they refer to affectionately as "Kin." To the Europeans, mostly Belgian, who put up with life in this depressing place because it is so profitable, Kin is known as Poubelleville, or Garbage Can Town.

Zaire is eighty times the size of Belgium—larger, in fact, than all of Europe—and the next day we flew a thousand miles in order to reach Goma, which lies on the frontier with Rwanda. At Goma airport, awaiting our baggage, we discovered that another Air Zaire plane out on the airstrip was the connecting flight to Bukavu, the only one that would leave before next week. Air Zaire at Kinshasa had not told us of this plane, far less booked us on it, though they knew we wished to go to Bukavu; perhaps they resented the intercession on our behalf by the *chef de base,* but more likely they knew nothing about it. The Goma agents would not discuss the matter until we had reclaimed our baggage, by which time the plane was filled, or so they said; we later learned from passengers who made this flight that a number of seats had been empty after all. The Zairois themselves refer to their national airline as "Air Peut-être" ("Air Perhaps") and estimate that the chances of any scheduled flight being completed are less than fifty-fifty, often for no better reason than a decision by the pilot, almost anywhere en route, that he has had enough flying for that day. "Sometimes they change schedules in midflight," one Belgian told me. "One never knows *where* they are. Perhaps this is why they are never hijacked." For the next five days, in any case, there would be no plane to Bukavu, nor (for want of fuel) was there a bus, nor a hired car for less than $350, nor any space on the Sunday boat south on Lake Kivu.

George Schaller's *The Year of the Gorilla* remains the best book I know of on this area. When Schaller came here in 1959, the year before Zaire gained its independence, Goma was still a neat and charming Lake Kivu resort, a "European center" for Belgian *colons* and tourists alike; by the time he left, in late 1960, the civil strife that would devastate the country had begun. Today the weeds have taken over the walks and formal gardens. The open-air cafés are gone, the pleasant pastels of the storefronts are sadly faded, there is nothing in the stores, and nothing works; the telephone is chronically out of order, the water system is breaking down, and nobody is left who can fix either. To escape the place, we decided to visit the Virunga National Park.

As early as 1889 Léopold II had set up reserves to save the elephants from black people in order that they might be killed by whites. Additional reserves were created by Prince Albert in 1890, but the Virunga Park—the former Albert National Park, in what was then the Belgian Congo—was the first true national park in all of Africa; it was established in 1938 on the recommendation of Carl Akeley, who had collected five gorillas here a few years earlier for the American Museum of Natural History. Since then the park has been considerably enlarged, before and after the independence of Zaire in 1960.

When I first came to Africa, in the early winter of 1961, it was assumed that the Albert Park and all its animals were

being ravaged and destroyed by the hordes of insensate
Africans who were making life so miserable for the coloni-
als; but this report turned out to be as exaggerated as many
others, and much credit should be given to the park's African guards, who went unpaid for several years and de-
fended what is now Virunga against the worst of the
depredations. At the park entrance there is a plaque com-
memorating the brave twenty-three who "died for the elephants" in those dark years. Jacques Verschuren, who
wrote a moving book about these men, is the former director of the Institut National pour la Conservation de la Nature (INCN), which administers Zaire's seven national
parks; these include vast forest tracts in the interior as well
as the group of beautiful reserves among lakes and mountains of the Rift. Because of a strong park tradition as well
as a small human population, all seven parks continue to do
well.

On Saturday morning we arranged a ride to Nyiragongo, the southernmost of the Virunga volcanoes, which
rise to the south of Ruwenzori or "Mountains of the
Moon," just below the equator between East Africa and
northern Zaire. Several of the "fire mountains" are still
active, and only a year before, on January 10, 1977, Nyiragongo quite suddenly erupted. As five coulees, or lava rivers, poured down its steep sides, the entire Bahutu village
of Bukuma utterly vanished and more than two hundred
people died. Destroying the prison and many other buildings, the flow reached the northern outskirts of the town of
Goma in just twenty-seven minutes, rolling within a half
mile of the airport, with its large depot of fuel; had the lava
touched that depot, it is said, half of Goma would have been
destroyed. The northward road into the Virungas vanished,
and not for a month did the lava cool sufficiently to carve
out the new road; a pretty graveyard in a grove of tall
mimosas not far east of the road was one of the few locations that was spared. A few scorched skeletons of trees still

stand in the shining fields, and these are being chopped for fuel by survivors of the cataclysm, who straighten here and there, in silhouette, to watch us pass.

Climbing the hill, we look across to dense plantations in Rwanda. This region of volcanic ash forms a rich and well-drained soil—one of the few good soils in all of Africa—and Kivu Province, despite civil wars and economic setbacks, continues to produce good crops of tea and coffee, bananas, cinchona, and pyrethrum. There is no smoke from the volcanoes, and on islets of high ground new gardens and banana groves have been established, but one day in the not far distant future, Nyiragongo—the mother of the spirit Gongo—will erupt again.

Augustus Gabula, the young Bahutu warden who guided us uphill on Nyiragongo, was near the summit when the 1977 eruption took place; his family in their village on these lower slopes had four minutes to flee before their hut was destroyed. Augustus himself ran down through a tongue of forest between lava rivers, his path broken by an elephant herd that was stampeding off the mountain. Perhaps because, as mammalogist Jean Dorst informs us, "Having the legs straight with the bones placed vertically one above another, they are quite incapable of leaping," not all of Nyiragongo's elephants survived. Augustus led us two or three miles up the main flow to a place where a group of six beasts had been overwhelmed; probably they were asphyxiated as this outpouring of lava burned up the oxygen across the mountainside. Among the hollows in the lava field are scattered a group of amorphous molds left by burnt hardwood trees and large white bones. A few liverworts and *Osmunda* ferns now prosper in these crannies. In one of the graves the whole form of the elephant is still discernible, even the holes made by its tusks (long since removed) and a sad, curved tube of stone where the trunk lay. These were forest elephants (once considered a distinct species), and some of them were young. Although there is no forage near the graves, only marigold, coarse bracken, and shrubby acanthus with pale lavender thorned flowers, a number of elephants have made their way out onto the cooled lava and communed for a time with the six encased in stone, to judge from the copious amount of dung around the gravesites.

Toward noon, clouds shift and rain comes blowing through the forest, leaving behind a hot and humid sun. The Kivu-Ruwenzori chain is the heart of the African highland-forest habitat, which has outposts in Ethiopia, in the Kenya highlands, and on Mount Meru and Mount Kilimanjaro in northern Tanzania, as well as far westward on Mount Cameroon. All of these places share many species of flora and fauna. At the lava's edge broad carpets of large pale yellow composites mark the transition zone, and within the forest the tree limbs are thickened by moist gardens, mostly fern and orchid. The flowers I recognize are pink *Impatiens,* peas, the gloriosa lily, and a large hibiscus with blossoms of a dark, sinister lavender. Strangely, butterflies are few, and other than elephant trails, with their fresh dung, there is little sign of animals. But a small troop of the beautiful L'Hoest's monkey barks at our appearance, then retreats with dignity across a tongue of lava; these semiterrestrial cercopithecines are shining black with a bright chestnut oval patch from the shoulders to the base of the long tail and with a striking mass of fluffy white whiskers, and one has an infant clasped to her belly. Compared with its relatives, the mona and blue monkeys, which are widespread in West and East Africa, respectively, the L'Hoest's monkey has an odd, small, scattered range, being confined to the mountains of eastern Zaire, Mount Cameroon, and the island of Fernando Poo, in the Gulf of Guinea.

Since most of my African travels have been made in the thorn scrub and savanna of the plains, I am not familiar with the highland avifauna and am happy to have Forbes-Watson as a guide. Alec has seen more species of African birds than anyone alive (not his own claim—I have heard it made for him by others), and on Nyiragongo we identify some forty species, more than half of which are new to me. Sarah Plimpton is delighted by the courtship displays of puffbacks and sunbirds, the wistful notes of flycatcher and cuckoo, the flocks of olive pigeons, high and dark, passing overhead. A strange, sad, single note is made by Lagden's bush shrike, which has the striking golden-yellow breast and belly of its East African relatives; we also take note of a regal sunbird—a sunlit male on a bare limb—a red-faced woodland warbler (not red-faced at all; it looks as if it had dipped its face into a peach), and a white-tailed blue fly-catcher, flaring the white outer feathers of its tail to catch up sun. For Forbes-Watson these four species are "life birds," as they are known to the bird fraternity, the first of their species he has ever seen, and Sarah and I feel privi-leged to see them with him; the last time Alec had as many as three life birds in a single day was years ago, on his first visit to Mount Cameroon.

Forbes-Watson is an East African colonial raised up in the "White Highlands," a veteran of the Kenya Regiment in the Mau Mau days, and a former game warden who likes other wardens and white hunters and is liked by them, yet is amused by the "old boy" element that takes its own romantic mystique so very seriously. I first met him in Nairobi eight or nine years ago, and though we haven't known each other well, we have many friends in common and find that we agree about almost all of them. "I grew up with these chaps, you see," Alec says gently, "and some of them are still trying to pretend that East Africa is like it was, and it just isn't." (Unlike many white East Africans, Alec speaks fluent ki-Swahili, not just the up-country kind used on safari; since he does not cling to the colonial mentality, he truly enjoys talking to Africans and feels quite at home in eastern Zaire, where Swahili is in common use.)

▼▼▼

On Sunday, when we rise at 5:30 A.M. to take the steamer
from Goma to Bukavu, people are descending toward the
lake with all sorts of buckets and containers; apparently the
waterworks is out completely. A little boy toting water back
uphill has been toppled by a jerry can that is much too big
for him, and two small friends try to lift it back upon his
head as he totters in a circle on the road edge. Beyond the
cove where the water is being taken, more crowds are
streaming alongshore toward the ferry. Many are passengers—one woman bears a very large, bright yellow suitcase
balanced on her head—but most of these must be mere
well-wishers. Or so we hope, since the old boat has no seats
at all and in any case will be loaded up like an aquatic bush
taxi with as many *citoyens* as can be crammed aboard.

Lake Kivu, at nearly five thousand feet, is the highest
of the central lakes that fill the depressions in the mighty
rift that splits the continent, and its ice-clear, dark blue
waters, set about by high mountains of Zaire and Rwanda,
make it one of the loveliest places in all Africa. The Zairois
claim that it is Africa's highest lake (Kenya's Lake Naivasha
and Lake Nakuru are both higher) and that, due to the great
amount of methane gas derived from rotting vegetation on
the lake bottom, its waters are poisonous and without life.
But this morning we saw that these waters may be used by
humans if need be, and some small tilapia at the dock pilings explain the activities of an African cormorant, seen
diving yesterday some distance off the shore. However,
these fish are not large enough to sustain any real fishery;
the few pirogues seen on the lake are mostly transporting
bananas and other produce from outlying islands and villages to Goma.

Soon the *Etoile* is passing close to the west shore of
Idjwi Island, a forested ridge, sparsely inhabited, that domi-

nates the center of the lake, and toward midmorning a brief
stop is made to drop off something at a mission village. In
a cove, under banana fronds, boys are fishing for the small
tilapia with wispy poles, and other boys dart forward in
pirogues to offer golden pineapples to the passengers.
Jokes, coins, and pineapples fly back and forth across the
rails, and in less than a minute the *Etoile* is under way again
along Idjwi's western shore, it high wake threatening the
numerous pirogues that harvest the island plantations; the
boatmen wave at us in fear and grandly we wave back.

On Lake Kivu the pirogue looks crude, and its paddle
is carved like a deep scoop that cups the water; the paddling
motion is a wild overhand that throws arcs of water forward
across the shoulders—an inefficient paddle and a poor
technique, or so it appears, suggesting the absence of a real
fishery tradition. (Most African paddles have the graceful
shapes of hearts or blades, as in the great basin of the
Amazon, and across the centuries the long pirogues of both
Congo and Amazon, sharp-pointed at both ends, have arrived at a near-identical, clean, pure design). Yet the Kivu
pirogues carry immense loads of bananas across wide
stretches of open water that are often roiled by squall and
wind; sometimes one can scarcely see the paddlers, three of
whom may be squashed into the stern.

Beyond Idjwi the *Etoile* returns to the mainland shore,
among myriad small, pretty channel islands. Two gray-
headed gulls, a distant stork, a white egret point up the
surrounding emptiness of sky and mountain; to the southwest rise Mount Kahuzi and Mount Biega. Then the *Etoile*
rounds the southernmost of five peninsulas ("a hand of
verdure dipped in the lake," the guidebook says) and docks
in the tranquil harbor of Bukavu.

Across the cove lies a collection of odd boats, retired
for reasons of old age or want of fuel. The largest and most
ancient craft, a wonderful old steamboat of the early century, is the retired lake ferry of colonial days, *Le General*

Tombeur, now renamed *Lt. Col. Potopoto.* Lieutenant Colonel Potopoto—whose name, in the local Lingala tongue, means "mud"—was one of the many heroes of the recent revolution, and his lettered name is the only new paint on this faded ship. Under the name *Lt. Col. Potopoto* the ferry has never left the dock.

The red roofs of Bukavu on its five peninsulas are strikingly inset in green plantations of tea and coffee, cinchona and pyrethrum, broken by forest stands of gum and pine on hills that rise perhaps fifteen hundred feet above the lake. Like Goma, the town lies on the border with Rwanda, which furnishes eastern Zaire with goods no longer available in this country. In Zaire fuel at the official price is not available, and even the government bureaus here must sometimes depend on black-market gasoline, which during one week in early April of 1978 rose from twenty-five to thirty dollars per gallon. At that price one might well wonder if gasoline or smuggled ivory or other contraband lies beneath those cargoes of bananas that are plied back and forth across the lake.

For want of gas no taxis have come down to meet the boat. Consigning our gear to three young boys, we walk slowly up into the town. The colorful broad boulevards of flowering cassia and coral trees are strangely empty, and so are the shops that, at the time of Schaller's visit in 1959, carried "the latest imports from Brussels, Paris, and Copenhagen." The paint has faded, all the street cobbling is coming up; there are no tourists and few cars. The shortage of gas has saved the life of a driver of a truck that lost its brakes on the incline of this street and rolled downhill backward, overrunning the gas pumps in the station. The garage roof now pins the truck in place; had those pumps been full, not only the truck but the Hotel Residence itself would be no more.

In other days this hotel was known as the Residence Royale, and though the statuary has been removed from niches in the marble stairwells, one may still contemplate the grandeur of days past in some old stuffed heads, huge portraits of the great buildings of Belgium, an antique elevator that can only be stopped by hurling the door open at the right floor, a dining salon in rococo plush, and other appointments of more spacious times. In our efforts to economize we take rooms in the *quatrième catégorie,* but even these have their own vast bathrooms and a lake vista or at least a prospect of the boulevard, as well as a view of the Pêle-Mêle Garage across the street.

Having got to Bukavu, we must now work out a way to cross the mountains of the rift and descend into the jungle haunts of the Congo peacock. According to Forbes-Watson the nearest village to the place where Chapin saw the peafowl is called Utu, which lies not far from Walikale, about a hundred miles to the northwest, along the jungle road to Kisangani (the former Stanleyville). This road descends from the Kahuzi-Biega Mountains, where we hope to make camp long enough to get a good look at gorillas. But since it costs twenty-five dollars simply to go out to the airstrip, we could scarcely consider hiring a car even if someone could be found to take us. Planes or supply trucks that serviced Christian missions at Walikale or the tin-mine station in the region, at Obaye, seemed our best hope, for only a large corporation or a mission could put together enough fuel for such a journey.

▼▼▼

A Catholic mission has a station out at Walikale, and we sought to befriend the *monseigneur* at the cathedral, which is located high on the hill above Bukavu, surrounded by candelabra cypress and the remains of flower gardens, turned over now to manioc and maize. The *monseigneur* (an African) assured us that the Walikale mission was not under his jurisdiction and that anyway, only the Protestants had planes. We sought out a Mr. and Mrs. Fred Bahler of the

Grace Mission, who proved hospitable, serving us coffee and cookies in their house above the lake and contacting the mission pilot on our behalf, but the pilot was already overbooked and could not help us. The Bahlers thought that we should see Adrien Deschryver, a former professional hunter who flew a plane for the national parks that might be chartered; and they repeated a story we had heard in Goma. A few years ago an American woman, Lee Lyon, had seen the Congo peacock in the wild and taken pictures of it, not at Utu but at Uku, which means "over there." Ms. Lyon had been killed a few years earlier by a young elephant while photographing an elephant-capture program in Rwanda, but Deschryver had been with her at Uku and could give us all the details of the story. Apparently Deschryver was away, but since he lived on the same road as the Bahlers, they would be happy to leave our message at his house.

Subsequently we talked to Citoyen Muzu, head of the local government bureau of mines, who sat with a number of unemployed friends in a huge office of the colonial period, under a high ceiling with big holes in it; like so many bureaucratic offices in the new Africa, this one makes plain that the real business is transacted elsewhere. Earlier Muzu had told us that he not only knew the Walikale area but had seen the famous *paon de Congo;* now he seemed less sure that this was true. By not repeating it, Muzu withdrew an earlier suggestion that he escort us in person to the peacock. No, he said, we must go to the Société Minérale de Kivu (Sominki), which actually ran the mines down in the jungle.

Partly because of Sarah's wide-eyed charm, the Belgian mine agents were very helpful; there was a truck that went down to the jungle every week, and we were welcome to ride upon it, on the condition that we would provide for ourselves and be ready to depart at the driver's convenience. But today was Monday, and the truck would not leave until later in the week, and time was running out; my visit to the jungle now depended, in effect, upon Adrien Deschryver, and no one knew when Deschryver would return.

That afternoon, for want of a better plan, we went down to the national parks office to talk to Citoyen Mushenzi, whose name means "mongrel" or "bastard" in Swahili. Mushenzi, an amiable and helpful man who gave us permission to camp at Kahuzi-Biega National Park as well as a note of introduction to its chief warden, is said to be amused by his own name, though we did not feel it was a joke that we should share. At the parks office there was an infant gorilla, apparently abandoned by its parents at Kahuzi-Biega; the young gorilla was completely trusting of human beings, and when it reached out to me, I took it up as one would a young human, cupping its small seat in my hand. It was entirely relaxed, astonishingly so, a solid little coarse-haired thing of no more than twenty pounds that leaned its head quietly against my chest as it gazed about, eliciting an unfamiliar surge of maternal feeling.

Jacques Goossens of the local travel office was kind enough to invite us out to his pleasant house for an aperitif in the late afternoon. On the way he pointed out a sort of monument, the tail of a white fighter plane sticking up out of a field. The downed plane had belonged to Jacques Schramm, the notorious mercenary for the international cartel that had attempted to separate the rich province of Katanga (now Shaba) from the new Zaire and thereby keep the copper wealth all to itself. As luck would have it, Schramm had not been aboard the doomed plane; somewhere in some warring African country, it was said, the man was still in his old line of work.

Goossens's house sits on the easternmost of the five Bukavu peninsulas, and the Rwanda border lies but a short distance away, across the swift Ruzizi stream that flows south into Lake Tanganyika. Except for a period in the late 1960s, when Belgians were made to feel unwelcome,

Jacques Goossens has worked in this country for forty years, and he speaks the equatorial Lingala tongue that is understood in most parts of Zaire. Unlike many former *colons,* Goossens would like to see the new Africa succeed, and although he met Patrice Lumumba once and didn't like him—"He was a big mouth," says the gentlemanly Goossens—he thinks that Lumumba had no choice but to fight the secession of Katanga and try to hold this country in one piece. Like most people in Zaire, both white and black, Goossens supposes that the CIA had its long finger in Lumumba's murder and that United Nations Secretary-General Dag Hammarskjöld was murdered, too, in the same year, for the same reason: international big money was at stake, and both men were in the way. Hammarskjöld directed the U.N. attempt to conquer Katanga and reunite Zaire, and people forget, our host observes, that Hammarskjöld's brother was a director of the cartel's competition, Anaconda Copper. Goossens shrugs. It has been a long time since anything surprised this charming, wise, and weary European.

In February of 1961, hitching rides south from Khartoum, I was stranded for some days in Equatoria. These were the bloody days that followed the Katanga secession, and Belgian refugees were streaming across the border into south Sudan; the small hotel at Juba was overflowing, and its grounds were littered with abandoned cars, broken down or out of gas. In mid-February I was at Nimule, across the border from Uganda, and, with two other whites met on the journey, came rather too close to being killed in the burst of anger that swept like a flash fire across Africa.

> Those days at Nimule I recall as the longest in my life. There was no point in trying to cross the border, as the nearest town was far away across an arid plain. For fear of missing the stray vehicle that might pass through, we waited forever at the guard post, and during this period—though

we never knew the reason for the crisis until days later, when finally we got away into Uganda—Patrice Lumumba, the firebrand of the new Africa, was murdered at Katanga in the Congo.

Overnight the friendly Sudanese became bitterly hostile. Guards and villagers gathered in swarms, their pointing and muttering interspersed with shouts and gestures. We could not understand what was being said, but it seemed clear that our crime was being white—so far as we knew, there were no members of our race closer than Juba, a hundred miles away—and that our fate was being decided. (Numbers of whites were killed that year in Africa; a thousand died in Angola alone.) Until then, the people of Nimule had been gentle and hospitable. The schoolmaster had offered us his hut, and even his own cot, and when our food ran out, the border guards shared their calabash of green murk and tripes into which three dirty white hands and seven or eight black ones dipped gray mucilaginous hunks of manioc . . .

After a day and night of dread, peremptorily, we were summoned once more to eat from the communal bowl. Doubtless the schoolteacher had interceded for us, though he had been at pains to seem as hostile as the rest. I knew we must accept the food to avoid discourtesy, and the South African agreed; bravely he gagged down his tripe, retiring immediately behind a hut to puke it up again . . . *

A fortnight later, on a plane from Nairobi to Bombay (I was off on an expedition to New Guinea), I found myself next to a mercenary pilot who was drinking hard, unable to get drunk; he felt threatened because he "knew too much" and was getting out of Africa as fast as possible. As I recall, this man was an Australian. He'd just come from the Congo, where he'd seen enough dirty work, he said, to last a lifetime; he described a recent episode in which some Africans had ordered him to fly a political prisoner to an

*The Tree Where Man Was Born (New York: Viking Press, 1972).

airstrip in Katanga, where the prisoner was first beaten and
then murdered; the killing bothered this man less than the
sadistic beating that preceded it. It was not until long afterward, when the circumstances of Lumumba's death became
known, that I took this tale as seriously as it deserved.

Considering the violence and rapine that have torn this
land from the bloody slaving days of the early nineteenth
century to that shameful period of recent years when Belgian interests, backed by international cartels, encouraged
the copper-rich Katanga province to secede and thereby set
one group of Zairois against another in a horrifying civil war
that made a travesty of the country's independence—considering that, it amazes me not that so many Belgians have
been permitted to return here—for the Zairois know all too
well that they need help from Europeans until a new education system can replace them—but that Belgians, French,
and white people in general are treated with such politeness
and forbearance. Perhaps, out of all their years of horror,
the Zairois have acquired a sense of identity, a national
purpose that transcends the tribalism of the past; perhaps
their acceptance of the white man's poor opinion of them
has been displaced by a more cynical opinion of the white
man. Since 1972, the Zairois call each other *citoyen* and are
encouraged to discard Christian or European names in favor
of "authentic" ones; thus, Alexandre Prigogine, a mixed-
blood Tusi nephew of the celebrated ornithologist and the
operator of a tour service in Goma, has dubbed himself
Negzayo Safari. The women in their elegant long caftans
braid their hair in marvelous patterns, while the men have
abandoned European shirts and ties in favor of the *abas-cost*
(*à bas le costume,* or "down with suits"), a light bush jacket.
T-shirts are popular with the nation's youth, particularly
shirts that advertise professional teams in the United States,
including a mysterious baseball club called the Boston
Giants. Despite hard times and a harsh regime, the people
appear happy, and perhaps they hope that the immense

resources of Zaire will one day be well organized to the profit and benefit of the Zairois themselves.

Most Zairians are wry about their president, Mobutu Sese Seko, whose somewhat foolish photographic likeness in big glasses, leopard cap, and leopard foulard presides over every public room and office in the country. At present his discredited regime is exceeded only by the governments of Equatorial Guinea and South Africa in the brutality of its political repression. The Zairois are beginning to resent this "leader" who is so fond of demanding sacrifices for the Popular Revolutionary Movement. The Belgians also bled Zaire, but at least they knew how to run the country.

Drink in hand, I listen contentedly to the evensongs of a tropical boubou and a robin chat, as Goossens speaks about the great days of the early 1970s, when the prospects for Zaire and for the Zairois seemed almost limitless. At that time, he was stationed at Banana, the seaport for Kinshasa and the only port on the short coast of this huge country. One day early in that year he received a wire from the ministry of tourism, instructing him to prepare accommodations for the forty-five hundred tourists arriving by sea for the world-championship prizefight between Muhammad Ali and George Foreman. Since Banana could scarcely accommodate five hundred, the news of the huge ship threw the town into panic; huts for the tourist hordes were thrown up on every side without regard for sewage disposal or the threat of plague. But the Great Boat for Banana was as illusory as prosperity for Zaire; it never appeared, and Goossens wonders whether it ever existed at all.

Returning from Goossens's house that evening, we passed the car of Adrien Deschryver, who turned up next day to meet with us in La Fiesta Bar. At thirty-eight, Deschryver is a husky, blunt, laconic man with short-cropped dark hair gone a little gray and the restlessness of somebody in pain; though courteous enough, he offers little, averting his flat, pale blue eyes and smiling a private knowing smile that he means you to see. As a young man Deschryver was trained in taxidermy by James Chapin and had assembled a collection of some seven hundred skins of local birds. All of these, together with his library, were lost during the period of the revolution; he has never had the heart to start again. *"C'est un homme bizarre,"* Goossens had told us, accounting for Deschryver's reputation for being difficult. "He has had a lot of trouble in his life. I don't know if that is a *good* reason, but it is a reason."

▼▼▼

Lee Lyon was with him several years ago, Deschryver says, when he saw two Congo peacocks, still alive, that were snared at Hombo; it was not true that she had seen the peacock in the wild. "She was never away from me," he adds enigmatically, "so I would know." He seems to doubt that Chapin saw the peacock, although Forbes-Watson loyally assures us that he did. (In *Birds of the Belgian Congo*, Chapin says that he hunted for the bird in 1937; he does not say that he found it. William G. Conway, the director of the New York Zoological Society, tells me that he once asked Chapin whether he had actually seen the bird and that Chapin said he had not. However, Chapin's notes record that on July 16, 1937, near Ayena, "I noticed something dark running under the bushes of the forest floor, and called to Anyasi. He pursued it, fired, and then I saw a fine male 'peacock' rise with noisy wingbeats and escape.") With Lee Lyon, Deschryver had hoped to film the peacock, but since her death he has lost heart for this project. However, our keen interest seems to reawaken his own; he agrees to join our party in the search. In Deschryver's opinion the best place to start is the region of the mine camp at Obaye. He will fly us there early on Friday and stay over until Sunday or Monday, when I must return with him to Bukavu and go to Rome. Meanwhile, we shall visit Kahuzi-Biega and spend two days—we hope—with the gorillas.

▼▼▼

Kahuzi-Biega is in the mountains twenty miles above Bukavu, and at seven in the morning a taxi was found with enough fuel to take us up there, though not back; the driver planned to coast down all the way. Before departing, he stopped to borrow the spare tire that is shared by Bukavu's old taxi fleet, and a good thing, too, as he had a flat not fifteen minutes out of town. Since his car had no jack, we found some villagers to help us hoist the taxi into the air while the tire was changed. Afterward we proceeded without incident uphill through the plantations, until the *Hagenia* trees appeared that marked the beginning of the montane forest.

Since arriving in Bukavu three days ago, we have not seen a single tourist and had hoped to have the gorillas to ourselves. But as luck would have it, two carloads of Belgian visitors turn up right behind us at the village of Bashi Bantu people by the park entrance. We have permission to camp here overnight, and the head warden, or *conservateur assistant,* has promised us our own guide for tomorrow, but today only one guide is available, and so all visitors must stay together. These six people who are to be *nos copains de safari* intend to take with them a very large brown-and-yellow plastic ice chest full of lunch. Rather than lug it up the mountain by its handles, the unfortunate African assigned to it steps into the bushes and with his panga cuts some strips of flexible green bark for "bush rope"; with this he rigs himself a tumpline in order to carry the big chest on his back.

Disgruntled, we walk through the Bashi village and follow a path cross-country on the mountain. Though still early, the day is hot and humid. Our little band, following the three small Batwa trackers—*les pisteurs*—pushes through tangles of coarse bracken, elephant grass, cane, and lianas between the tall trees and the overgrown plantations. Since there is little forage in unbroken forest, the gorillas are drawn to the abandoned fields of the Bantu peoples' shifting cultivation, where the sun encourages a variety of leafy growth, and are often found too close to the villages for their own good. The trackers descend into swampy streams and up again into the forest, investigating the paths made by the apes and the freshness of their droppings; since gorillas are entirely vegetarian and must eat vast amounts by way of fuel, the droppings are abundant, large, and rather greenish, with a mild sweet smell.

In midmorning there comes a sound of cracking limbs from a tree copse on the far side of a gully; the small *pisteurs* are pointing with their pangas. But one of our *gaie bande,* a silver-haired man who looked flushed even before he started, has not kept up; he is back there doubled up over a log, suffering heart flutters, attended not by his own party but by Forbes-Watson. "I thought I had a corpse on my hands," said Alec later; he was unable to persuade the man to remove the cameras that were dragging down his neck. Meanwhile, I am warning his compatriots about nettles, about the sharp spear points made by panga cuts on saplings, about false steps, mud slides, safari ants—

"*Ngaji!*"

The first gorilla is a large dark shape high in a tree, a mass of stillness that imagines itself unseen. Then, near the ground, a wild black face leans back into the sunlight to peer at us from behind a heavy trunk, and the sun lights the brown gloss of its nape. Soon a female with a young juvenile is seen, then—*le gros mâle! Voilà!* There is high excitement as a huge silver-backed gorilla, rolling his shoulders, moves off on his knuckles into the tangle. The shadows close again, the trees are still. In the silence we hear stomach rumbles, a baboonlike bark, a branch breaking, and now and then a soft, strange "tappeting" as a gorilla slaps its chest; this chest slapping is habitual and not usually intended as a threat.

▼▼▼

▼▼▼

Midday has come. The gorillas have retired into deep, hot thicket, and no one thinks it a good idea to push them out. The dapper *conservateur assistant,* who likes to be called M. le Conservateur, has come up with more guides, and trackers, leading a highly colored troop of tourists that also includes a group of adolescents. Vivid as a parakeet in a suit of green, M. le Conservateur strides up and down before the silent thicket, warning the whites of the dangers from great apes while declaring himself ready to assume responsibility. Clearly he senses a threat to his authority from a dashing Belgian in his group, whose playsuit, as bright blue as his own is green, has assertive brass studs up and down the fly; this fellow's fingers are hooked into his belt whenever his arms are not akimbo. Frowning deeply to indicate the seriousness of the situation, the Belgian joins the *conservateur assistant* in peering meaningfully in all directions; their stance declares their intention to defend the women and children from attack by incensed gorillas that might come at us suddenly from any quarter.

And so the apes doze in their bush, while the human beings wait dutifully in the damp sun. Pale children fret— and doubtless a few black hairy ones, back in the bush, are fretting, too—and a mother distracts her youngest child by swathing it like a mummy in pink toilet paper, thereby enhancing the festive colors of this jungle scene.

A Klaas' cuckoo sings, long-crested hawk eagles in courtship sail overhead, and from the thicket comes the sweetish chicken-dung aroma of gorillas, accompanied by low coughs and a little barking. It is a standoff. On one side of this big thicket perhaps thirty large and hairy primates are warning the restless young among them to be quiet, and on the other, a like number of large, hairless ones are doing the same thing. But all at once the suspense is broken by the ceremonial opening of the plastic ice chest, which incites a rush upon the lunch; the meat sandwiches and hard-boiled eggs that appease the hairless carnivores assail the platyrrhine nostrils of the hairy herbivores back in the bush, for there comes a wave of agitation from the pongid ranks. The thickets twitch, shifting shadows and a black hand are seen; the humans stop chewing and cock their heads, but there is no sound. The gorilla, like the elephant, is only noisy when it chooses, as in the definition of the true gentleman, "who is never rude except on purpose"; and the sad face of a juvenile, too curious to keep its head low as it sneaks along a grassy brake, is the first sign that the apes are moving out.

Gorilla gorilla goes away under cover of the bushes, easing uphill and out across the old plantation and down again into dark forest of blue gum, leaving behind a spoor of fine, fresh droppings. Up hill and over dale comes *Homo* in pursuit, but *Gorilla* is feeling harassed now, and *Homo* is driven back from the forest edge by the sudden demonstration charge of a big-browed male who has been hiding in a bush. An oncoming male gorilla of several hundred pounds, with his huge face and shoulders and his lengthy reach, commands attention, and when the black mask roars and barks, showing black-rimmed teeth, we retreat speedily. The gorilla sinks away again into the green. To a branch just above comes a big sunbird with long central tail feathers—"Purple-breasted!" cries our dauntless birdman. "*That's* a new one!"

Finding their voices, the frightened guides yell at the gorilla, "*Wacha maneno yako!*" a Swahili expression often used to silence impertinent inferiors; loosely it means, "Don't give me any of your guff!" One of the Bashi, Seaundori, is scared and delighted simultaneously; grinning, he first asks eagerly if all had seen the charge of the gorilla, and then, imagining he has lost face by betraying excitement, he frowns as deeply as M. le Conservateur himself and fires nervous and unnecessary orders. The visitors, too, are bab-

bling in excitement; only the small Batwa trackers, grinning
a little, remain silent. They follow the gorillas, never rushing them, just flicking steadily away with their old pangas
in the obscuring tangle of lianas. Even when the creatures
are in view and no clearing is needed, the trackers tick
lightly at the leaves as if to signal their own location to the
gorillas and avoid startling them and provoking a panicked
charge. This is the only danger from gorillas, which are as
peaceable as man allows. Though a leopard has been
known to kill an adult male, *Gorilla* has no real enemies
except for *Homo*, and after years of protection at Kahuzi-
Biega two of the three gorilla troops that are more or less
accessible have placed an uneasy trust in man's good inten-
tions. For the second time they permit us to come within
twenty feet before the bushes start to twitch and tremble,
a sign that the ones still feeding in plain view might be
covering for those that are withdrawing. And though our
views are mostly brief, there comes a time when *Homo* and
Gorilla are in full view of each other for minute after minute,
not thirty yards apart. The apes are more relaxed than we
are and also more discreet, since they do not stare rudely
at our strange appearance; on the contrary, they avert their
gaze from the disorderly spectacle that we present, lolling
back into the meshwork of low branches of big leaves and
staring away into the forest as they strip branches of big
green leaves and push the wads of green into their mouths.
At one point a dozen heads or torsos may be seen at once
in a low tier of green foliage just below us; the black woolly
hair is clean, unmatted.

I count twenty-six white human beings and ten black
ones in a loose line on the steep slope, slipping clumsily on
the slick green stalks cut down by the *pisteurs;* at the fore,
amateur *cinéastes* are jockeying for position, while from the
rear come muffled cries of pain. Once again our path has
crossed that of the safari ant, *siafu,* which is biting the hell
out of women and children alike. Forbes-Watson and I try

to move the tourists from harm's way, but supposing us to be competing for a better snapshot angle, they keep on milling until it is too late. By now Alec is reduced to desperate oaths, apologizing to Sarah for each obscenity and vowing that never, never again will he observe wildlife under such conditions: I wonder what my friend George Schaller, who pioneered gorilla observations when gorillas were still considered very dangerous, would have made of this peculiar woodland scene. To cries of "Silence!" from the adults, much louder than the original disturbance, unhappy children fret in the dark forest, and the *conservateur assistant,* gazing at the sky, makes an erroneous forecast of hard rain by way of an inducement to depart.

In the confusion the gorillas sink again into dense thicket. Departing, they must cross the path made by the trackers in trying to head them off, and at least fifteen pass in view, including *le gros mâle.* With a sudden roar he rears up, huge-headed, from the green wall, as the nervous Bashi guides yell, *"Rongo!"*—"Bluffer!"—and the whites fall over one another in the backward surge: the head of the adult gorilla is so enormous that it seems to occupy more than half the width between the shoulder points. But the threat display seems perfunctory and rather bored; *le gros mâle* regards us briefly before turning to give us a good look at his massive side view and the great slope of his crown. Then he drops onto his knuckles once again and shoulders his way into the forest. From neckless neck to waist he is silver white.

▼▼▼

The apes are gone, and man troops down the mountain. Despite the frustrating indignities of this hot day, Alec, Sarah, and I are exhilarated and excited, but for our companions their first sight of the wild gorilla was *"très fatiguant"* and even *"un peu décevant,"* or so they write in the park register; one took advantage of this opportunity to register

a public complaint about the high price of film here in
Zaire. Part of the group identifies itself as "*la famille Pois-
son*," and it may be that the others were "*la famille Boeuf.*"

Before leaving Zaire I crossed paths again with these
inheritors of King Léopold's bloody legacy. At Goma airport, their voluminous luggage had been increased by
enormous crates of vegetables, one to each person, and
they were abusing Air Zaire's black agent for charging them
overweight; had they traveled this primitive airline for two
weeks only to be repaid with his stupidity? ("*Merci, messieurs,*" the agent said.) Tourists would *never* come back to
the Belgian Congo as long as they received such ungrateful
treatment! The Belgians slap their money down, they
wheel, they rant: "*Ça* non, *monsieur!*"

▼▼▼

Next morning we return again to the realm of the gorillas,
taking a direction south and west and moving higher on the
mountain. Still unsettled by the throngs of yesterday, we
had suggested to the *conservateur assistant* that we would be
happy to make do with a single tracker and no guide, but
this antihierarchical idea upset his sense of order very
much. (*Les guides ne sont* pas *les pisteurs! Il y a le Conservateur—
c'est moi!* Puis, *les guides!* Puis, *les pisteurs!*") As special visitors
with a letter from le Conservateur Mushenzi, we were entitled to two *guides* and three *pisteurs,* and that was that.

I had assumed that the small trackers were Batwa or
Twa, the name used by Bantu speakers for all of Africa's
small relict peoples, including the Bushman and the Pygmy.
But these *pisteurs* are called Mbuti by the guides, and Adrien
Deschryver later told me that they are apparently Bambuti
or Mbuti hunters from the Ituri forest to the north who
were hunting gorillas in these mountains even before colonial times and maintain a small, separate village about five
miles away from the nearest Bashi. Perhaps a certain mixing
has occurred, for these little people are not "yellow," as the

Mbuti Pygmies of the north are said to be, and may even be a little larger, though none of the three *pisteurs* has attained five feet. They have large-featured faces—big eyes, big jaws, wide mouths, and wide flat noses—in heads that seem too big for their small bodies. But it is the way they act and walk that separates them most distinctly from the guides, for their bearing is so cheerful and self-assured that one is soon oblivious of their small size; they move through the undergrowth and with it, instead of fighting the jungle in the manner of white people and Bantu. In the presence of the guides the leader of the three identifies himself as Shiberi Waziwazi; *waziwazi*, in Swahili, signifies one who comes and goes and is rather derogatory. But later he murmurs that Shiberi Waziwazi is the "African" name given to him by the Bantu, and that his true name, his "forest" name, is Kagwere. At this, the one called Kahuguzi says eagerly that he, too, has a forest name: it is Mukesso! And the forest name of the third Mbuti is Matene. Kagwere's left hand has been shrunken to a claw by fire, and he and Matene have the incised scars between the eyes and down upon the nose that are a mark of the Mbuti. All three have lightly filed brown broken teeth and small, neat, well-made legs, which stick out from beneath diminutive olive-colored raincoats and disappear into olive-colored rubber boots so old and torn that one wonders what might serve to keep them on. This *pisteur* uniform, with rain hats to match, is a sign of high prestige, to judge from the fact that they wear it over rough sweaters in this humid heat even while hacking at the torpid thickets with their pangas. The color hides the Mbuti in these forest shadows, through which, like the gorillas, they know how to move in utter silence, even in these ragged rubber boots.

Before entering the forest the Mbuti set up a kind of altar of sharp sticks stuck upright into the earth; they kneel before it, chipping at the soil in a strange manner with their pangas and crying out some sort of invocation, then pluck

▼▼

fresh leaves and press them down in seeming offering. Yesterday Alec dismissed this ritual as some sort of nonsense
folklorique for tourists, comparing it to the "Chika dances"
in Kenya's Embu region, but later our kind friend
Semesaka, headman at the Bashi village and a former soldier in the rebellion (known locally as the *Vita ya Schramm*,
or "War of Schramm," after that last and most notorious
mercenary in Kivu Province), assured him that it was sincere, and so, today, we pay the ceremony more attention.
Afterward Forbes-Watson asks some questions, but because he does so in front of the two Bashi, Kagwere is
apparently embarrassed. He says what we had already supposed, that the ceremony is to help in locating the gorillas
and to keep the trackers safe; pressed, he says in a false,
wheedling tone that the *mungu* they are praying to is Jesus
Christ. I watch Mukesso and Matene; they stare at Kagwere,
look shy, then begin to laugh, and Kagwere is trying very
hard not to laugh himself. We laugh, too, as Alec answers
in Swahili, "Oh, come on, now, I'm no missionary!" At this
all three Mbuti laugh much harder, but they cannot change
the story now, not in front of the Bashi, who look from the
whites to the Mbuti and then back again, sullen and mysti-
fied. So Forbes-Watson asks what the ceremony meant
before the missionaries came into the forest, and the quick-
witted Kagwere says, "How could I know? I wasn't here!"
At this all three of the little men roll on the ground, and
even the two Bashi laugh, and the whites, too.

▼▼▼

The trackers point their pangas at high forest to the south,
consulting in a rapid murmur as they roll thin cigarettes
with makeshift papers. Then they set off up the mountain
in a small-stepped amble that reminds me of the Hadza
hunters of Tanzania, checking gorilla droppings, following
the gorilla paths in search of some fresh sign of feeding; a
place is marked where the gorillas have exposed a whole

large bed of small white woodland mushrooms, and these will be gathered on the return journey. Tambourine doves hurtle down the path, and from the forest all around come their long, sad, falling notes; we climb onward as a green-blue stretch of Lake Kivu comes in view, down to the east.

Mukesso stops short, he has heard limbs cracking. We hear nothing. But Mukesso is sure, and Kagwere and Matene do not doubt him; the Mbuti strike off into dense jungle, making no effort to keep down the noise, and have not gone a hundred yards when they cross the gorillas' path. The guides are nervous in this tangle, and even the trackers seem uneasy. They stop to listen every little while, ticking the vines and branch tips with their pangas to let the hidden shapes know where they are. One whistles to the others, backs away a little. There is a big dark movement in the nearest bush, only feet away. We see the branches move, glimpse shifting blackness. Then the apes are gone, and the Mbuti do not follow. This place is dangerous, we must wait a little to see which way the apes will go.

Not so long ago, we had been told, a gorilla had killed one of the Mbuti and carried the body about with it for several days, but like the story of the exotic past of the old steamboat *Lt. Col. Potopoto*, this exciting story is not true. It was a Bashi who was seriously bitten, not so long ago, when a panicked gorilla charged past him in making its escape, and this may account for the nervousness of the two guides. Most of the time Seaundori and the other guide, Rukira, are sullen and officious; no doubt they know that we don't feel we need them in the forest, for the *conservateur assistant* is not tactful with his staff, to put it mildly. To track gorillas, to hack paths through the forest is Pygmy work; since the guides carry no rifles, like true askaris, they must know that they serve no purpose here whatever. Like people all over Africa who have lost touch with the old ways, they live in mixed fear and contempt of the wild animals. Seaundori yesterday, Rukira today, were unnerved by the threat display of the great apes, although both must have observed it many times, and so, to save face, they shout a lot of senseless orders and answer questions in querulous, aggressive ways.

Eventually, though we hear nothing, Kagwere jumps quickly to his feet and heads away into the forest, hacking and clipping, with Mukesso and Matene close behind. They trace an old path for perhaps a half-mile, following it around the east face of the mountain, pausing to listen, moving on again. The creatures are now well below us, working their way slowly up the hill; the Mbuti have anticipated their route of forage, we have only to ease along the mountainside, they will come to us. And soon the Bashi, growing bored, stop ordering us about, even let us walk ahead so that we may observe the Mbutis' deadly tracking. "Real bushmen," Forbes-Watson mutters. "I love being with people like this." I do, too, there is nothing I like better.

Soon a young gorilla comes in view, climbing high into a tree. From a point a little farther on, a vast female is visible, sprawled in a comfortable crotch, in sun and shade, perhaps fifteen feet above the ground. Avoiding our stares, she stuffs big, broad leaves into her mouth and pulls a thin branch through her teeth to eat the fresh light bark.

Slowly we sink down into the foliage. Through the wind light of the canopy the sky is blue, and to the nostrils comes the pungence of crushed leaves, the fresh green damp from this morning's rain, the humus smell of the high forest. Overhead a honeyguide, a tinkerbird sing fitfully; in the thrall of apes we pay them no attention. Observing the big female as she eats, a big male leans back into the vines on the ground behind her; probably he is too heavy now to climb. And seeing his vast aura of well-being, one understands the Africans' theory that the gorilla was formerly a villager who retired into the forest in fear of work.

Young gorillas come, still curious about the forest;

they play with each other and with the trees, using their
opposed toes to brace their climbing. One juvenile lies
belly down over a branch, all four limbs dangling; he rolls
over and down, to hang by one hand in the classic pose and
scratch his armpit. He has wrinkled gray bare fingers and
gray fingernails. Briefly he roughhouses with an infant, who
flashes a little pale triangle of bare rump that I had not seen
before, and the Mbuti laugh, mopping the sweat from their
wet faces with handfuls of fresh leaves. For a time the young
ape hangs suspended by both arms like a toy gorilla; lacking
the discretion of his elders, he leers at man in a thin-lipped,
brown-toothed grimace that matches his brown eyes, those
eyes with the small pupils in a flat and shining gaze that
does not really seem to see us. The gorilla face looks cross
and wild and very sad by turns, though scientists assure us
that no primate but man is capable of emotive expression.

To sweet-scented dung, like rotted flowers, comes a
yellow butterfly; somewhere unseen the flies are buzzing,
and a tambourine dove calls. From the undergrowth come
deep contented grunts, then stomach rumblings and the
sharp crack of a branch that does not break the rhythmic
sound of the females' chewing.

Soon the last of the gorillas has swung, climbed, lolled,
chewed, cleaned its bottom, beaten its chest in those soft
tappeting thumps in different series, lowered to the ground
the bellyful of vegetation that makes gorilla legs look small
and thin, and vanished once more into the forest. We have
watched them for an hour, and we are delighted; we talk
little, for there is little to be said. On the way home the
Mbuti cut themselves packets of bark strips for making bush
rope and gather up the small white mushrooms to take
home.

▼▼▼

Deschryver had said he would come around on Thursday
evening to confirm departure plans for Friday, and when he

fails to appear, we find ourselves fretting once again, in this continual frustration about transportation; even Alec, who has stayed calm throughout all the delays and difficulties, grows a bit morose. Neither of us is used to traveling in this helpless way, entirely dependent on expensive, uncertain transport, and we vow that it will not happen again. I keep on saying hopefully that Deschryver must have got in late and is sure to turn up in the morning; now it is 9 A.M., and still he has not come. We are just looking for a car to go in search of him when he turns up at the door of the hotel. He is ready to take us to Obaye, he says, but he cannot stay, since later today he must fly government dignitaries from Goma north into the Ruwenzori. Since otherwise I shall be stranded, I have no choice but to return with him to Goma, on the first leg of my departure.

At the airport entrance, under a big sign reading TOUS POUR MOBUTU, MOBUTU POUR TOUS, a number of ragged Africans are chopping weeds. As we arrive, the airplane of the U.S. embassy is coming in, and we wonder aloud why the United States maintains consulates in such out-of-the-way corners as Bukavu and Lubumbashi, in Shaba. "There is the CIA plane," Deschryver remarks, and I ask if he shares the popular opinion that Lumumba was murdered at the instigation of the CIA, that CIA agents are merely errand boys for international big business. Deschryver shrugs as if to say, What does it matter?

Deschryver is worried about the weather, which looks heavy toward the western mountains; in this season the good flying hours are in the morning. We are airborne a little after ten, circling slowly in the single-engine plane before climbing westward toward Kahuzi and Biega. The plane will cross between these peaks, which, unlike the Virungas, are not volcanic but granitic, a part of the great central rift of Africa. The highland forest of great trees, many of them now in flower, gives way with increasing altitude to the light feathery greens of the bamboo zone;

somewhere below, hearing our motor, the gorillas may pause briefly in their chewing, though I doubt it. On the western slope, white torrents cascade steeply down into the Congo Basin, setting out on the long passage to the sea. To the north, leaning over at an extraordinary angle, a mass of granite rises out of the deep greens like a stone whale; otherwise the green extends unbroken as far out to the west as the eye can see. This is the Maniema Forest, a stronghold of cannibalism until after World War II, when measures such as execution may or may not have put the practice to a stop.

At lower altitudes a few Bantu huts appear; penetration of the forest here, Deschryver says, is very recent. He picks up the road that crosses the mountains and follows it north and west toward Walikale, less for purposes of navigation than because it is the only place to land in case of trouble. "Otherwise you are finished," he remarks, gazing out over the green expanse and making a cutoff motion with his hand. He points down at the small village of Hombo where several years ago, in the company of Lee Lyon, he had bought a snared *paon de Congo* for about two dollars. "They sold it to us like a chicken. I gave it to the international research station at Bukavu, but it died."

In 1949, as a young boy, Deschryver was brought by his Belgian parents to Bukavu. He was always interested in animals, he says, and after he completed school, he became a professional hunter—a very good one, it is said. But perhaps because of his training with James Chapin, he remained concerned with conservation, and in 1965 he requested that his hunting block at Kahuzi-Biega be made a national park; this was finally done in 1975. Though a few elephants still occur there, his main concern was for the gorillas, which were being killed by Africans for food. The gorilla's range extends into these lowlands, and in 1975, at Deschryver's urging, the boundaries of Kahuzi-Biega were considerably enlarged; the park now extends all the way

west to Utu and to Uku, in a vast tract that includes much
of the known range of the Congo peacock. Meanwhile, Deschryver has been featured in two television films on the
gorillas, both widely distributed in the United States and
Europe.

In 1967, at the time of the *Vita ya Schramm,* Deschryver
was forced to leave the country. When he returned about
six months later, his house and property had been destroyed. "I lost everything," he says, "everything," and as
he speaks, that sad and bitter mask tightens his face.

Deschryver had been acquainted with Jacques
Schramm, who had a coffee plantation in this region before
he became a mercenary, but Schramm had never been a
friend. "He wasn't doing what he did only for money,"
Deschryver remarked suddenly, after a silence; he made a
forward pushing movement with his clenched fist. "No, he
was *hard*!" He nodded. "He was too hard." Yes, he had
heard that Schramm was still a mercenary in southern
Africa—he shrugs again. "Who knows where that man is?
He just disappeared."

▼▼▼

The airplane crosses the brown Lua River. The lone road
has degenerated to a thin brown track with a grass strip
down the middle, a sign that vehicles are very few—we have
not seen one. A brown scar in the forest to the north,
surrounded by thin, isolated smokes, is Walikale. Here the
Lua flows into the Loa, and the land is flat, for the white
rapids of the highlands have disappeared. "The Loa is full
of crocodiles," remarks Deschryver, coming as close as he
ever comes to satisfaction. Not far to the west of Walikale
the Loa will join the upper Lualaba, once called the Congo.

Under the plane the forest is primeval, without a sign
of track or hut or smoke, green green green green as a
green ocean, with here and there a glint of river under the
islets of white cloud. The jungle stretches away under the

leaden sky two thousand miles to the South Atlantic and beyond, along the Gulf of Guinea, to the westernmost African rain forest in Guinea.

The strip at Obaye is no more than a minute tear in this green fabric. It is already in view when Deschryver says, "I don't know whether my calculations are right or not, but Obaye should be just here." Soon he is circling the strip, and he makes a false landing to clear it of Africans, who are already running in from all directions. The roar scares up a number of big white-thighed hornbills that sail away among the strange umbrella trees, *musanga* (almost identical in appearance to a South American forest tree of an entirely different family and therefore a remarkable botanical example of the phenomenon called parallel evolution).

The smiling people at the airstrip are Banianga, who as recently as twenty years ago were famous cannibals, selling off their excess captives to like-minded tribes; they practice the shifting cultivation of those early Bantu who came down out of Cameroon in the first centuries A.D. Standing tall among them is a big white man with glasses and neglected teeth who has been out here since the cannibal days as manager of the tin mines for Sominki. Victor Delcourt is surprised to hear of the quest for the *paon de Congo*. "Why, I have *eaten* it!" he exclaims. "Very good, too!" Yes, but has he seen it in the wild? "*B'en oui! Je l'ai tué moi-même!*" Twenty years ago he had seen one by the roadside, stopped his truck, and shot it. There seems no reason to doubt a man so innocent of his own accomplishment.

I leave Sarah and Alec in the hands of the only white man ever known to have seen, killed, and eaten *Afropavo*. We part with regret, for we have got on very well; there is talk already of another expedition, perhaps to one of the three avian regions left in Africa that Alec does not know. But since all three—Namibia, Angola, Ethiopia—are presently in a state of war, it is hard to imagine when this expedition might take place.

Deschryver is anxious about the weather; it is time to go. When the plane takes off again, the children run behind it, down the airstrip, and the big hornbills with white patches on their wings rise once again to flap and sail to far umbrella trees.

On the eastward flight Deschryver opens up a little and even speaks out once or twice of his own accord; when he chooses, he has a pleasant smile and a good laugh. But heavy weather is closing in behind us, and by midday, as Adrien had predicted, the weather has changed suddenly for the worse. Due to rising heat and moisture—the transpiration of this vast expanse of humid jungle—the rain clouds build up steadily all morning, and now they are bursting all around us, as rain comes in a hard patter on the windshield. Deschryver, frowning, forced off course, feels his way around the thunderheads, emerging finally well south of his intended route, at the northern boundary of the Kahuzi-Biega Park. A beautiful waterfall comes and goes in a mist of gray and green, and then we see that enormous rock, like a leaning tower, that we had passed on its south side on the trip west. "We are near Wagongo," Deschryver says, and he points to the heavy cloud mass not far south that shrouds Kahuzi. "If I flew there"—and once again he makes that cutting gesture with his hand—"then we are finished. When pilots get lost out here, that's it. So it's very good that I know just where I am." At Goma we would learn that due to weather his charter to the Ruwenzori had been canceled; we might as well have stayed there at Obaye.

The plane drifts along the western shore of Kivu, with its beautiful islets and sheltered coves hidden by the green steep walls of drowned volcanoes. The water turns in patterns of pure blues, deep, dark, and pale—whether cloud shadow or sign of depth it is hard to tell. Already wind streaks gather in the silver sheen that will form into gray chop this afternoon. At the north end of Kivu, where in 1912 broad coulees of lava boiled the lake, small craters guard the shore, and one of these is far out in the water, forming an emblematic U just off the mouth of a hidden harbor. Nyiragongo comes in view, a dim shadow in the heavy weather that is closing off the north, a specter of the fire mountains, quite unreal, and once again I am struck by the great beauty of this heartland of a continent, exclaiming aloud that it must be one of the loveliest regions in all Africa. Deschryver nods, as if this fact were tragic; despite his Zairian wife and children, he is not permitted to become a citizen. I ask if he intends to spend his life here. "Why not?" he says, turning to look me squarely in the face for the first time since I have known him. "What else am I to do?" (He died in 1989, still in his forties.)

A few weeks later I received a letter sent from Paris by Sarah Plimpton. George had joined them, and although they had not actually seen the Congo peacock, they believed they had heard the *gowé-gowah* that Chapin had recorded. According to Charles Cordier the cock calls loudly in the night—*ko-ko-wa!*—to which the hen responds—*hi-ho, hi-ho*.

PYGMIES AND PYGMY ELEPHANTS: THE CONGO BASIN
(1986)

 On the last evening of 1985, the all-but-empty flight from Dakar-Monrovia-Lagos to Nairobi is crossing the lightless forests of the Congo Basin, passing at midnight over the Central African highlands of the Zaire-Rwanda border, where the earth's last bands of mountain gorillas sleep in their nests. Down there in the dark, the outraged Africans who are thought to have murdered the gorilla researcher Dian Fossey are still in hiding; Fossey is being buried there this very evening. On the screen is a South African movie, *The Gods Must Be Crazy*, a simple-hearted tale (though politically disingenuous, with its slapstick guerrilla squad of foolish blacks led by a caricatured Cuban). It's easy to follow without the soundtrack, and I especially enjoy the wistful grace of the Kung Bushman, whom I knew as Komsai seven years ago when his band was living in Botswana's Tsodilo Hills. Komsai had worked in South Africa's mines, he spoke the South African lingua franca called Funhalarou, and perhaps this is why he was chosen for this movie. When I crossed

his path, he had gone back to the Kalahari and he was a
hunter, with a newly killed eland in his camp, and the huge
fresh lyre horns of a kudu bull, both taken with his bow and
poison arrows. Somewhere I have heard that since partici-
pating in the film, Komsai has died; perhaps this is not true,
perhaps the gods are not crazy after all.

At 2 A.M. in the new year, I am met in Nairobi by the
savanna ecologist David Western, a husky, trim, and well-
kept Kenyan citizen of forty-two. Dr. Western is the resource ecologist for the New York Zoological Society, best
known for its Bronx Zoo and New York Aquarium; he is also
pilot of the NYZS aircraft in which we shall embark the day
after tomorrow on a survey of the rain forests of Central
Africa, paying special attention to the numbers and distri-
bution of the small forest elephant, which may be seriously
threatened by the ivory trade. As Dr. Western—known
since a small boy as Jonah—wrote me in a letter last September, "We still know remarkably little about either the
forest elephant, which now accounts for sixty per cent of
the ivory leaving Africa, or the Congo Basin, an area including about twenty per cent of the world's tropical equatorial
forests. The forest elephant is something of an enigma, and
reason enough for the entire trip."

The African elephant, *Loxodonta africana,* has been seriously imperiled by ivory hunters; recent analyses of market
tusks show that the poaching gangs, having reduced the
savanna or bush elephant, *Loxodonta africana africana*, to less
than a half million animals, are increasingly concentrating
on the much smaller forest race, *L. a. cyclotis.* Unlike *L.a.
africana,* which is easy to census by light plane, *cyclotis*
spends most of the daylight hours hidden in the forest, and
estimates of its numbers have been mainly speculative.
Proponents of the ivory trade maintain that the forest canopy hides very large numbers of small elephants, while
ecologists fear that in this inhospitable habitat the numbers
have always been low. It is generally agreed that an African

elephant population of two million or more animals could probably sustain the present slaughter for the ivory trade, which until very recently, at least, has produced about seven hundred and fifty tons each year. However, computer analyses indicate that if fewer than a million elephants are left, as many authorities believe, then the species is already in a precipitous decline in which half the remaining animals will be lost in the next decade. The future of *Loxodonta* may depend, in short, on an accurate estimate of the numbers of the forest race, which would lay the foundation for a strong international conservation effort on behalf of the species as a whole.

"There will be a large gap in our understanding of the forest elephant until we understand the forest better," Western's letter said. "That is one of the purposes of this survey. The truth is, we know very little about forest ecology. Only in recent years, with the realization of how rapidly the rain forests, with their great abundance and variety of life, are disappearing, especially in South America and southeast Asia, have we come to realize that the forest is a very important biome that cannot be ignored by anyone committed to conservation and the future of the earth. Because of its inaccessibility and low human population, the Congo Basin is still largely intact, but there is no reason for confidence that it will stay that way."

As for me, I am interested in both the forest and the forest elephant, and I enjoy the company of biologists, who teach me a great deal that I wish to know about the origins and structure and relationships of the natural world, which have filled me with awe and fascination all my life. Throughout our journey we shall be working with ecologists already in the field, and an elephant biologist will meet us in Central Africa and accompany us throughout the first part of the journey. Later we shall accompany okapi biologists and Mbuti Pygmy hunters into the Ituri Forest of Zaire.

Since our main destinations will be wilderness regions of the Central African Republic, Gabon, and Zaire, we will travel nearly seven thousand miles, from Nairobi, in Kenya, to Libreville, on Gabon's Atlantic coast, and back again. So far as Dr. Western knows, this transcontinental forest journey has never before been made in a light plane, but the feat interests us much less than the discoveries we might make along the way. With luck, for example, we shall learn more about the mysterious "pygmy elephant" in C.A.R. and Gabon, widely reported for almost a hundred years. With the exception of the mokele mbembe, an elusive dinosaurlike denizen of the vast swamps of the Congo Basin, the pygmy elephant, *Loxodonta pumilio,* is regarded as the last large "unknown" animal in Africa. In a forest of such size and inaccessibility, it would be unwise to dismiss the pygmy elephant out of hand; the gorilla was reported for nearly a century before its existence was scientifically accepted, and the okapi, a large forest relative of the giraffe, eluded detection entirely until 1908.

▼▼▼

Dr. Western and his wife, Dr. Shirley Strum, the distinguished social anthropologist and student of the baboon, have a new baby and a new house that faces across the Mbagathi River, which forms the boundary between the Nairobi National Park and the Kapiti Plain, in Masai Land. Driving out the Langata Road, passing the demolished car of a New Year's celebrant, Jonah assured me that early in the morning I might see black rhino from his guest-room window.

Calls of the ring-neck and red-eyed doves reminded me as I awoke that I was once again in Africa. Now it is sunrise, and I see no rhino, but there are eland, impala, and giraffe, and a small herd of buffalo on the thorn landscape, still green and fresh after December's short rains.

The bureaucracy in the new Kenya is under stern instruction from President Daniel arap Moi to serve the people rather than abuse them, as has been the popular custom on this continent, and preparations for our air safari go quite smoothly. But this morning the Directorate of Civil Aviation was down to a single airport clearance form, though six were needed, and all the copiers in the ministry were out of service, and by the time we filled out the long form and took it downtown to be copied, and completed the strict airport preparations and procedures, and passed through customs, it was already two in the afternoon, with a long flight across Kenya and Uganda into northern Zaire to be made by nightfall.

The New York Zoological Society's aircraft is a single-engine Cessna 206, which normally can go six hours without refueling. It has been specially fitted with a cargo pod and extra gas drums to give us a range of fourteen hours, very critical in the vast reaches of Central Africa where sources of fuel are few and undependable. This heavy-duty blue-and-silver plane is the sole survivor of a group of three that were formerly attached to the European Economic Community's Jonglei Canal Project, designed to bypass the Great Sudd of the south Sudan and carry Nile water more efficiently to the Muslim north. The southern tribesmen—Nilotic pastoralists of the Nuer and Dinka tribes—dispute what they see as continuing Muslim aggression at their expense. In recent years, the spear-carrying "rebels" have been supplied with modern arms by Ethiopia, and not long ago they blew up two of the Jonglei planes. The remaining one was sold to the NYZS. Its former pilot, a Kenyan citizen named Gwynn Morsen, was held hostage by the rebels for more than a year. "Spent most of my time thinking up ways to strike back," he told us this morning at Wilson airport, "and I think I've settled on a plague of rinderpest. Can't infect them with cholera or human plagues because they have all that already, so I'll hit them where it *really* hurts—their cattle!" Two years ago, when Jonah and I first discussed this journey, we planned to look at the great herds of kob antelope on Sudan's Boma Plateau, and the beautiful small park on the White Nile at Nimule where I first saw white rhino in 1961; but now one cannot land safely there, nor in Uganda, so pervasive are the civil wars on this sad continent.

"You're leaving too late," Shirley remarks when she comes to see us off, and we both know this, but by now we are frustrated, anxious to get going. Jonah, an experienced bush pilot of thirteen years' experience, reckons that we will still reach the airstrip in Zaire's Garamba Park before dark. There we will refuel the aircraft from our spare fuel drums and spend a day with Kes and Fraser Smith, who are studying the last northern white rhinos. The following day we will head west to our first destination in the Central African Republic.

Leaving Nairobi, the plane turns northwest across Kikuyu Land and the Rift escarpment, heading up the great Rift Valley between the Mau Range and the Aberdares. As it crosses Lake Naivasha, I peer down upon the bright white heads of fish eagles and a shimmering white string of pelicans; off the white soda shores of Lake Nakuru is a large pink crescent made by thousands upon thousands of flamingos. Then we are crossing the equator, droning northwestward over the Kakamega Forest, the easternmost outpost of the equatorial rain forests that extend all the way into West Africa. Off to the north rises Mount Elgon, on the Uganda border, as a great migratory flight of European storks passes south beneath the plane, on their way, perhaps, to winter range in the Serengeti.

The high winds of the new monsoon, blowing out of Chad and the Sudan, have shrouded the rich farmlands of Uganda in a haze of dust. The sun looms, disappears again, behind bruised clouds that are thickened by the smoke of fires in this burning land. The rebel forces of Yoweri Museveni might bring peace and stability to this bloodied

country—in early January of 1986 still under the control of
the violent soldiery of the beleaguered Milton Obote, who
is now known to have presided over the tribal slaughter of
even more thousands of his countrymen than did his prede-
cessor, Idi Amin. (Even among African countries, Uganda
seems unusually beset by bloody-minded tyrants, who were
already ruling when the first explorers came up the Nile; in
the days of Henry Morton Stanley, the despotic ruler was
a man named Mwanga, for whom Idi Amin named his son.)
The long red roads are strangely empty of all vehicles, for
the countryside below, so green and peaceful in appearance, is in a state of utter anarchy and fear, with all communications broken down and the hated, vengeful army of the
latest tyrant in retreat across the land, looting and killing.

The broad morass of lakes and swamps called Lake
Kyoga, with its primitive island villages, is utterly roadless
and indeterminate in configuration, like some labyrinthine
swamp of ancient myth, there are no landmarks for calculat-
ing a precise heading, and the monsoon wind carries us just
far enough off course so that we pass east of the Victoria
Nile, which we had intended to follow down as far as Murchison Falls. By the time we correct our course, we must
backtrack across the Albert Nile to the Victoria, following
whitewater rapids to the extraordinary chute where the torrent hurtles through a narrow chasm and plunges into the
broad hippo pool below. Twenty-five years ago, when I first
came here, hitchhiking south from the Sudan into East
Africa, this park (renamed Kabalega but now Murchison
again) was famous all over the world for its legions of great-
tusked elephants and other animals. Today most of the
animals are gone, cut down by the automatic guns of ma-
rauding armies, including the Tanzanian forces that helped
to depose Idi Amin. In February of 1961, this pool was
fairly awash with hippopotami; now there is not a single
hippo to be seen. The park's twelve thousand elephants are
now three hundred. We see none. The only animals in view

are a few kob antelope that scatter wildly at the coming of the plane. The booming white falls of the Victoria Nile, descending from Lake Kyoga, thunder undiminished in an empty and silent land.

From Murchison Falls, we take our final bearing for Garamba. The day is late, the skies in all directions dark with haze and smoke, as we set out across northeastern Zaire. Air charts of Zaire are out of date, therefore misleading, and Jonah, frustrated, must resort to my small relief map for his navigation. On this large-scale map, in the poor light, we confuse the town of Arua, on the Uganda side, with Aru in Zaire, so that none of the scarce roads and landmarks seem to fit, and the light fails nearly an hour earlier than expected as the sun sinks behind a dark shroud of smoke and desert haze off to the west. We are now disoriented, with only a very rough idea of our location. Small clusters of huts below, in the old fields and broken forest of rough hill country, are already dimming in the shadow of the night, and suddenly we know without discussion that we will not arrive this evening at Garamba, that even a forced landing in rough country is much better than finding ourselves in the pitch dark with no place to come down. (Not all pilots, as he told me later, feel confident about landing in the bush, and some tend to hesitate until the light is so far gone that *any* landing becomes very dangerous.)

The dirt roads are narrow and deeply rutted, and we must choose quickly among rough shrubby fields. Jonah banks for a quick approach, and slows the plane to stalling speed. Because coarse high grass hides the ground, and the field is small, he is forced to touch down quickly. Nose high, we settle into the stiff grass. The plane strikes the bricklike laterite with a hard bounce and hurtles through bushes with a fearful whacking of stiff branches against metal. Missing the hidden termite hills and ditches, it suffers no worse than a few dents in the tail planes.

To make such a wild landing without mishap is exhilarating, and I congratulate Jonah on his skill, grateful to be wherever the hell we are still in one piece. All we have to do, I say to cheer him, is refuel the wing tanks, lay out our bedrolls, and be off again at dawn. But this is the first time in thirteen years as a bush pilot that Jonah has been lost at nightfall and forced down, and though he is calm, with scarcely a blond hair out of place, he is not happy. As a man who neither drinks nor smokes and is before all orderly and neat, he takes pride in his preparations and efficiency, and he has not yet figured out where things went wrong. "Getting off again, Peter, may be quite another matter," he says stiffly, descending from the plane and staring about him, hands on hips.

From every direction, Africans come streaming across the country; we had seen some running toward the scene even before the airplane touched down. Within minutes, they surround the plane in a wide circle, and a few come forward, offering long, limp, cool, callused hands. They touch the wings, then turn to look at us again, eyes shining. Everyone is scared and friendly—the children run away each time we move, women smile and curtsy. "It is like an apparition to them," one young man tells me gently, in poor French, there by separating himself discreetly from these hill peasants who have never seen an airplane before.

Many of these Bantu folk of the northeastern region known as Haut-Zaïre (Upper Zaire) have some French or Swahili, and so we are able to converse freely, and a good thing, too. The first group of several dozen shy onlookers has swelled quickly to a noisy crowd of hundreds—at least seven or eight hundred, by the end—all of them growing more and more excited in that volatile African way that can lead very quickly to irredeemable gestures, and sometimes violence. Politely but firmly, our well-wishers warn us to move away into the dark, to let the people calm themselves a little. We are told that we have landed near the village of

Dibwa, and soon the village headman, who is drunk, asserts his authority by demanding to see identification. An ad hoc committee, heads together, draws our passport numbers on a scrap of paper amidst random officious shouts and cries of suspicion and bewilderment.

In 1903, when the first Baptist missionaries penetrated this huge region west of the Nile—said to have been the last region without whites in the whole Dark Continent—it was known to other Africans as "the Land of the Flesh-Eaters," due to the rampant cannibalism of its inhabitants, and the reputation of these local Azande people (of northeast Zaire, southwest Sudan, and southeast Chad) has not improved much since that time. After the Belgian Congo achieved independence (became Zaire in 1960), there began a six-year struggle for power, and Haut-Zaïre was pillaged by waves of undisciplined soldiery, guerrilla bands—the Simba rebels—and South African and Rhodesian merce-naries. Because of this recent memory of bloodshed and famine, and because Zaire is surrounded by unstable, often hostile African states, the Zairois are highly suspicious of unidentified white foreigners. But as in most Africans, their excitability is offset by a great courtesy and gentleness, and we were treated well by almost everyone in this remote community.

Now it is dark, but the people do not disperse. Increas-ingly it becomes clear that we will not be permitted to sleep here at the plane, that we are, in fact, to be taken into custody. "After all," my confidant explains, when I protest, "our people are very simple, they do not know why you have come here suddenly like this, or what you will do during the night." I look over at Jonah, who is getting the same message in Swahili. Having no choice, we agree to be escorted to the nearest hut, a quarter mile away, where in a yard swept bare as a defense against night snakes, granary rodents, and mosquitoes, a fire is built and well-made chairs of wood and hide provided.

"We *have* to keep you here, we *have* to report you!" the headman explains, somewhat mollified now that we have decided to come peaceably. We sit surrounded by admirers, who wish to hear our story over and over. Soon we are shown inside the hut, where cane mats have been spread for us on the earth floor. "This is not what you are used to," one man suggests shyly, not quite sure of this, and eager to inquire about our customs. Two men ask to borrow my flashlight and have yet to bring it back when, still in good spirits, I close my eyes.

▼▼▼

Toward midnight we were woken up and led outside. Someone had run across the country to fetch some sort of district secretary, and we gathered once more at the fire. Once again we produced our passports and told our story, which was duly recorded. The secretary had walked here from six miles away to gather this information. "I have done it for the security and welfare of my people," he informed us.

Another herald had been sent by bicycle to the town of Aru, almost twenty miles away, to notify the district commissioner, who arrived in a van with his aides and soldiery about one-thirty in the morning. This time a gendarme in green uniform banged into the hut, shouting abusively, shoving Jonah, and loosening his belt, as if in eagerness to whip us along faster, Outside, the calm, cold-faced commissioner had already been seated, and the foreigners were led to two chairs placed directly in front of him. Once again we showed our passports and accounted for ourselves, but this time the passports were not given back. Though we said we wished to stay nearby, to watch the plane, the commissioner informed us that a soldier would be assigned to guard it, and that we were to be taken back to Aru.

Under armed escort, we were marched across the fields toward the road. Without my flashlight, I could not see the hard-baked ground; I made a fatal misstep at the edge of a ditch, and tore my ankle. I fell to the hard earth with a mighty curse, aware that at the very outset of this trip, which would involve a lot of forest walking, I had resprained an ankle already injured in cross-country skiing. The pain was so violent that I did not notice the safari ants that everyone else was slapping: I simply hobbled ahead while I still could, gasping in anger and shock. Not until I was inside the van, seated opposite a sullen African with a machine pistol and another with two carbines, did I feel the *siafu* attacking me under my pants. I dealt with them all the way down the rough road to Aru.

Beside me, Jonah seemed as stunned as I, and we did not speak. Jolting along in the dead of night, with no idea what was coming next, there was little to say. With each new development, our predicament seemed to be worsening. We had no clearance for landing in this region, only at Kinshasa, where we were scheduled to arrive a few weeks later, and Zaire, with its reputation for violence and corruption (it is sometimes referred to as a "kleptocracy"), was no place to have one's papers not in order. Also, an investigation might identify me as the author of an article about a previous visit, a few years before, in which I was sharply critical of Zaire's puppet dictator—reason enough in this feverish climate to be arrested as an enemy of the state, if not a suspected mercenary or spy.

Twenty-five years ago to the very month, scarcely a hundred miles east of this place, on the Sudan border, I had also been in custody, under much worse circumstances (the murder of Zaire's prime minister, Patrice Lumumba, in January of 1961, had inflamed Africa, turning Sudanese friends into fierce enemies), and I had no wish to repeat any such experience.

In Aru, to our great astonishment we were not locked up—we could go nowhere, after all, without passports or airplane—but were dropped off almost casually at the quarters of a British pilot for the United Nations' High Commission for Refugees, which is kept very busy in this part of the world. Our host, routed out at 3 A.M., kindly showed us where we might lie down, observing in passing that Zaire was paranoid these days about "mercenaries," which has been a dread word in this country since the anarchy and massacres of the 1960s. Rumors had implicated Zairois soldiers when seven French whitewater boatmen who had entered the country without permission disappeared on the Zaire River a few months ago. The government revealed that they had perished in the rapids, though their boats were found intact and right side up, and the one body that turned up had been beheaded.

The pilot was flying to Nairobi at daylight, now two hours away, and Jonah, fearing that our friends at Garamba might radio an alarm when we failed to appear, sent off a message to his neighbor Philip Leakey to notify his wife that we were fine.

At 8 A.M., the pilot's Ugandan assistant drove us around to the district commissioner's house to inquire about our passports. We were referred to the chief of immigration, who referred us to the chief of police, who said he had reported our arrival to his superiors in the regional capital at Bunia and could not return our passports without their permission. Surely Bunia would decide to check our identities at Kinshasa, and, since it was Saturday, it now appeared that we might be detained here through the weekend.

Meanwhile, the authorities had no objection if Dr. Western brought his airplane to Aru; they assumed that he would not vanish, leaving me and his passport behind. As Jonah wished to take off with an empty plane, the obliging police chief returned with him to Dibwa, where the people were ordered to chop brush, knock down termite hills, and fill up ditches while the plane's extra fuel and other cargo were unloaded for ground transport to the strip at Aru. As

it turned out, the pair who had absconded with my flashlight the night before had used it to off-load all they could
find in the unlocked cargo pod under the fuselage, including three jerry cans of fuel, a computer printer destined for
Garamba, and a duffel containing all my clothes and personal belongings. The duffel, minus some of its original
contents—toilet kit, malaria pills, spare flashlight, sneakers,
sweater, hat, and every pair of socks and underwear—was
retrieved eventually, but the fuel and the printer were gone
for good.

Jonah made a skillful downhill takeoff and followed the
road into Aru. By the time he arrived there, word had come
to let us go. (Apparently Bunia had learned from Kinshasa
that our visit was expected by the minister of national
parks.) By early afternoon, we were in the air again, and
headed north.

▼▼▼

Nagero, on the Dungu River, forms the southern boundary
of Garamba National Park. At its small airstrip, we were met
by Alison (Kes) Smith, a pretty woman in her thirties with
dark red hair. Dr. Smith, born in England and now a Kenyan citizen, is the biologist on the Garamba Northern White
Rhino Project, which is funded by various conservation
groups and private donors. Her husband, Fraser Smith, is
in charge of restoring to good operating order the logistical
system of Garamba, which was the first of Zaire's parks,
established by the colonial authorities in 1938. Accompanied by their infant daughter, the Smiths escorted us in the
afternoon to the flat rocks by the hippo pool where they had
been married just a year before in a roaring and blaring
serenade from these hundred hippos. The silver limbs of
the dead tree across the Dungu were decked with a winged
red inflorescence made by companies of carmine bee-
eaters, which, with their blue heads, cobalt rumps, and long
streaming tails, are among the most splendid of African

birds. With them were some smaller, only slightly less spectacular red-throated bee-eaters, and by its nest on a high
tree sat a thickset white bird, the palm-nut vulture. Already
we were far enough west so that endemic bird species of
East and West Africa were overlapping; I had last seen this
peculiar bird in Senegal.

Fraser Smith had constructed a small house on the
banks of the Dungu, and the household presently included
a large dog (a second dog had been taken by a crocodile),
two cats, and a banded mongoose, which had enjoyed the
run of the camp before taking up a habit of attacking people; its victims included its mistress, severely bitten twice.
Since Dr. Smith had mentioned its bad character, I was
unpleasantly surprised to see the snout and beady eyes of
this large weasel relative appear beneath the wood stockade
of the outdoor shower into which I had limped just before
dusk. There was no mistaking the intent of its opened
mouth, which was to bite me as speedily as possible, and
sure enough it whisked into the shower and nipped my heel
before I could take defensive action.

As anyone knows who recalls Kipling's Rikki-tikki-tavi,
a mongoose is much too quick for any cobra, let alone a
crippled man in a cramped shower slippery with soap. With
my inflamed and swollen ankle, I was already a bit rickety
on the wet uneven bricks, and this evil-tempered viverrid,
renewing its attack, had me at enormous disadvantage.
Jonah and Fraser were away from camp, refueling the airplane, so I called to Dr. Smith, more or less calmly, that she
could find her mongoose near the shower. She had meant
to take "Goose" for a walk, she said, and commenced to call
it. The mongoose ignored her, darting in and out of sight
under the stockade. I flicked hot water at it and made fright-
ful growling noises, all to no avail; it backed out of view,
came in swiftly from another angle, and sank its teeth into
my toe, eliciting a sharp cry of vexation. "Is Goose biting
you?" his mistress called. "So sorry!" It seemed that she

was nursing her baby, but would come and fetch the mongoose in a minute.

For the nonce, I seized up a steel bucket and banged it down in front of my tormentor. This drove him back a little but did not deter him. Hopping mad, he dug furiously at the sandy earth—what field biologists call displacement activity, in which strong emotions are vented inappropriately. My toe was bleeding, my ankle hurt, and I, too, was full of strong emotion. Though loath to execute a household pet by bashing its brains out with my bucket, I was considering this last resort when it darted out of sight, made a flanking maneuver, and shot in again from yet another angle, affixing itself to the top of my left foot with a terrific bite. There it remained until I kicked it free, emitting a wild oath of rage and pain.

Perhaps afraid for her pet's life, my hostess appeared almost at once, joining me in the shower without warning. On the soapy floor, her legs flew out from under her, and she landed on her bottom, careening into the stockade as the mongoose disappeared beneath. Looking up, soaked by the shower, she found herself confronted by the nudity of her amazed guest, covered a bit late by the bucket. "Sorry," she said, starting to laugh, and I laughed, too. "I have no secrets," I said, groping for a towel. "Just remove that mongoose." I pointed sternly at my bloody foot. And with suspicious speed, or so it seemed to me—as if, in this camp, an emergency mongoose-bite repair kit was ever at the ready—Dr. Smith was back at the shower door with bandages and disinfectants. "Sorry," she said. "Better take care of that. Might turn septic quickly in this climate."

The mongoose episode occurred exactly twenty-four hours after the forced landing at Dibwa, and considering all that had taken place so early in our journey, I felt the need of a stiff whiskey, in which Kes joined me. I asked her first of all to explain her nickname (it's from "Kesenyonye," or "Live in Peace," a name given her by Masai tribesmen when she and her first husband, Chris Hillman, who was working on an eland study, lived in Masai Land south of the Ngong Hills) and, second, for details of the white rhino project— specifically, why she felt so strongly that such a large international effort should be expended in a probably doomed attempt to save the last seventeen animals of the northern race, when the very similar southern race is well protected, and the species as a whole not currently in danger.

Among all land mammals on earth, white (from the German *"weit,"* or wide-mouthed) rhinos are second only to elephants in size. Dr. Smith pointed out that the southern white rhino (the originally described race, *Ceratotherium simum simum*) was already endangered by the turn of the century and virtually exterminated in the 1920s by South African hunters; it was reduced to a remnant hundred animals before its protection was seriously begun. This number has now been increased to approximately three thousand, most of them in South Africa's national parks; white rhinos have also been reintroduced in Botswana, Zimbabwe, and Mozambique (though it seems unlikely that the Mozambique animals have survived that country's wars). This recovery lends at least faint hope for the recovery of the northern race, which is worth saving not only for itself but as a symbol of the conservation effort. (By spring 1989, the population has increased to twenty-two animals.)

The northern white rhinoceros was originally found in far northwest Uganda and northeast Zaire, the southern savannas of Sudan and Chad, and the Central African Republic, throughout suitable habitat north of the rain forest and west of the River Nile. In 1938, when Garamba was established, several hundred rhino were located by surveys, which until recent years have all been made on foot. By 1961, when I first saw these huge placid animals in the small park at Nimule, in the Sudan, an estimated one thousand to thirteen hundred white rhino were living in Garamba.

Not long thereafter, the Simba rebels, protesting the murder of Lumumba and the ascendance of a pro-European regime, took control of most of Haute-Zaïre, including the Garamba Park. In the next few years the Simbas slaughtered ninety percent of the white rhinos solely for their horn, the proceeds from which were used for the purchase of more weapons. In 1969, parks control was restored, but by 1977, when the rhino's numbers had increased to about five hundred, lack of government funding and logistical breakdown had removed all protection from the park's animals, which were now attacked more or less at will by organized poaching gangs from Uganda and Sudan, armed with automatic weapons from both countries' wars. By 1981, just thirty-six animals remained, and a survey two years later would locate less than twenty. The Garamba population has not increased in the years since, and everywhere else the northern race has probably been exterminated. The few lone animals that may still wander the empty eastern reaches of the Central African Republic will die without contributing to the population, since any meaningful increase in this remnant group would have to be achieved quickly, before the gene pool and breeding potential are further reduced by scattering, accident, or senility.

As the one certain defense against poaching, removal of these sixteen animals to a safer area has been considered, but there is no other safe, suitable habitat in Zaire, whose president-for-life Mobutu Sese Soko has decreed that these "Zairian" rhinos shall not leave his country. Instead he has promised help to the rhino project that has not been forthcoming. For the several months prior to our visit, Garamba's faithful guards and rangers had not been paid; they grew gardens by their huts in order to survive.

The Garamba rhinos might conceivably be protected in a small fenced area, but there are no funds for such confinement, which would introduce a whole new set of problems. As a last resort, they could be transferred to a zoo. Mark Stanley Price, a young biologist we spoke with in Nairobi, was involved in a successful program to restore a captive population of the white Arabian oryx to the Oman deserts. On the evidence of successful zoo propagation of the southern white rhino—there are now two hundred in world zoos—he does not doubt that these northern animals could also be raised successfully in captivity and thereby "saved." But reintroduction—a far more lengthy, expensive, and complicated process than mere release—is quite another matter. Even if a safe and suitable habitat still awaited them, the slow-breeding animals are huge and difficult to manage, and the ultimate irony might be that new veterinary regulations or new laws against international transport of wild animals might forbid the return of the saved species to its own environment.

▼▼▼

Kes Smith, whose own plane was out of commission, was anxious to go on an air survey of Garamba, which she had been unable to make in several months. In the early morning, before breakfast, we flew north with Jonah across a vast plain of savanna grassland, already browning in the dry season, interspersed with shining, languid rivers. In the grassland stand large isolated trees—mostly the sausage tree, *Kigelia*. The more permanent watercourses are enclosed by gallery forest—sometimes called "finger forest," because it penetrates deep into the savanna in long fingerlike extensions of the rain forest that lies farther to the south. The rich green strands, which shelter many forest animals and birds, are set off by lovely lavender leaves of a combretum liana that here and there climbs to the canopy.

In comparison with the East African savanna, which has many medium-size animals, including zebra and antelopes, both large and small, this northern grassland has very few, a discrepancy mainly attributable to climate.

Equatorial East Africa has two rainy seasons of about three months each, with corresponding dry seasons in which herbivores can crop back the new grasses, whereas in this northern savanna, with its mixed woodland, a single long rainy season produces and sustains a high, rank, thick-stemmed grass ten to fifteen feet tall. Such grass cannot support herds of small herbivores, being not only unpalatable but too coarse to be managed except by large browsers with big guts; there are no zebra, and the few antelope species resort to flood-plain grasses and burned ground.

Human beings and domestic animals, or the lack of them, are also factors. In East Africa, the pastoralists, with their diet of blood and milk, can encourage calving in the rainy season and still have milk throughout the dry, whereas in this region, calves born in the long rains are weaned off long before the dry season, which is harsh and long. Thus, the Sudanic pastoralists such as the Nuer and the Dinka must eke out their milk diet with sorghum and millet and savanna game, or "bush meat." Farther west, in these woodland savannas, the presence of tsetse is inimical to livestock, and the use of bush meat is much heavier, with a corresponding wildlife decline. Especially in West Africa, where the savanna belt between rain forest and the near-desert known as the Sahel is very narrow, and the human population very high, the need for animal protein has all but eliminated the wild animals.

On the flood plain are fair numbers of antelope—tiang, kob, and waterbuck—together with buffalo and warthog and a few small herds of elephant. The Congo giraffe is also here though we do not see it. Kob and buffalo are by far the most common animals, and large black herds of buffalo may be seen along most of the many streams that flow south to the Garamba River.

The northern region of the park, which adjoins the meaningless Lantoto Park in Sudan, is rocky and hilly country, with only a small animal population, vulnerable to poachers. Unlike elephants, which are wide-ranging, rhinos are sedentary and are very easily tracked and killed, and the horn can be bashed off with a stone in a few minutes. Ivory poaching, on the other hand, is always risky and considerably more difficult and requires an efficient organization, since time is required to remove the tusks from a fresh carcass, and tusks are heavy to transport through roadless country. But the park rangers have not been provided with the means to patrol this remote area, with its poor roads, rivers, and precarious log bridges, and such animal protection as exists is concentrated on a thirty-two-square-mile area in this southern third of the park, entirely composed of savanna and slow watercourses. This region contains almost all the remaining rhino, but even here they are threatened: a captured poacher recently admitted having killed two rhino in 1983 and another two in 1984, effectively eliminating, all by himself, any increase that the animals might have made.

In an hour's flying, we count ourselves lucky to spot three white rhino, a lone male and a cow with calf; seeing our plane, the calf moved closer to its mother, which raised her head toward the sky but did not run. The huge, calm, pale gray creatures with their primordial horned heads might have been standing on the plains of the Oligocene seventy million years ago, when they first evolved. Except for a lion rolling on its dusty mound, they were the only creatures at Garamba that did not flee at the airplane's approach. Kob scattered widely through the tall coarse grass, and the buffalo herds, panicking one another, rocked along aimlessly in all directions, and the big bush elephants of the savanna, wariest of all, hurried along through the high grass in their stiff-legged, ear-flapping run.

▼▼▼

Toward midmorning, Jonah and I head west across the Garamba River, on a four-hundred-mile flight to Bangas-

sou, in the Central African Republic. We have left the rivers
that flow toward the Nile; the Garamba is one of the many
headwaters of the Congo (now the Zaire River). In the
nineteenth century, when the Zanzibar slaver Tippu Tib
sent his expeditions up the tributaries of the Congo, and
Arab slavers came westward from the Nile, this savanna belt
at the north edge of the rain forest was a great slaving
region, and captured tribesmen carried ivory tusks back to
the coast. Stanley's journals from his 1887 expedition—
part of which was spent traveling with Tippu Tib—draw
early attention to the devastating cost of the ivory trade:

> There is only one remedy for these wholesale devasta-
> tions of African aborigines, and that is the solemn combina-
> tion of England, Germany, France, Portugal, South and East
> Africa, and Congo [Free] State against the introduction of
> gunpowder into any part of the Continent . . . or seizing
> upon every tusk of ivory brought out, as there is not a single
> piece nowadays which has been gained lawfully. Every tusk,
> piece, and scrap in the possession of an Arab trader has
> been steeped and dyed in blood. Every pound weight has
> cost the life of a man, woman, or child, for every five pounds
> a hut has been burned, for every two tusks a whole village
> has been destroyed, every twenty tusks have been obtained
> at the price of a district with all its people, villages, and
> plantations. It is simply incredible that, because ivory is
> required for ornaments or billiard games, the rich heart of
> Africa should be laid waste . . . that populations, tribes, and
> nations should be utterly destroyed.

The region was all but emptied of human beings, and
the few that were left, infected with syphilis by the slavers,
were beset by an infertility that has kept the population low
to the present day. More recently, the withdrawal of the
colonial administrations and their clinics has brought a re-
surgence of sleeping sickness to both Sudan and C.A.R. For
these reasons and others not well understood—supersti-

tious memories of the dark era and fear of Azande witch-craft as well as cannibalism may have kept other groups from moving in—most of Haut-Zaïre and eastern C.A.R., with its immense woodlands and savannas, swamps, and rivers, shows no sign that man has ever been here.

In the great silence that settled on the land, the ele-phants prospered, and long after King Léopold II's Congo Free State was taken over by the Belgian government, this region remained the greatest ivory-hunting country in all Africa. Because it is remote, without roads or towns, its herds were unmolested even when, in the late nineteen-sixties, the price of ivory escalated, and wholesale slaughter of elephants throughout East Africa began. The amount of ivory exported from Kenya rose eighty-six percent in a sin-gle year between 1970 and 1971, eighty-one percent more the following year; within five years, Kenya had lost half of its elephants, or about sixty thousand animals, and by 1980 Uganda's elephants were all but gone. In Somalia, northern Tanzania, Zambia, Mozambique, Angola, and throughout West Africa, the populations were reduced by fifty to ninety percent. (Zimbabwe, Botswana, and South Africa, which were farthest from organized poaching gangs and ivory depots, were much less affected.) Inevitably the poachers turned to Sudan, in which the herds were reduced from a hundred and thirty-five thousand animals in 1976 to fewer than thirty thousand in 1983. In recent years, the pressure has intensified in Chad, Zaire, and C.A.R., from which the bush elephant is rapidly disappearing. Here as elsewhere, corrupt regimes have encouraged and controlled the trade in ivory.

The eastern two-thirds of the Central African Repub-lic, like northern Haut-Zaïre, is classified by ecologists as "Guinea savanna," after the broad belt of grass and wood-land extending eastward from northern Guinea, in West Africa, all the way across the continent into south Sudan and Ethiopia. North of the guinea savanna—a rolling pla-

teau country up to three thousand feet high—lies the Sahel,
a dry grassland which, in the great drought that began
about 1970, has been steadily invaded by the Sahara Desert.
To the south lies the tropical rain forest, which extends
from southern Guinea along the West African coast to
Cameroon, widening out in the great Congo Basin and
spreading eastward to the highlands of Central Africa.

This broad savanna with its sinuous reaches of riverine
forest, stretching away north toward the Sahel, is entirely
beautiful and awesome, and yet the great silence that re-
sounds from a wild land without sign of human life, from
which all of the great animals are gone, is something ominous. Mile after mile, we stare down in disbelief; we are not
prepared for so much emptiness, for such pristine and undamaged desolation. Beyond Garamba we had encountered a few elephants, but these must have strayed out of
the park, to judge from their great scarcity farther west. In
hundreds of miles of unbroken wilderness, without so
much as a distant smoke in sign of man, we see no elephant
whatever, nor the elephant trails that give away the presence of these animals even from high in the air.

With its notably sparse population of human beings
(the whole country has less than three million people, and
a third of these, by present estimate, have crowded into the
few cities and towns), C.A.R. would seem an ideal environment for elephants. Before 1970, there were thought to be
well over a hundred thousand in this country, and as late
as the mid-seventies, when elephants were disappearing
almost everywhere else, it was hoped that this region in the
heart of the African continent would survive as a last
stronghold of the species. Instead, the animals were exposed to unrestricted slaughter, and official exports of ivory
from C.A.R. jumped from four tons to a hundred and sixty-
five tons in a single year. In just five years, here in the east
part of the country, it is thought that four-fifths of the
elephants were killed.

Jean Bédel-Bokassa, the "emperor" of what he called the "Central African Empire" until he was deposed in 1979, is said to have ordered the slaughter of thirty thousand elephants by helicopter gunships and other means. He wished to support his family enterprise, La Couronne, in its near-monopoly on ivory exports, which, according to the elephant biologist Dr. Iain Douglas-Hamilton, who made a continental survey of African elephants in 1979, were largely based on ivory illegally imported from Zaire and the Sudan. (Zairian elephants, he discovered, were also being massacred by government troops.) In 1980, after Bokassa was deposed, bans on ivory exports were announced in both C.A.R. and Zaire, but neither was meant to be enforced, and the slaughter continued unabated. With official reopening of the ivory trade in 1981, as Douglas-Hamilton pointed out in a paper presented at a wildlife conference at Bangui in late 1985, C.A.R. was the only country left in Africa in which ivory hunting was "entirely legal, authorized, and operational."

In addition to the local people, the massacre attracted tough poaching gangs from Sudan and Chad that had run out of elephants in their own countries. The Sudanese favored camel transport and automatic weapons scavenged from the wars all around the region, while Chad's wild desert horsemen stuck to traditional methods, riding up on the great beasts from behind and ramming their sides or crippling their legs with long sharp spears. (Out of thirty-two animals examined by a Peace Corps group in 1983, twenty-five had been cut down by spears.) Already "big ivory" was hard to find, and between 1982 and 1984, exports declined from two hundred tons to forty. In 1984, an air survey of C.A.R.'s northern parks sponsored by several international conservation organizations could locate no more than forty-three hundred elephants, indicating a decline of nearly ninety percent in just four years. As Douglas-Hamilton observed at Bangui, "What happened in northern C.A.R. was caused by regional crises involving not only C.A.R. but Chad, Sudan, and Haut-Zaïre. Ten years ago this regional resource was beyond compare, five years ago it was in serious danger, today it is largely destroyed." In recent years, Sudan, Gabon, and C.A.R., responding to international pressure, have ordered an official ban on ivory export, but nobody thinks that this has slowed the killing.

Ivory hunters and others also killed every rhinoceros they came across, since the price of rhino horn had risen from thirty-five dollars a kilo in 1974 to five hundred dollars in 1979. In 1970, there were twenty thousand black rhino in Kenya; today there are five hundred fifty, and figures are similar all over Africa; four of the black rhino's seven geographic races are as precarious as the northern white rhino. In 1982, it was supposed that three thousand black rhino roamed the C.A.R.—the only significant population left in all of West and Central Africa. Two years later, the air survey noted above was unable to locate a single one. A few black rhino in Cameroon are the last of their species in Central and West Africa.

A parallel drastic decline in buffalo and Derby eland is partly attributable to a rinderpest plague brought by the starving livestock herds from Chad and Sudan that overran the northern parks as a fifteen-year drought all across Africa moved the Sahara ever farther south. Whatever the reasons, a great silence has descended on one of the last redoubts of wildlife on the continent.

Already much of the recent harvest was coming from the smaller forest elephant, whose straight tusks are composed of a harder, whiter ivory that is easily detected in the shipments. Ian Parker, a wildlife entrepreneur based in Nairobi and a student of the world ivory trade, was maintaining that about sixty percent of the ivory turning up in Hong Kong and Japan, much of it illegal ivory being exported through Burundi, came from the forest elephant.

Yet Parker, a longtime participant in the trade, was also claiming that elephants were still so numerous that tusks harvested from natural mortality alone would adequately support the ivory commerce, which handled an annual average of seven hundred and fifty tons in the ten years between 1975 and 1985; except locally, he said, there was no such thing as an elephant crisis, since at least three million elephants were still at large in Africa. Douglas-Hamilton, on the other hand, had estimated a population of 1.3 million, and was convinced that *Loxodonta africana* was already endangered as a species.

Dr. Western believes that even the smaller figure may be too high; the most recent analyses of ivory-trade records indicated that elephant numbers can no longer exceed one million, far less three. Between 1979 and the present, he says, the average weight of marketed tusks declined by one half, which meant that roughly twice the number of animals had to be killed to maintain that 750-ton harvest. It also meant that more than half the slaughtered animals were females, which in the old days were rarely shot at all. Analysis of ivory exports indicates that the average tusk weight is about three kilos, in an animal that formerly produced tusks of thirty-seven kilos each; computer analysis has shown that once average tusk weight falls below five kilos, a collapse of the entire population is at hand. The main source of these little tusks are juvenile males between five and ten years old—well below the age of reproduction—and mature females, twenty to twenty-five years old. Not a single tusk came from an animal over thirty-five years old, in a species which may attain four times that age. If there really were three million elephants, as Parker claimed, why was no one shooting mature males? And why did the tonnage drop off drastically in 1985 to four hundred and eighty tons, despite dedicated killing by ivory hunters all across Africa?

By using an arbitrary equation that correlates elephant

density with average rainfall, Ian Parker concludes that very large numbers of forest elephant—about two per square kilometer—are hidden by the forest canopy, a figure higher than the highest density found anywhere in the savanna. Dr. Western, whose own data Parker borrowed to construct his estimates, reminds me that elephants may eat three hundred pounds of fodder in a day, and defecate fifteen to eighteen times in the same period. "If you think of Parker's density figures in terms of a dung fight," he says wryly, "I can only say that you would never be out of reach of ammunition."

As Western had written to me in September, "The discrepancy hinges on the different estimates of forest elephants in Zaire, and to a lesser extent in Congo Republic and Gabon. There is very little disagreement elsewhere." If densities in primary forest are as low as he believes, then the African elephant as a species is in serious trouble.

The main hope of this expedition is to resolve that discrepancy once and for all. It is not that we are anxious to prove that the forest elephant is an uncommon animal—how much more exciting it would be to prove the reverse!—but that this proof, by dispelling self-serving data and wishful thinking, might lay the groundwork for a new era of responsible elephant conservation.

▼▼▼

Bangassou, on the Mbomou River, described as a center of cotton, coffee, oil palm, lumber, and diamond production, is the only town in eastern C.A.R. (which together with Chad was known as Ubangi-Shari after their great rivers, in the days when both were still a part of French Equatorial Africa). We put down quickly to refuel at the Bangassou airstrip—we have no clearance—then take off again and continue west across savanna and forest to our next landmark, the Ubangi River. Below the Kouimba rapids, the Ubangi makes a great loop north. We do not follow it but maintain our course, crossing the river and flying three hundred miles over the jungles of northern Zaire in order to meet the Ubangi once again where it sweeps south on its last descent to the Zaire River. On this leg of the journey, like the one before it, there is scarcely a sign of human presence—no tracks, no huts, no smoke, near or far— though an artificial city has been built for Zaire's billionaire president somewhere off there to the south, at Gbadolite. Nor are there tracks of animals, nor visible life of any kind except huge black hornbills with broad white patches on their wings, flapping and sailing over the forest canopy and slow green rivers. Then the forest opens out on the great Ubangi, where a few pirogues hold more human beings than we have seen in the eight hundred miles since we left Garamba.

The river slides south to a great bend, and here rocks part it into rapids presided over by Bangui (the Rapids), the small capital of the erstwhile Empire of Central Africa. According to my trusty map, this pretty town inset in small steep hills lies just upriver from two villages, Bimbo and Zongo.

▼▼▼

A French trading post established in 1889, Bangui, with its fine river prospect, is a typical colonial town turned capital city in the new Africa. Its decrepit villas, European cars, and more or less modern commercial buildings housing the remnants of colonial enterprises are set off by potholed red-earth streets, fragrant markets, head cargoes, traditional peasant dress, radio music and impromptu dancing, flowers and colors, and, everywhere, a restless proud humanity in bright clean clothes, streaming along under the trees to quarters that, for more people than not, will be tin-roofed shacks without electricity or plumbing.

The capital is set about with triumphal arches erected in his own honor some years ago by Emperor Bokassa, for

whom the imperial boulevard into the city from the grandiose and empty airport was also named. It is now called the
Avenue des Martyres, after the two hundred schoolchildren
who were slaughtered on imperial whim, with the emperor's own wholehearted participation. Because Bokassa
was a "charismatic" Francophile (he once presented a gift
of diamonds to French premier Valerie Giscard d'Estaing),
this by no means isolated episode disappointed his many
French admirers, who for investment reasons had supported him long after his bloodthirsty predilections became
known. When the schoolroom adventure drew international attention, the emperor and most of his country's
money were hurried off to La Belle France, where he was
living in the greatest comfort and "was very popular," or so
we were told by his bewildered countrymen. (In October
1986, of his own accord, Bokassa returned to C.A.R., where
he was tried for arthropophagy as well as multiple assassi-
nations. The following June he was sentenced to death, but
the sentence was commuted to life imprisonment, apparently in the basement of the presidential palace, where he
lives today.)

At Bangui, where we spent two days conferring with
wildlife officials, we resided at the Hotel Minerva, a more
modest establishment than the Rock Hotel (which boasts a
bar called "Scotch Club du Rock"), yet very lively, especially at noon when the offices close, most of them for the
remainder of the day. The bar just inside the front door
fairly swarms with elegant *poules de luxe* with high heels, long
legs, liberated breasts, and sumptuous steatopygia, waving
hard-puffed cigarettes in long cool hands. One young
woman affects jeans and a T-shirt inscribed CHICAGO COS-
MIC, but most are attired in wide-open blouses and transparent skirts. The colorful ladies are well known to the
colons and sullen-faced paratroopers in harsh haircuts who
represent France's small "military presence" in its "special
relationship" with its former colonies in Africa. These men

squeeze the ladies' hands as they enter the bar—*Ça va bien!
Et toi?*—and meanwhile the women are boisterously ad-
mired by their tattered young compatriots, who await the
rare tourists outside in the street. The young men sell eth-
nic wood stools, dried forest butterflies, and bows and arrows said to come from the Babinga Pygmies in the south.
My fren? My fren? You wish a bow, a arrow?

Perhaps in frustration, a young peddler teases a beer-
bellied *colon* as he leaves the bar, and the big man whirls
with a threatening gesture, causing the boy to back away.
The white man waves contemptuously at the youth's wares,
his poverty, his whole African being. "You think you are a
somebody, is that it?" Offended, the other Africans crowd
forward and the man retreats, slamming his car door—*Ça
non, messieurs!* The youth appreciates my disgusted reaction, though his face is sad. "*Champion fistique,*" he explains.
"He does not know how to laugh."

▼▼▼

Our main business in Bangui is to urge the creation of a
national forest park and promise the New York Zoological
Society's cooperation to Raymond Mbitikon, minister of
waters and forests, fishing and hunting, who asks us to
prepare a survey and recommendation while we are down
in the Bayanga region. The park was originally proposed
last year by Richard Carroll, a former Peace Corps volunteer in C.A.R., now a doctoral student doing his thesis on
lowland gorillas. Monsieur Mbitikon kindly dispatches a
ministry vehicle for Bayanga with a week's provisions and
drums of aviation fuel. The journey is about five hundred
miles and fourteen hours over a rough road, and the truck
will meet us there tomorrow.

To venture very far outside Bangui, according to a
brochure of travel in these parts prepared some years ago
by Air Afrique, "it is necessary to equip oneself seriously
and be prepared for rather long delays." Since we are flying

out tomorrow to Bayanga, in the far southern corner of
C.A.R., we have seriously equipped ourselves with traveler's checks, to pay not only for provisions but for aviation
fuel, for fuel comes very high indeed in what people living
here believe to be the most expensive city in the world. We
have lunch on the Ubangi River with the kind and helpful
ambassador and officers of the American embassy, and the
ambassador's wife, Katia de Jarnette, escorts me to a Peace
Corps clinic, where my mongoose bites are thoroughly
cleansed and a tetanus shot administered by a cheerful
nurse appropriately christened Kandi Christian.

We are also "prepared for rather long delays," and a
good thing, too. At the airport next morning we find that
the compressor on the gas pump has broken down, and that
gasoline in drums that cost three dollars a gallon yesterday
will, for unmysterious reasons, cost five dollars today. We
protest this piracy, and wait, and eventually the compressor
is resuscitated. Before the plane can be refueled, however,
a general failure of airport electricity knocks out the gas
pump for a few more hours, and not until three-thirty in the
afternoon, after flight clearance from the airport tower,
customs, and immigration, do we clear the ground. We are
accompanied on this flight by the British elephant biologist
Richard Barnes, who made all the arrangements for us here
in Bangui, and also by Gustave Doungoubey, director of
management of wildlife, who is kindly escorting us to
Bayanga.

Immediately southwest of Bangui, the plane crosses a
huge palm-oil plantation and heads out across the rain forests of the Congo Basin. There is no savanna anymore, the
rare patches of swamp are small, the scarce red tracks are
narrow, shrouded by trees. Except for the rivers, which are
not always in view, there is no place to come down in one
piece. Some years ago in eastern Zaire I flew over this
Congo Basin forest in a light plane, from Bukavu to Obaye,
then north to Goma, and the sight of its monotone expanse

of green, undulating in all directions to the green horizon, is just as disturbing now as it was then.

Even so, the rolling foliage is magnificent. Forest green and gray-green, jade, emerald, and turquoise, pond green, pea green—all the greens of the world unroll below our wings, set off by bright fire red leaves of the *azobe* (or *bois de fer* or "ironwood"). Here and there in the wet sloughs is a strand of raffia palms, said to be a favored haunt of pygmy elephants. Just once in the whole flight between the Ubangi and the Sangha do I see a sign of human habitation, two poor huts in a clearing near a forest stream.

The first glimpse of the Sangha River is a silver sliver among darkening hills in the late afternoon light. The plane swings south over slow rapids, the trees of the river islands mirrored in the silted water, and then the river opens out onto broad sandbars that in the dry season appear in front of the Bantu village called Bayanga.

Bayanga lies in the Lobaye Forest, in the farthest southern territory of C.A.R., surrounded by forests of the Congo Republic and Cameroon. Originally our plan had been to swing well east over the Congo Republic and count the elephants along the swamps and rivers, but M. Doungoubey received word this morning that Congo soldiers were crossing into C.A.R. in a border dispute, and might shoot at a small circling airplane, not realizing that elephants and not themselves were being studied. (Later we learn that the Congolese soldiers have withdrawn to their own border post, down the Sangha River, which flows due southward through that country to its confluence with the Zaire. "They put up their flag in our territory and we take it down again," said a C.A.R. soldier.)

Bayanga is named for the Sangha or Yanga fishing people ("Ba"—"Wa" in East Africa—is a Bantu prefix signifying plural man or "people") attracted here by Slovenia Bois, a Yugoslav lumber concession whose mill lies at the south end of the settlement, and whose acting manager,

Janez Mikuz, is kind enough to meet us at the airstrip and refresh us with cold beer at the company mess overlooking the river before installing us at a comfortable guest house in the compound. But to our embarrassment our friend Gustave Doungoubey and his cousin, Monsieur Babisse, who has arrived with a soldier-driver in the truck, are installed separately in lesser quarters. Gustave, a bright, equable fellow who permits nothing so small as this to trouble him, seems not to mind; he has many friends here, all of whom come to embrace him. Next morning at breakfast, there is more discomfort when Monsieur Babisse and the local forestry official polish off a half bottle each of Slovenia Bois's good Côtes du Rhône white wine, pouring it into man-sized tumblers and drinking it straight off like spring water. Our friends show no effects of their glad refreshment, then or later, but the Yugoslavs, who do not seem fond of Africans (Jonah remarks that this tends to be true of most Eastern Europeans), are irritated, plainly regretting that the natives of this country must be permitted at their European mess. However, they are civil to the Africans, and kind and hospitable to the whites throughout our stay.

▼▼▼

From the settlement a bright red road runs southwest through the forest, crossing a bridge in a big thicket of bamboo and climbing a steep hill to a forest ridge. Manioc and long papaya fend for themselves in the thick weeds grown up around the unbranched columns of black skeletal trees a hundred and fifty feet in height. Like all forest Bantu, the Yanga practice the primitive slash-and-burn agriculture that has already destroyed most of the rain forest of West Africa. Often a forest garden is abandoned and a new one started even before the poor soil is depleted, since slashing and burning is easier than keeping up with the fierce weeds. In regions of dense population, such as West Africa, primitive agriculture leads inevitably to total degradation of the forest together with the disappearance of the animals, but in Central Africa, where the human population is so low, the random agriculture, by encouraging second growth, makes forage more accessible, and, where not intense, may actually increase wildlife populations.

The dust of the road is broken by the shifting soil prints of thick vipers, and the snake patterns are interspersed with tiny human prints of Babinga Pygmies (sometimes called Ba-Aka, after their Aka language). Lost in the weeds between road and field are the Pygmies' low leaf-thatched huts, which are woven of a strong latticework of saplings stuck into the earth to form the walls, then bent over and lashed together as the roof, giving great tensile strength to a light structure while obtaining the maximum space of a rounded dwelling. (Huts constructed on this principle are also made by the Turkana and Masai and are in fact found all over the earth. Even the Inuit igloo is quite similar, including the long tubular entrance on one side, and so are the modern tents we carry with us.) Though the huts are scarcely four feet high, the tiny sleeping platforms of bamboo are often set one above another, in order to keep more people clear of the earth floor.

The middle-size descendants of those Babinga who have interbred with their Bantu neighbors have inherited few of the fine points of either race, seeming neither as handsome and husky as the Bantu nor as alert and merry as the forest people. By our rather narrow Western standards, most Babinga are unprepossessing, seeming stunted and bent rather than small, with scared, uncomprehending faces and the slightly averted gaze of uneasy animals. At a roadside camp, three naked little boys, feeling behind them with their hands, withdraw into the foliage in the slow way of wild things not wishing to be seen, and one drops to all fours before disappearing into the leaves, peering back at the huge white men over his shoulder.

Last night after dark we listened to Babinga drums, and

this morning near the airstrip we hear raised voices, a simple wistful three-note descending chorus, *dee-do-do*, like a
human echo of the sad sweet song of an emerald green bird,
Klaas's cuckoo, which I watched this morning at the forest
edge. According to the Bayanga people, the Babinga come
here only in the dry season, to take advantage of old manioc
plantations and perhaps work in the lumber mill. They
erect their leaf huts outside the mill and the Yanga village.
They are thought of as forest demons, not quite human, by
the Bayanga. Like most Pygmy groups, they have a certain
interdependence with their Bantu neighbors, who live
mostly in rectangular wattle-and-daub huts, with tin roofs
brought in by the lumber company, and are served by
makeshift shops and a small bar. (Outside the Bar Patience
is a decrepit jitney bus on which is painted SANGHA EAGLE.
As a parting shot to those left in its dust, a message painted
on the rear end reads GOOD WILL NEVER! It has been quite
a while since the Sangha Eagle traveled anywhere. How it
got here or where it used to go has been forgotten.)

▼▼▼

Early in our visit to Bayanga, I accompany Drs. Barnes and
Western on a reconnaissance flight across the "Dzanga-
Sangha Reserve" proposed by Richard Carroll, which
would include an area of twenty-seven hundred square kilometers. We hope to persuade M. Mbitikon to enlarge Carroll's proposed reserve with the idea that in the future,
when the timber leases have run out, it might be given the
fully protected status of a national park.

    After a few preliminary circles at high altitude, we de-
scend again to a few hundred feet above the forest canopy;
the trees flow down to the gallery forests along the Sangha
River, bursting and shimmering with morning light. The
ironwoods are burning bright in the sea of greens, and the
strange semaphore of white-winged birds turn out to be

groups of the huge brown-cheeked hornbills, crossing the cool glades of the forest.

To our surprise, not all these trees are evergreen, though there are many less deciduous species than one sees farther north. Even here near the Equator, the Congo Basin, unlike the upper Amazon and Borneo, has fleeting dry seasons, like faint echoes of the long dry seasons to the north and south, but what is probably more important to its ecology are the extended climatic changes, recorded in lake sediments as well as in fossil pollen and termitaria, that have occurred here ever since the Tertiary. These wet and dry periods were more extreme and of greater frequency than in Southeast Asia and South America, which have been largely undisturbed since the Cretaceous. The last great dry period, ten thousand years ago, entirely eliminated the forests of the central basin in what is now Zaire. The forest was limited to relict areas to east and west, known to ecologists as "Pleistocene refugia," from which fauna and flora spread out again as the rain returned. By comparison to the refugia, however, the central region remains "impoverished forest" to this day, although a pygmy chimpanzee is found there that does not occur anywhere else.

Our first forest elephant, a bull seen in a slough near the Dzanga Pan, shakes its head at the banking airplane as if in disapproval, but it does not run—a sign that ivory poachers must be rare here. Another good sign is the almost total absence of forestry scars other than narrow logging roads already overgrown. Later we learn from Slovenia employees that this advanced lumber operation, which exploits only four of the myriad tree species (three red hardwoods are cut for export, and a white wood is used in local construction), rarely removes more than one tree every few acres.

Selective logging, excellent in principle, often does great damage to the forest because of the network of forestry tracks and roads required to remove the trees, but, to judge from the minimal effects observable from the air, Slovenia Bois is taking unusual pains. By opening many small new clearings, this selective operation may have the same beneficial effect as the fall of ancient trees, which from the air look like giant skeletons on the forest floor. The sunlight streaming down through the tear in the forest permits a burst of second growth, providing accessible browse for many animals that cannot reach the nutrients high in the canopy.

▼▼▼

Richard Barnes, who did his master's thesis on the bush elephant in Tanzania's Ruaha Park, is being sponsored by the NYZS in a study of techniques for censusing the forest elephant, which is very difficult to observe. Until now, the vague estimates of its numbers have been influenced by the bias of the guessers, and a much more accurate census will be needed before international conservation efforts can be mustered on its behalf. Dr. Barnes's study area, which we shall visit, is in the Ivindo River region of northern Gabon, perhaps three hundred miles southwest of Bayanga, and before he is finished he will have made the first comprehensive census of forest elephants in Gabon, the methods of which can then be applied to the African rain forests as a whole. "We haven't worked out precise figures as yet," Barnes informs me in his usual precise tones. "There are certain anomalies in our dung-density data having to do with dung decomposition rates. But it is already safe to say that rain-forest populations will work out to less than one animal per acre, even in this region where elephants are reported to be common."

Dr. Western nods. "And this is the region, southern C.A.R. and Congo, south Cameroon and north Gabon, where *cyclotis* populations are apparently highest. I'm told that elephants are already scarce in eastern Zaire, as I think we'll establish when we visit the Ituri, and it must be assumed that in large tracts of the Congo Basin there are scarcely any."

At Bayanga, Dr. Barnes will use his techniques to arrive at some estimate of elephant densities in both primary and secondary forest, and after the reconnaissance flight on our first morning he and Dr. Western, with Monsieurs Doungoubey and Babisse and three Babinga trackers, set off on the first of his foot transects, in which elephant droppings over a predetermined distance provide the main basis of the count.

At Bangui the nurse had warned me that I must not walk more than absolutely necessary until my spectacular ankle swelling had gone down, and since I wish to be more or less fit by the time we arrive in the Ituri Forest, I decide to limit my forest walking to the afternoon. Slaus Sterculec, the man in charge of Slovenia's local construction, has kindly offered to accompany me to the Dzanga salt pan, a haunt of elephants perhaps two miles by forest path off an old logging track. Mr. Sterculec, a lifelong bachelor and wiry jungle veteran of a breed less often seen these days in Africa, has been out here since the founding of Bayanga thirteen years ago, and he has not left the forest in the last five years. He turns up to fetch me with two Babinga hunters, Bisambe and Lalieh, who are markedly smaller than the three who have gone off with the other party. Bisambe, the elder of the two, is yellowish and hunched, with a big head, and both have incisors filed down to sharp points.

I am not displeased that Mr. Sterculec has brought along his rifle. "It is not for hunting," he explains disarmingly. "It is for my fear."

▼▼▼

At supper the night before we had discussed the pygmy elephant (*Loxodonta pumilio*), which is known to the native peoples throughout the tropical forest as a creature even smaller than the small forest race of the African elephant that we are here to study. Richard Barnes tells us that in Gabon nobody doubts the existence of this reputedly pugnacious little elephant, which is called *assala*. *A Field Guide to the Mammals of Africa*, published in 1977, provides a detailed description of this creature and cites its widespread reputation for aggressiveness. However, it notes that "the existence of a species of pygmy elephant is not generally recognized; the animals described are believed to be small members of the Forest Elephant."

The first description of a "pygmy elephant" appeared in 1906, based on a small animal (1.2 meters at the shoulder) taken in Gabon the previous year and shipped to the New York Zoological Society's Bronx Zoo. The would-be discoverer, Theodore Noack, a German professor, claimed it as a new subspecies of the African elephant *Elephas [Loxodonta] africanus pumilio*. Unfortunately it had doubled in size and was a normal forest elephant when it died nine years later—still an adolescent—but by that time it had been forgotten, its place in the scientific limelight having been usurped by a second "pygmy" of an allegedly separate subspecies, *E.a. fransseni*, collected in 1911. There was also a well-received report of a herd of five miniature elephants from the same locality on the north bank of Lake Leopold II, in the Congo, where the exciting new animal was known as the "water elephant," and was alleged to have amphibious habits, like the hippopotamus. Two more small elephants killed there in 1923 were identified as pygmies by no less an authority than the New York Zoological Society's celebrated director, Dr. William Hornaday, and in 1936 another pair of "midget pachyderms," arriving alive in New York City, caused a great stir in the press and among the populace. One of these was still alive in 1947, by which time, like Dr. Noack's specimen, it had grown remorselessly to full forest-elephant dimensions.

Nevertheless, reports by reputable observers continued, although the pygmy appeared to share almost the entire known range of the forest elephant, and did not seem to occur where the latter was absent. The local Africans in all equatorial rain-forest countries without exception agreed that there were two distinct elephants, the smaller of which was notoriously less wary and more aggressive than the larger. Furthermore, they said, it made a different sound, had more sedentary habits, and generally preferred swampy terrain, often in association with raffia palms, leading some authorities to speculate that even if it was not a separate geographic race, it was separate ecologically, and therefore entitled to subspecific status.

Those who doubted the existence of a separate race of "pygmy elephant" pointed not only to the tendency of captive specimens to grow up in captivity but to the absence of dependable sightings of juvenile animals in reports of pygmy herds. But if the existence of such a creature was unproved, so was the statement that it did not occur where the forest elephant was absent. Or so claimed its partisans, including a controversial Belgian zoologist, Dr. Bernard Heuvelmans, author of *On the Trail of Unknown Animals*, in which he states that "to deny that the pygmy elephant exists, even as a subspecies of *Loxodonta cyclotis* [*sic*] is absurd." Also, the late W. D. (Karamoja) Bell, among the most celebrated of all African elephant hunters, described a herd of pygmies from Liberia. Bell made a drawing of these animals from memory, and the drawing revealed a female pygmy with a baby alongside. Others had also reported evidence of baby pygmies—the afterbirth of a killed female, a female in lactation—to which the naysayers retorted that evidence of sexual reproduction was no evidence of maturity, and that these reproducing females would continue growing and exceed the six-foot limit usually applied to the hypothetical adult *pumilio*.

On our trek into the forest, I ask Bisambe if he knows about the pygmy elephant, and he says he does. Asked if it was *"plus méchant"*—nastier, more aggressive—than the others, he murmurs, *"Ils sont tous méchants!"* at which both he and Lalieh burst out laughing.

The trackers wear ancient shorts and child-sized and decrepit red plastic sandals, but on entering the forest both go barefoot, carrying their sandals with great delicacy between their fingertips. Bisambe, who takes the lead, stops frequently to listen, poising right in the middle of a step, foot off the ground, turning his head to pick up some fleeting sound or smell amidst the raucous squawk and hooting of turacos and hornbills, the pungent dung and foliage aromas of the forest. *"Moku"* he whispers, or *"gandi,"* with a slow mysterious smile, eyes dancing with delight. *Moku* is monkey (*which* monkey is the question; there are thirteen different species of diurnal primate in this forest, including the gorilla and the rare red colobus) and *gandi*—to judge from his deft mime—a species of duiker, a small forest antelope. Like many traditional hunters, the Babinga communicate in the bush with what seems to be a kind of soft ventriloquy; sometimes Bisambe, twenty yards ahead of me on the leafy path, murmurs something in his deep, soft voice without bothering to turn his head, and there comes an answering soft sound from Lalieh, twenty yards behind.

Dancing ahead of us along the narrow path are male diadem butterflies with big white dots on black wings (the female, very different, has her own name: yellow pansy) and big cobalt-and-black striped daneids. Smaller forms have cobalt spots or are entirely cobalt, and the same brilliant color—perhaps the one that shows up best in the forest darkness—flares again in the rump and tail of a green-breasted pitta, a secretive bird of the forest floor which I feel very fortunate to see.

Nearing the Dzanga Pan, Bisambe stops short again, and a moment later the snap of a heavy branch, like a pistol report, cracks the green silence, signaling the presence of a browsing elephant or a gorilla. Bisambe remains motionless for a little while, long fingers pointed like antennae. Then he moves on in dead quiet to a place where the thick canopy opens out, and afternoon sunlight pours into an open pan, perhaps four hundred yards in length and a hundred across. There he turns his big head with a smile to end all smiles, his hand pointing straight ahead between the trees.

From the west end comes a family group of elephants, a cow and three juveniles, and to the east a female with small calf and a large bull skirted each other. To my astonishment, the large bull has the high shoulders, huge ragged triangular ears, and heavy forward-curving tusks of the bush elephant. Another gathering of perhaps ten animals is far down at the west end of the pan. Directly in front of us, two very small male elephants with disproportionately big tusks are snuffling deep in a mudhole in the pan, which is broken by shallow pools of stagnant water.

I have scarcely focused on this odd pair with my binoculars when I see the faces of two Africans in the trees behind them. *Poachers!* I think, but a moment later I pick up a white face behind binoculars, and then another, observing the same two little elephants. Richard and Jonah, completing their transects through the forest, have been led into the Dzanga Pan from the far side. Just prior to my arrival, they tell me later, one of these feisty little tuskers had actually skirmished with the large savanna bull. Though there are other elephants in the pan, these small males with outsized tusks turn out to be the most intriguing of all the elephants we are to see throughout our journey.

In the near-windlessness, the female with three young has caught our scent and led her small group without hurrying into the forest, as Gustave Doungoubey and his armed men, spotting our Pygmies for the first time, come hurrying across the pan, suspecting poachers. Slaus and I step out into the open, eliciting sheepish grins from our African friends, and soon Jonah and Richard come across the pan to compare impressions of our first forest elephants, in particular the big "bush elephant" and the two small males.

Just as the forest elephant may follow the river trees into the savanna, and sometimes is observed in open country, the bush elephant penetrates deep into the forest. Richard Carroll had also seen "bush elephants," assuming that they were fugitives from the ivory trade slaughters to the north, but Jonah thinks it is the savanna genes that have penetrated so far south; this particular animal, in all likelihood, has never seen the open grasslands.

The other elephants, in varying degrees, display the characters of the forest race, *L.a. cyclotis*, in which the highest point of the body is behind the middle of the back, and the head tends to be held lower, so that the small rounded ears on the small head (which make them look like very young bush elephants) do not reach higher than the neck. In *cyclotis*, the tusks tend to be narrow, straight, and pointed straight downward. Presumably the low head and small ears are adaptations for forest travel, but the function of the vertical tusks, like so much else about *cyclotis*, is not yet known. (I speculate that straight tusks might be used for digging tubers, in the way that the walrus uses its straight tusks for digging clams, but Jonah appears unimpressed by this brilliant theory.) Nor is it known why the forest race lacks pronounced sexual dimorphism; in the bush elephant, a big male may be twice the size of an average female.

"I suspect," Jonah says, "that dimorphism in elephants, as in other polygamous species, is related to male competition for females. In the savannas, which are strongly seasonal, herds aggregate during the rains, females come into estrus fairly synchronously, and bigger males will of course win out. Here in the equatorial forest, the seasons are much less pronounced, and food and water are more evenly spread. Under these conditions, we suspect, female elephant herds are tiny and more evenly distributed, and probably breed all year round. If this is true, males would also be widely spread, and would not compete so strongly in one place and at one time, so that the advantage of size is less."

Richard, in his reserved, taciturn way, is discernibly elated by these interesting elephants, seen in the open, at close range. Never before has he had such a look at forest elephants, and this is only the second time he has been able to get photographs. "In Gabon," he had told me over breakfast, "they are always hidden, sometimes only a few yards away. We can be right on top of one and not know he's there. And even when we *are* aware of them, we make noise to drive them off, because"—and here he shrugged, as the relentless candor that is one of his likable qualities overtook him—"because, well, I'm *afraid* of them. I'm not prepared to take the risk of approaching strange elephants in the forest, and my fiancée has extracted a promise from me that I will not do so."

Unlike Jonah and I, who go about in shorts and sneakers, Richard spends every day out in the forest, and therefore feels he cannot afford our casual attitude toward such jungle afflictions as thorns and biting insects. In this very hot and humid climate (though the forest is much cooler than the clearings), he is fortified by a tight-buttoned and tight-belted dark green khaki field jacket, baggy trousers with large extra pockets, gaiters, and boots, together with a full compliment of canvas bags, canteens, and compasses, bags of dust to test the wind, binoculars, camera, and other useful and less useful accoutrements. Peering out through owlish glasses from beneath his heavy-gauge rain-and-sun hat, he brings to mind old photos of nineteenth-century naturalists, with whom he shares an old-fashioned meticulousness and dedication that is most impressive.

If Drs. Barnes and Western were surprised to see a "pure" bush elephant so deep in the forest, they were positively astonished by the tusk size of the two young males just in front of us, which, to judge from their height—no more than five feet at the shoulder—are probably about five years old. These creatures answered perfectly the description of the "pygmy elephant," even to an aggressive nature, displayed when the larger of the two had instigated that brief skirmish with the savanna bull, which was several times its size. But a few minutes later, the same little male had approached a female in the large group at the west end and engaged in unmistakable filial behavior. Thus in an instant he had demonstrated that he was not a mature elephant of pygmy dimensions and outsized tusks but an extraordinarily independent young forest elephant. The reason for that independence may well lie in the complete absence of lion, hyena, and wild dog, the only predators that might attack young elephants of this size in the savanna (the leopard is simply not large enough to bring one down). Freedom from predators permits a very early independence from the mother, and might account for the obstreperous groups of juvenile *cyclotis* that are reported as "pygmy elephants."

Though an adult male is only eight feet high while his counterpart in the savanna may be well over ten, forest elephants are thought to have a shorter life span than the bush form, and probably reach maturity much faster, tusks and all. "In the bush elephant," Jonah says, "you *expect* to find big tusks, because the male is so much bigger. But in the forest elephant, without dimorphism, such tusks are striking, even though male tusks grow much faster relative to age." If this animal and his companion are specimens of "pygmy elephants," as we suppose, there remains a certain enigma in those tusks, and their precocious development in at least some of young male *cyclotis*.

It is encouraging that these elephants are comparatively tame, a sign that they are harassed little if at all—a point to be made in our recommendation of this place as a national reserve. The foresters say that elephants are more plentiful farther south, and that gorilla and bongo, though difficult to see, are common in the region. What Dr. Western will probably recommend is a park far larger than the proposed reserve, occupying the whole triangle of C.A.R. that lies between Congo and Cameroon, with contiguous reserves or parks in those two countries—the first international forest park, preserving hundreds of square miles of undamaged habitat.

Since we have flashlights, Slaus and I, with Lalieh and Bisambe, decide to remain here until dusk, when we might hope to see bush pig or bongo, or possibly the giant forest hog. Our friends have scarcely disappeared when four more elephants, golden yellow with caked clay from another bathing place, walk out of the deepening evening greens onto the east end of the pan. Soon they are joined by the big gray savanna bull, whose size, color, and configuration make him look like a different species altogether. All five cross over to our side and reenter the forest, and we wonder if we will encounter them on the way back. Another elephant comes and goes. Then, quite suddenly, the Babinga are gesturing.

The vanished five have reappeared at the edge of a grassy swale just to our right. Not catching our scent, they keep on coming, passing too close as they head toward the center of the pan, where they bathe and drink for a little while before the female catches our scent in a subtle shift of wind. She lifts her trunk high, then directs it straight at us like a blunderbuss. Silently, in unhurried hurry, the elephants move out of the pan, and the sand plovers, the green sandpipers from Europe, and some blue-winged, chestnut-colored ducks shift just enough in the wash of mud and water to escape being flattened by the great round feet. I have never before seen this beautiful forest duck (labeled Hartlaub's duck through no fault of its own), the nest of which has never been located. "Faunistically," as Jonah says, in uncharacteristic resort to eco-jargon, "the rain forest of the Congo Basin is very little known."

Two days later, while Richard continues with his transects, Jonah and I return to Dzanga Pan, arriving at two in
the afternoon so as to be ready when the elephants come
in; we are interested especially in large-tusked "pygmies."
The day is hot, the pan dead still: I watch a sun bird, a green
shiny lizard, and a pair of chortling gray parrots catching
the sun in their red tails. (This species is the loquacious
favorite of caged-parrot fanciers and therefore threatened
in the wild.) Not until midafternoon does the first group of
elephants appear, looming suddenly out of deep green
shadows in the forest wall across the pan, lifting their trunks
to sniff the air, swinging a forefoot several inches above the
ground, ears uncoiling, thin tails switching, in the constant
"flowing" of the elephant, even a calm one. "The first ones
in are always suspicious," Jonah whispers.

This first group, which appear to be almost "pure"
cyclotis, is scared away by two Babinga hunters who emerge
from the forest to the southwest with big leaf-wrapped
packets of fresh meat and whack a tree hard with a panga
to clear out the elephants before crossing the pan. Twenty-
two elephant come in once they are gone—mostly hybrids,
with pronounced bush characters such as bulging brow,
long back, and sharp-cornered ears. The sole young male
is smaller than our "pygmy elephants" and lacks their heavy
tusk development, yet he is even more independent in behavior, coming into the pan early, all by himself, traveling
the length of it past other groups, and departing the pan,
still entirely on his own, in another direction. "On the
savannas," Jonah says, astounded, "elephants are eight
years old before they leave their mothers. That one can't be
more than three! In the savanna he wouldn't last one day!"

▼▼▼

The forest west of the Sangha River is entirely roadless,
stretching away across an unmarked boundary into Cameroon. Perhaps for want of firsthand knowledge, blacks and

whites agree that the gorilla is most plentiful in that region, which is dense and treacherous, so Gustave says, and ridden with swamps aswarm with crocodiles. Its only inhabitants are Pygmies, but no local will accompany us, since they say that these Pygmies, who come in from Cameroon, are "*très méchant.*" (Cameroon is the westernmost territory of the Pygmies, who are thought to number about two hundred thousand altogether. The largest group—about twenty-five thousand—and the one most culturally intact, are the Mbuti, whom we shall meet in the Ituri Forest of Zaire.) International boundaries are of no concern to Pygmies anywhere, but possibly the Sangha River is a natural barrier between Pygmy nations. Or perhaps, being people of the forest, they are afraid to cross such a broad water at the mercy of the Yanga fishermen, who stand in the stern of their pirogues to paddle their narrow leaflike craft up and down the currents in the shadow of the gallery trees.

Under the circumstances, Jonah and I will set off on a gorilla hunt alone. Since the pirogues are too delicate and leaky to carry two big passengers, Slaus Sterculec offers to take us across the Sangha in his riverboat, a decommissioned metal landing craft from World War II. Soon we are rounding the broad sandbars that appear in midriver in the rainy season and crossing the heavy current to a break in the forest wall where elephants come occasionally to water.

Slaus is concerned that without a tracker we may lose ourselves in the dense forest, and on the far side he conscripts a young Yanga fisherman, Aliende, who agrees to guide us. Heading inland, Aliende skirts a broad and grassy marsh, perhaps an ancient oxbow of the river, and arrives at an overgrown, treacherous swamp perhaps a hundred yards across, all tussocks and tangled undergrowth, rotten footing and hidden holes, into which we sink well above the knee. On the far side, the rain forest has been much modified to their own advantage by the elephants, to judge not only from plentiful droppings but the numerous small

clearings with abundant second growth that provides them
fodder. This browse is also very useful to gorilla and the big
forest antelope called the bongo, and before long we come
upon gorilla sign—beds, feeding areas, old droppings.
(There are thought to be several thousand gorilla in this
southwestern forest of C.A.R.) Continuing westward perhaps two miles more, we find fresh green droppings and a
sweet whiff in the air left behind from the night before. But
the gorilla, who rarely shows himself until he wishes to have
a look at his observers, remains hidden in the rank and
heavy cover.

From the north, across the river, comes a shot; four
more ring out in the next half hour. Aliende stops and
shakes his head; any animals nearby are sure to flee. He is
not a Pygmy, and he grows unsure as he goes farther from
the river, for there are no paths. He has marked our course
rather casually with panga flicks, and two or three times on
the way back, we see him misread his own signs even before
he backtracks to pick up the trail. Near the river, there is a
sudden burst of rufous animals out of a thicket in the grassy
swale—Bohor reedbuck, an antelope we know well from
East Africa.

At the river, Aliende slips away in his pirogue, and,
waiting for Slaus, Jonah and I sit on the bank gazing out
over the water. So far we have gotten on extremely well,
perhaps a bit better than I had expected, though we have
been friends for fourteen years. Increasingly we can laugh
at each other and have fun, and since, on this journey, we
share many interests and concerns, we are rarely short of
conversation. There by the river, splitting an orange, we are
full of well-being and contentment. Jonah tells me about his
father, a British building surveyor and city planner who
worked for the colonial administration in Dar es Salaam
thirty years ago. In his spare time, Arthur Western was a
hunter, but, like many hunters in East Africa, he was also
a conservationist, and he was instrumental in the establish-

ment of Mikumi National Park in what in those days was still Tanganyika. He was also an "honorary ranger" who was sometimes called upon to dispatch dangerous rogue elephants, and he was killed by such an animal in the Kilombero Valley, north of the Selous Game Reserve, in 1958, when Jonah was fourteen.

Jonah, who was born in England, returned there in 1961 to find work and complete his studies. "I was only anxious to get back to Africa," he says. In 1967, he took up residence in Amboseli Park, in Kenya, to complete his thesis ("The Structure, Dynamics, and Changes of the Amboseli Ecosystem"), and for the next ten years he lived mostly at Amboseli, under Mount Kilimanjaro, which he still considers home.

▼▼▼

On a reconnaissance flight on our last afternoon, we are sorry to see no elephants whatever in the pans to the south near the Congo frontier, and only a single herd of forest buffalo. But once again there are elephants at Dzanga, which seems to attract most if not all of the local population.

During the flight over the forest, the plane develops a mysterious whine, as some sort of minor oil leak from the propeller films the windshield. I notice that on the return flight Jonah crosses over to the Sangha River and follows it back upstream to Bayanga. On the ground, as we refuel and prepare the plane for tomorrow's four-hour flight, I ask if coming back along the river had been a precaution, and he said it was. He tells me that that whine is nothing serious, the motor was overhauled completely before we started on this voyage, perhaps we will have it checked in Libreville.

Jonah seems preoccupied and even downcast; he says he is fighting off an achy flu. Walking down the twilight road toward the village, we discuss for the first time the fine points of a forced landing in these jungle rivers. "No mar-

gin for error out there, is there?" Jonah murmurs, manag-
ing a grin, and I nod, relieved that he realizes this, too, and
feels relaxed enough to say so. He describes how Douglas-
Hamilton once conked out over the forest, and, with the
usual amazing luck that has rescued our friend from one
scrape after another, peered down to see the only clearing
in the region, which he glided into.

Since Jonah is nothing if not stiff-upper-lipped, he
rarely mentions the awesome inhospitality of the equatorial
forest from the perspective of a single-engine plane, perhaps because there is nothing to discuss: in the event of
engine failure or forced landing, unless a swamp or river is
within gliding range, a light plane would disappear into this
greenness like a stone dropped from the air into the sea.
(Even if by miracle the plane managed a pancake landing
on the canopy without disintegrating or exploding, there
are no low limbs on the forest trees, and the injured passengers might find themselves confronted with a jump of at
least a hundred feet into the gloom below.) It would do no
good to worry people by telling them our course, which is
usually remote from radio contact, even if radio contact
would be useful. One's best hope, all things considered,
would be death on impact, since survivors could never be
found, far less assisted. In short, why talk about it—the less
said, the better.

▼▼▼

The morning is hazy, and we do not take off until 9:30 A.M.,
after bidding adieu to our cheerful C.A.R. associates and
kind Slavic hosts. Climbing above a lens of cloud, the plane
heads southwest, crossing the invisible frontier and drifting
out over Cameroon. An hour later, by rough estimate,
Cameroon's border with northwestern Congo falls behind.
Occasionally we glimpse the green snake of a slough or a
dark gray-brown jungle river, the scar of a burned clearing,
or even an overgrown red road with the glint of a tin roof

at the end. (Later Jonah estimates that we were in sight of a swamp or river or some other such place to attempt a landing about a third of the time—optimistic in Richard's opinion and my own, and not heartwarming odds in any case, quite apart from one's prospects during and after such a desperate measure.

In Congo, we peer down at Souanké, a human outpost perhaps an hour from the Karagoua River and two hours from the Gabon border, at the bitter end of the most remote road in all the world. We cross the northernmost province of Gabon, then the southeast corner of Río Muni, a former Spanish colony currently known as Equatorial Guinea. Then we are back over Gabon again, crossing the steep green Monts de Cristal, from which fierce whitewater streams course down to the Atlantic. The Gulf of Guinea comes in sight within the hour, a dull streak on the gray tropical horizon. A rough crust on the sea edge is Libreville, the capital of Gabon, where we must seek permission to visit Makokou, in the tropical forests we have just flown over.

▼▼▼

Makokou, on the Ivindo River of northeast Gabon, lies less than fifty miles north of the equator. The Makokou Institut de Recherche en Ecologie Tropicale, founded originally by the French, seems just the place for Richard Barnes to perfect the techniques for censusing the forest elephant, a task in which he is cheerfully assisted by his fiancée, Karen Jensen; Ms. Jensen has trained herself carefully in analysis of dung, which provides forthright and honest evidence of elephant numbers. An easygoing and informal young American from Long Beach, California, where they are to be married in July, she appreciates Richard's rather formal personality (and vice versa) and suits herself up in full jungle regalia for their expeditions, just as he does.

Richard and Karen met a few years ago at Dian Fossey's

gorilla camp at Karisoke, in Rwanda, where Richard was
director of research and Karen was a research assistant.
Both were impressed by Miss Fossey's fierce commitment
to and thorough knowledge of gorillas, and both were
alarmed by her misanthropic personality, which expressed
itself most disagreeably in her violent prejudice against
Africans, including her own cowed and frightened staff.
"They lived in dread of her return," says Richard, "and
when she arrived, the morale went all to pieces. She liked
to abuse and humiliate African men, and because they had
families, and jobs were scarce, they had to take it. We were
told she would have poachers stripped, then thrash them
head to toe with nettles; when she was drunk, she fired her
pistol over people's heads."

One cannot question the veracity of Dr. Barnes, who
goes out of his way to be conservative in his opinions, and
Miss Jensen supported him in all he said. "At the end," he
told us, "she rarely went out into the field unless camera-
men or reporters were in camp. She loved gorillas, perhaps,
but she had no love for human beings. We were certain
there was going to be violence, with which, on moral
grounds, we didn't wish to be associated. It never occurred
to us that she might be the victim until we spoke with the
American ambassador, whose comment was, 'One of these
days, they're going to come after her with pangas, as they
did Joy Adamson.' Finally I went to the authorities and
advised them strongly not to renew her visa. They had
already heard how serious things were, but they said she
attracted tourist income to Rwanda, which was badly
needed, and they couldn't refuse her. Under the circumstances, we resigned; we felt we could not work there any
longer."

Karen Jensen nodded her agreement; she has unpleas-
ant memories of her own. That a colleague who started out
so well (and won the admiration of such peers as George
Schaller and Jane Goodall) should have come to such an

ugly end was very upsetting, but their impressions of the last years of Dian Fossey are widely shared by others who had dealings with her. At a primate conference in 1985 in San Diego, Miss Fossey informed Dr. Western that the only meaningful approach to conservation in Africa was to hand out condoms. "I thought I was talking to a crazy person," Jonah says. "I told her I didn't think we had much to talk about, and walked away. She was spitting mad."

In his years at Amboseli, Jonah worked continually with Africans, in particular the Masai, whose cattle competed with the wild animals for the scarce grass, and he is convinced that conservation that does not cooperate with the local people is of limited value, confining the preservation of animals to the artificial limits imposed by the boundaries of a national park. "Putting a boundary around Amboseli did not protect it. If you work with the people, show them the benefits that may come to them, show them the compatibility of human use and conservation, they will support what you are doing, even help with antipoaching. This way, wildlife conservation can extend beyond park boundaries." Jonah shrugged. "Things still go wrong, of course. The Masai *morani* are forbidden to kill lions these days, and so last year, to prove themselves, they killed forty elephants instead. Nevertheless, cooperation with the other interests, with the farmers or pastoralists, or with the foresters, is far more effective in the long run than fighting everyone as Dian Fossey did. For one thing, the governments can support both interests instead of always having to choose."

▼▼▼

One day we join Richard and Karen in a walk of ten kilometers through the forest, led by an old Ba-kota hunter named Bilombi. Though popularly supposed not to be a Pygmy, Bilombi is so small that much of the day is spent ducking under vines that the old tracker does not slash aside because he himself passes easily beneath them. This is not a failure of courtesy but of spatial apprehension, for he is an amiable old man. For a Bantu, he seems very easy in the forest, and familiar with all the nuts and fruits consumed by forest inhabitants, including man. One fruit the size and color of an orange comes from a liana called *mbolo*, which also produces a white sticky resin sometimes used in rubber manufacture. The *mbolo* climbs hundreds of feet to the top of some great tree in the canopy, where its bright fruits are consumed by monkeys. "Monkey candy," Bilombi says. Another small fruit, the *atanga*, is shiny purple-blue, and Bilombi stops to gather up a pocketful, which he wraps carefully for his family in the wide thin leaves that characterize the light-starved plants of the forest floor. "Everybody eats it!" Bilombi exclaims, with an utterly open smile of delight, as if in approval of all life. Then he says, "If you wait here, all the antelope will come!"

Bilombi is referring to the small forest duikers, but the sitatunga is also here, deep in the marshes, and so is the bongo of the elegant lyrate horn. Crossing a marshy stream, Bilombi points out the print of a larger antelope, which he says has been made by a sitatunga. Jonah shakes his head—"not long enough." And a swift green snake with a red belly which shoots from the leaf litter into a log Bilombi calls a mamba, though it is not. Probably Bilombi is mistaken in much of the information that he offers us, and tends to err on the side of what his white companions wish to see, but all the same his eye is sharp and his bushcraft expert. And so we learn about native medicines such as this tree sap which, when boiled, will deal with urinary mischief in all women, and this peculiar paste with thin white fibers, created somehow by a tortoise eating mushrooms; he draws our attention to a strangely swaying bush where a departing mandrill has not eluded his keen eye. At one place he whacks free a three-foot section of rattan that he calls "water liana," from one end of which, miraculously, a small but steady stream of pure good water flows into one's mouth. At another, the old man stops short and commences a weird nasal honking, used by the forest hunters to call duiker, and sure enough, a small blue duiker, large-eyed and delicate-limbed, hurries in across the narrow shafts of sun before whirling to flee with a great thump and scatter.

Today we are recording all elephant sign seen in each kilometer of our walk, footprints and scrape marks on trees as well as droppings, which Karen, compiling her "dung-density data," is very good at assessing as to age. Most of the droppings found today are old ones and well scattered, scarcely more than a round dark shadow of soft soil. "There are a lot of bush pig here," says Richard, "and they do a hell of a lot of rooting in this *tembo* dung. For that reason, our dung-density data"—and here he gives Karen an affectionate, sardonic glance—"may depend more on the density of bush pig than it does on the density of *tembo*." (Richard's use of the Swahili word for elephant, an echo of his days in Ruaha Park, is respectful and not an affectation; a man with fewer affectations would be hard to find.)

That elephants were here last month is borne out by the droppings, but there is no question that they are scarce here. "Soils and plants determine where an elephant *can* live," Richard says, as we pause to inspect the remains of a cooking fire near a stream where people have been fishing, "and man determines where an elephant *does* live." Elephant scarcity at Makokou is attributable to scarce fodder as well as to the occasional hunters from the Makokou settlement who make camp in these glades. (The men go hunting while the women fish the slow, dark forest brooks by constructing rough mud-and-log dams, braced with upright sticks, braced in their turn by long Y-sticks planted at an angle.)

Of all the countries in the Congo Basin, Gabon is thought to be the most intact, with the highest percentage of undisturbed forest and the least disrupted wildlife populations. Even so, wildlife seems scarce compared to the plentiful life in the savanna. "I'm not a forest man," Jonah says later, "but it seems to me that the available food produced here is much less than the food produced in the savanna, even if the mass is counted that is far out of reach of the elephants, up in the canopy. And much of the food that *is* within their reach is unpalatable, having developed secondary compounds—bad-tasting chemicals not related to the plant's growth—to keep elephants and other creatures from eating it. Richard is unwilling to give out premature figures, but from what I've seen, both here and in C.A.R., he's getting about one-point-five droppings per kilometer of walking, which—allowing time for decomposition—works out to a rough count of one elephant going by each month.

"I doubt if this will improve very much anywhere in the equatorial forest, whether the region is occupied by man or not. According to Ian Parker's figure of five elephants per square kilometer, there should have been two thousand animals in that area we investigated at Bayanga, which includes the high-density concentration around Dzanga Pan as well as a number of smaller pans and watercourses. I very much doubt if there were two hundred altogether, and the average across the Congo Basin must be far less. Perhaps there were more originally, but I don't think forest elephant numbers were ever as high as people wished to think."

It is here near the equator that we thought a pure population of *cyclotis* would be found. We were mistaken. A young male shot yesterday by local authorities as an alleged crop raider was immediately butchered and eaten by the people, but enough was left to determine that it was a hybrid, with bush tusks extending well forward, and round, small cyclotiform ears.

▼▼▼

In the dry season, when rocks emerge and its water is a clear dark tannin brown, the Ivindo reflects the huge paletrunked trees of the gallery forest, the flowering lianas and fire red of the new leaves. It is very beautiful, especially among the rapids and rock islands down the river, where collared pratincoles and the exquisite white-throated blue swallows are the common birds. We see no crocodiles. A few years ago, a French hide trader gave rifles to the Ba-kota, who killed every crocodile in the Ivindo on his behalf, and the same pattern was repeated almost everywhere throughout Gabon, which has almost no crocodiles left. The rifles are still here and the Ba-kota still hunt the river in their delicate pirogues, with the result that the monkeys have withdrawn from the gallery forest where they are ordinarily most easily seen.

Away from the river, monkeys are still common; we see the talapoin, smallest of all African species, hurrying along low limbs from one tree into another, and the white-nosed guenon, making a wild twirling leap forty feet down onto the understory, and DeBrazza's monkey, a handsome creature that we saw earlier at Garamba, in Zaire, at the east end of its broken range. All three are of the great guenon tribe, the cercopithecines, which extends all the way across Africa, from the mona monkey in Senegal to the blue or Sykes's monkey of East Africa. (It also includes the vervet or green monkey, only known source of virus-free polio vaccine, and also the carrier of the viral source of the very dangerous "green monkey disease," which is a close relative of the AIDS virus.) Some authorities—Dr. Western is one—regard the cercopithecines as mere geographic races of one great superspecies, despite their differences of size and color and their striking varieties of whiskers and beards.

Jonah's opinion would surely be anathema to Dr. Jean-Pierre Gauthier, a friendly and expansive primatologist who has worked out of this research station for many years. Even at breakfast, Dr. Gauthier is given to comical gorilla imitations, and also the fascinating coughs, moans, and long-distance shouts of the great guenon tribe that is his specialty. Sounds of aggression or warning may be shared by different species, he says, but the cries, the hooting of the males, the gathering calls and murmurings that keep the troop together in its travels through the forest, are so specific to each species that it is impossible for a juvenile of one species to successfully imitate the vocalizations of another. In fact, vocalization patterns in the five guenon species he has studied are directly related to the evolution of the various cercopithecine types.

Perhaps increasingly with the coming of man, forest monkeys have acquired new defenses, and many species in this brash and noisy group are largely silent. Others, such as DeBrazza's, are largely terrestrial, and when threatened, simply leap out of the trees (where they might be shot) and scamper off. The little talapoin may roost in low branches over water, and even a female carrying an infant will dive off the branch and swim away beneath the surface, a tactic that may have evolved first to frustrate the leopard. All such defenses demonstrate how difficult it is to capture these intelligent and wary creatures. Many hundreds of hours, Dr. Gauthier says, are ordinarily devoted to every monkey darted or trapped and fitted out with a radio collar for further study.

Dr. Gauthier, who lives in Paris, has returned to Gabon to investigate what he believes to be a new cercopithecine species. It was first described in 1985 by British primatologist Mike Harrison from the Région des Abeilles (Bee Country), about one hundred miles south of Makokou, where the strange monkey, known locally as *mbaya*, was first seen slung over a hunter's shoulder. The *mbaya* is most closely related to L'Hoest's monkey, and is said to be the wariest of a very wary lot, though this trait may be less significant in its avoidance of discovery than its limited range in a remote and largely uninhabited forest.

▼▼▼

The rain-forest communities are the oldest on earth, with hundreds of insect species specific to each of the many species of its trees. Almost half of the earth's living things, many as yet undiscovered, live in this green world that is shrinking fast to a small patch on the earth's surface. Man has already destroyed half of the rain forests, which disappear at an ever-increasing speed, and a mostly unknown flora and fauna disappear with them.

Therefore, at every opportunity, we explore the forest, and often I go out alone, for walking in solitude through the dim glades, immersed in silence, one learns a lot that cannot be taught in any other way. The canopy of huge trees is closed, so that even at midday its atmosphere is cool and dark, too dark—too *mysterious*, it almost seems—for photographs. The forest silence is impermeable, entirely undisturbed by the soft bell notes of hidden birds, the tick of descending leaves and twigs or soft thump of falling fruit, or even the far caterwaul of monkeys. From far above come the unearthly squawks of great blue turacos, hopping and clambering along the highest limbs like *Archaeopteryx*.

Increasingly uneasy in one's own intrusion, moving ever more quietly so as not to wake things, one grows aware of immense harmony. The dust of the world spins in cathedral light in the long sun shafts falling from on high. The light touches a brilliant bird feather, an armored beetle, a mighty bean pod husk, silky and red, or hard and shiny as carved wood. The silent processions of the army ants, in their myriad species and deadly strength, glisten in dark ribbons on the forest floor; the taut webs of jungle spiders shine and vanish. High overhead, a bright orange *mbolo* fruit swells with sun in a chink of blue sky like a clerestory. But this underworld is brown and green, and green is the color of the stifled air.

Man hunts in this forest, and few creatures are still left—monkeys, mandrills, squirrels, duikers, tree hyrax, several pangolins—to sustain the leopard whose scat I found yesterday near a forest pool. The scat was too old to attract butterflies, which lose all caution and are easily caught when feeding on the protein in carnivore dung. Like a beautiful lotus growing out of mud was the strange blossom of elusive life that we came upon one day on the forest path, cobalt and red and black and forest green. The blossom opens as the butterflies palpitate, drawing their life, their very color from their reeking feast. And they are hurrying, for in a climate that permits ceaseless reproduction, certain butterflies may begin and end their days in a single month.

All along, an enormous sound has resounded through the silence, and suddenly it transfixes one's awareness. It is the fierce wing shriek of cicadas, each shriek as painful to the ear as a blade sharpened on stone, yet joining with thousands of others in electric song and smoothing out in a wild ringing from the canopy high overhead. The thick-bodied, green cicadas are ventriloquial, Jonah says, and I wonder if this is not also true of those hidden forest birds whose beautiful voices seem impossible to trace. Most of the birds remain high in the canopy, but bird armies, or "ejaks," of mixed species—leafloves, wattle-eyes, malimbes, greenbuls—come flitting through the understory, and if one stands still long enough one of the hidden singers will appear.

Late one afternoon the yellow-cheeked trogon, a shy, uncommon forest dweller with emerald mantle and crimson breast and yellow spots behind the bill, flew from the shadows and perched dead still on a limb over the path. Like a spirit of the forest, it remained motionless even when we walked beneath it, and it did not turn its head to watch us go.

▼▼▼

The Ivindo River, which flows south from the border region of Cameroon and Congo, drops off the high plateaus
below Makokou in a series of white waterfalls and rapids to
join eventually with the great Ogooué, which flows west
past Lambarene to the sea. Like the Sangha, the Ivindo is
one of many Congo Basin tributaries that are larger than
any river in East Africa, or any river on the Indian Ocean
except the great Zambezi and possibly the Ruvuma, on the
Tanzania-Mozambique border. Nevertheless our attempts
to follow it on our southward journey are thwarted by low
clouds that almost turn us back. "That wasn't a good situation," David Western mutters, after making a tight circle
back and gaining altitude before resuming his course. "The
ceiling got lower and lower as we neared those mountains,
and before you know it the aircraft could have been trapped
down in some valley between hills, unable to see where it
might climb out."

At the Ivindo's confluence with the Ogooué, we head
west, making a landing at the Lope airstrip, between the
Ogooué and the brave new Trans-Gabonais railroad designed to open up Gabon's unexploited interior to timber
and mineral development. A few years ago, when the railroad up the Ogooué was being constructed, this Lope region was very hard hunted to provide meat for the crews.
Today it is a wildlife reserve, and the animals are coming
back, with buffalo and elephant now quite common. One
day, perhaps, Lope-Okande, as it is known, will be a true
national park, but for the moment it still issues timber
leases. (Virtually the entire rain forest of Gabon, C.A.R.,
Congo, Cameroon, and much of Zaire has already been
sold in logging units to European countries and the Japa-
nese; already about one-fifth of Gabon's foreign income
comes from wood.) And since the nation's oil, which fi-

nanced the new railroad, is drying up, and since Gabon's mineral reserves are less extensive than was at first believed, the country's small population and its low rate of increase may prove to be a blessing. Even so, the people are officially exhorted to produce more children and occupy the wilderness regions to the east. Whether foreign investors or the Gabonnais themselves will profit from this exploitation remains to be seen, but in view of the headlong scary rate at which the earth's rain forests are disappearing, there seems no doubt that humanity will be the loser.

Richard Barnes, who has accompanied us from Makokou, has kindly made arrangements for our various visits in Gabon, and we are picked up at the airstrip by Lope's warden. M. Sambouni drives us through the open savanna hills under Mount DeBrazza, named after the French explorer who discovered the Ogooué River and gave his name to the distinguished monkey as well as to Brazzaville, the present capital of Congo Republic. The extensive grassland in this region, in an odd pattern up and down the hills, seems to bear no relation to the ecological topography, and although M. Sambouni says that the savanna has always been here, he also says he must burn it each year to keep the forest from encroaching.

David Western is convinced that the savanna is "derived"—created, that is, by man's impact; in fact, he disputes the widespread notion that the great wildlife savannas of East Africa are a natural ecosystem, mysteriously unaffected by the presence of pastoral man for three thousand years. Since it has never been forested in present memory, the grassland must have been established in earlier centuries of Bantu settlement, perhaps as early as the first migrating waves of Bantu peoples, who are thought to have followed the rivers south perhaps fifteen hundred years ago in response to long-term drought or overpopulation in the savannas. Throughout this region, the patchwork grassland is so widespread that settlement must have been much more extensive than it is today, and only the depredations of the slave trade, and the fierce intertribal slaving wars that followed, seem to account for the great emptiness of this broken landscape.

▼▼▼

In less than an hour, we arrive at the quarters of Dr. Caroline Tutin, a young British primatologist whose airy camp on a savanna hilltop overlooks the Lope-Okande forest. For a year and a half in the early seventies, Dr. Tutin, a small, trim young woman with green eyes and red hair, worked with Jane Goodall at Gombe Stream in Tanzania, after which, for a number of years, she pursued her own chimpanzee research at the Parc de Niokolo Koba, in Senegal. It was there that she first met her associate, Michel Fernandez, a genial French pilot, mechanic, and logistical expert who constructed and maintains their present camp. (Tutin and Fernandez remind me that we met in 1979, when I visited Niokolo Koba.) Dr. Tutin says that she finds field work in Gabon exciting not only because most of its forest is intact but because this high western region of the equatorial rain forest was a Pleistocene refugia, where a very large, complex, and diverse flora and fauna survived the widespread cooling and drying on this continent that occurred during the Ice Age, ten thousand years ago, when most of the rain forest disappeared. Little is known as yet about this fauna, and even less about the flora, and she suspects that new species may yet be found. She agrees with her colleague Dr. Gauthier that the *mbaya* is a distinct new species of cercopithecine, despite its very limited range of one hundred square kilometers across the Lolo River to the east.

At Lope, Dr. Tutin is studying the behavior of chimpanzee and lowland gorilla, both of which, she says, were first reported from Gabon by American missionaries. Though she is still partial to the chimp—"Everything in its social organization encourages the development of high intelligence"—she is at present concentrating on the gorilla. In her first two years, she has located and censused five separate groups, not counting two or three lone males, but none of these animals are as yet habituated to human beings, and the big silverback males (the French also like this term, saying "seelvairebok moll") are still given to roaring display charges that will cause even elephants to back up.

The great majority of gorilla threat displays stop well short of physical contact, but a year ago, on December 24 ("I remember the date well," says the victim), a lone silverback rushed out of the thicket and bit Fernandez on the calf. The gorilla took him for another male, he thinks. "If he'd wished to kill me or seriously hurt me, he could have done so very easily," Fernandez told me, a surprised expression on his face, "but he didn't even bite me with full force."

Since male gorillas are equipped with large, sharp canines, this gentle bite left holes in his leg, the scars of which are still impressive. Similar bitings have occurred at Dian Fossey's camp at Karisoke, in Rwanda, and at Kahuzi-Biega, in eastern Zaire, where I observed gorillas a few years ago, but none have been fatal despite the huge strength and fearsome aspect of what all authorities regard as a gentle vegetarian creature. "Imagine one of these great hunters shooting down a silverback!" Caroline Tutin says with quiet indignation. "It's hard to imagine a less sporting shot!"

The mountain gorilla of the Central Highlands, which is regularly shot by poachers for tourist "trophy heads" (the young are taken illegally for zoos, a process which usually involves shooting the adults), is now in serious danger, its population having been reduced to about four hundred, but, like the northern white rhino, it is regarded as a geographic race, not a true species, despite marked morphological differences in the two forms. (At present a third race is recognized—the eastern lowland gorilla, now reduced to a few small ranges in eastern Zaire. Between twenty-five hundred and forty-five hundred of this largest of the three gorillas, which include the animals at Kahuzi-Biega, are thought to remain.) Worldwide alarms of gorilla extinction that were sounded a few years ago were based on rough estimates that the combined populations of the mountain and the lowland races did not exceed five to seven thousand animals, but in a recent development—quite the opposite of what we now anticipate for forest elephant—Dr. Tutin and other researchers have discovered an estimated thirty-five thousand gorilla in Gabon alone, and other healthy lowland populations as far west as Cameroon. (Richard Carroll's more conservative figure is thirty thousand to fifty thousand western lowland gorilla in all five countries of the western Congo Basin—Cameroon, C.A.R., Gabon, Congo, and Equatorial Guinea.) As in the case of the northern white rhino, this raises the question of whether so much conservation effort should be spent on a remnant and perhaps doomed geographic race—the mountain gorilla—when the species as a whole is not in danger.

With Jonah, I accompany Dr. Tutin on an afternoon trek into her forest, which appears far more modified by elephants than the forest at Makokou. Because the gorillas are still shy, she thinks it unlikely that they will show themselves, and she turns out to be right, although we encounter a large number of fresh droppings. Dr. Tutin deftly collects one in a polyethylene bag for food analysis. "Some of these smell quite nice," she says, and at this point she glances up at Dr. Western, aware that his wife, Dr. Strum, is a noted baboon authority. So gently that Jonah doesn't notice he is being teased, she whispers with a shy sly smile, "Better than baboons'!" (Remarkably, the best known primate researchers—Goodall, Fossey, Biruti-Galdikas [the orangutan researcher in Borneo], and more recently Drs. Strum and Tutin—are women. The first three—known irreverently in primate circles as "the trimates"—were protégées of Louis Leakey, who felt that women had more patience for prolonged study, but this does not fully account for the phenomenon, for which no behavioral theory has been advanced.)

On a forest ridge, our coming provokes a crashing flight through the dense undergrowth. "Large duiker," Dr. Tutin whispers. "Yellow-backed, I should think." We also startle a mustached monkey, one of three guenon species that share this forest with gorillas, chimpanzees, mandrills, gray-cheeked mangabeys, and black colobus. Dr. Tutin says that primate species are even more numerous in south Cameroon, at the northern end of this Pleistocene refugia, which extends all the way down to the coast; she has seen gorillas on the seashore at Mayumba, in southwest Gabon.

The ridge opens out on one of the large rocks that jut up from the forest floor, and here we sit still for a little while, hoping to hear the chest thumping and other noises that might betray the whereabouts of the gorillas. What we hear instead is the strange "pant-hooting" of an approaching troop of chimpanzees, each animal's harsh cries joining with others in a wild ululation that rings and wanders through the trees. "They've found something good to eat, or they've run into another subgroup, perhaps both," Caroline murmurs, turning to listen with the same smile of unabashed wonder and approval that is so affecting in the hunting peoples. We cross the ridge to the far side, following the sound of the chimps feeding, but already the apes are falling quiet, all but hidden in the canopies of leaves. "They're settling down now for the night," Caroline says, smiling again. "I'll be here the first thing in the morning."

▼▼▼

In the course of his African elephant survey in 1979, Dr. Iain Douglas-Hamilton saw a troop of little elephants on the sea beach at Iguela Game Reserve, here in Gabon. Douglas-Hamilton's escort, Claude Pradel, the director of the hunting preserve of President Omar Bongo at Wonga-

Wongue, and a veteran of thirty-three years in this country, told Iain that these elephant were *assala*, which is the local name for "pygmy elephant." If we wanted a look at the mysterious *assala*, the wild tract of thirty-five hundred square kilometers at Wonga-Wongue, extending inland from the coast, seemed very promising, since elephants were more protected there than anywhere else in this casual country.

Not without difficulties and delays, Richard Barnes and his friend Dr. Aart Louis, the director of the national herbarium, have received permission for a brief visit to Wonga-Wongue, and on January 22, accompanied by Dr. Louis and another Dutch botanist, Dr. Jan Reitsma, and escorted by a soldier of the president's guard, we fly about seventy miles south of Libreville to a tranquil region of forest and meadows parted by clear streams that flow down from high grassy plateaus to the sea. Without much question, Wonga-Wongue, surrounded by vast marshes and lacking road access—one can only come by boat or plane—is one of the loveliest reserves in all of Africa.

M. Pradel lives year-round at the president's camp on a wooded hill well inland from the coast, together with his wife, Nina, his nineteen-year-old son, Norbert, a German assistant, an African staff, four Bengal tigers, five puma from South America, a young chimpanzee, two zebras, and a very large monitor lizard, which resides in an empty swimming pool by the main house. Most of these creatures are the property of President Bongo, who is usually accompanied here on his rare visits by some other head of state who is anxious to shoot something. Thus Wonga-Wongue is exposed to hunting, as are Lope-Okande and Iguela, but the hunting here is as limited as it is infrequent. From the animals' point of view, at least, it comes closer to a true national park than any wild area in Gabon.

Monsieur Pradel is away in Ivory Coast at the time of our visit, but Madame Pradel, a handsome redhead from

Toulouse, is very hospitable in her husband's absence. She presides over an exotic living room lined with stuffed birds and monkeys, kudu and sable horns, a monkey-skull fetish, artificial flowers, photographs, amateur paintings, curios, and three saddles mounted on racks; one of the saddles is an ornate cowboy model acquired last year on a visit to Texas, where she also acquired the University of Texas T-shirt worn by young Norbert. The Pradels keep horses here but have not had much luck with them because of sleeping sickness and other, undiagnosed, ailments. "We've never kept a horse alive more than four years," she says. "It's very sad, watching them die."

All three Pradels pilot their own airplanes, but Madame Pradel, who sees to Wonga-Wongue's administration, has not left the reserve for the past two years. "What is there to do in Libreville?" she inquires, throwing her hands up in fine Gallic disdain. "I'm better off here. I don't wish to *die* here, but . . ." She shrugs. The first few years of her sixteen in Gabon were spent at Makokou; she describes to Richard the gigantic Makokou elephants that are now all gone. But what she remembers even better than the elephants are the huge Goliath and rhinoceros beetles in the forest.

Madame Pradel confirms the presence of *assala*; just the other day she has seen a troop with a tiny infant "no bigger than a toy." The presence of the infant does not fit our theory that pygmy elephants are nothing more than maverick young forest elephants, with or without precocious tusks, and neither does her account of a sick *assala* from Wonga-Wongue which after its death had been stuffed for display in President Bongo's palace back in Libreville. Judging from the worn condition of its tusks, everyone who saw this little animal, say the Pradels, agreed that it was at least sixty years old. But inspecting the photograph that Madame Pradel shows us, we see what looks like a four-year-old forest elephant, even to the body hair found on young animals. "The tusk wear doesn't mean a thing," Jonah says later. "Juvenile tusks often get chipped and worn, and look like tusks of older animals." What we wish to do as soon as possible is to inspect these *assala* in the field, and dispel the mystery once and for all.

Norbert Pradel offers to guide us around Wonga-Wongue during our stay. Dressed in camouflage fatigues and cap, packing a pistol, Norbert maneuvers the family's bush vehicle as rapidly as possible over the red sand roads. We flush one sitatunga, which has wandered up into the grasslands from the marshy lakes, but the only animals seen in abundance are red forest buffalo. Like the forest elephant, the forest buffalo is of the same species as its savanna kinsman, and it, too, is half the size of its savanna race and very different in appearance, carrying its much smaller horns as duikers do, swept back and tight for forest travel. Like their large relatives, the forest buffalo wheel to the four winds when panicked, nostrils high, ears wide and ragged, hummocking along on random courses that often carry them across the path of whatever it is that they are fleeing.

Some years ago, young Norbert's father was nearly demolished by a *bouffle* that rose and pursued him after his bullet dropped it, and gored him twice before plunging off into the forest. "And that one was *dead*," exclaims Madame Pradel later, ladling buffalo meat onto our plates; she tells us about a woman worker on the reserve plantation who recently survived a severe goring.

Because of its remote location and lack of access roads, Wonga-Wongue is virtually free of all but local poachers, who hunt for meat, and even these (from what Norbert views as a deplorable weakness in the tribal character) are betrayed by their fellow villagers at the first whisper of trouble. Only lately have commercially inclined outsiders started to appear. One such fellow was apprehended with forty-three decaying monkeys, which he hoped would still be pleasing to his customers in Libreville after a journey of seventy hot miles in his pirogue. Much more serious, Norbert relates, was an episode in which a white pilot in a military aircraft gunned down a troop of elephants with rockets. The carcasses were bulldozed under by a confederate on the Wonga-Wongue staff, to be exhumed again when the ivory had rotted free. These people were eventually traced and arrested, thanks to Claude Pradel, who has earned a reputation for enforcing game protection in this country where protection is, at best, a quaint idea.

Even on the highest plateaus, where the grass blows to the horizon, remnant isles of trees rise from the tawny land. The botanists agree with Western that all this country was once forest, and that this vast empty savanna, like the one at Lope, was originally cleared and farmed by Bantu peoples who later fled the pillage of the slave trade. The ancient soil, its minerals leached out by sixty million years of rain, was weakened further, Dr. Louis believes, by erosion caused by primitive cultivation, so that the forests were unable to return. As in the savannas north of the forest, the impoverished grasses, which provide supplementary bulk to the large animals, are too coarse and poor to support the smaller herbivores; even the zebras of President Bongo seem to disdain them. These uplands have attracted some of the same bird life that one sees in the savannas of East Africa—eagles, larks, and swallows, the Senegal plover, the nightjars and spotted eagle-owls of the night roads—but by comparison, the birds are few, and of few species.

By the roadside I see the gleam of a large python, but unfortunately Norbert sees it, too. He yanks the vehicle onto the shoulder and runs it over, nearly losing control of the car in the jolt of the impact. Astonishingly the snake slides away. "Python," he says, disgusted. "Maybe three meters." I ask him rather sharply why he wished to kill it, and hearing no criticism, he answers cheerfully, "Because I do not like it. *Sont les sales bêtes*."

In the late afternoon, a few elephants come carefully from the forest. Their usual habit is to feed all evening and through the night in the grasslands along the forest verges, returning into the green wall at break of day. Toward twilight, in a dusky sun, seven or eight are moving steadily through sand-colored grass along the distant trees. A solitary cow appears, then a young male, and, finally two cows accompanied by small young and a half-grown female.

Our young guide does not slow down when elephants are sighted, being of the opinion that the pesky things will head straight for the forest, no matter what, and that our one chance is to head them off with the speeding car. Given their chronic exposure to this technique, it was certainly likely that they would head straight for the forest, and all we see are baggy gray hindquarters being swallowed by the trees. But the last group is caught out in the open, and Norbert, cutting across country, rides right up alongside the fleeing animals. They wheel and scream, ears and tails lashing, and head back in the opposite direction, as we assure him we have seen enough. Unquestionably these are adult females with calves bouncing at their flanks, and they are by far the smallest elephants we've seen, not six feet high.

"*Assala*," says Norbert Pradel, pleased he has shown us "*éléphant pygmée*" at such close range. I ask him if these little elephants were average size for the *assala*, and he says they are, reminding us that "big elephants" also occur here.

Next morning, in dense dry season mist, with chimpanzees howling from the forest, we approach on foot a lone adult male at least seven and a half or eight feet high, by Jonah's estimate. This elephant, too, has round small ears and lacks the protruding brow of male bush elephant, which would stand two or three feet taller at the shoulder, but his large ivory has the pronounced forward curve of the savanna race that we had noted even in one of the diminutive elephants seen up close the previous evening.

We had thought to encounter pure *cyclotis* rather quickly upon entering the equatorial forest, whether just north of the equator at Makokou or just south of it at Wonga-Wongue. What we had not expected was this very broad zone of hybridization in which large and small elephants coexist.

Traditionally paleontologists have believed that the bush elephant was the ancestral form, since its ancient bones have been found in the savanna. But bones don't last long in the damp forest (or researchers either), and since there were no savannas in pre-Miocene times, the African elephant must have evolved as a forest animal; either *cyclotis* is the original elephant or it evolved from the original, with the bush elephant appearing later. The nonadaptive and inappropriate bush habit of destroying trees while feeding was adaptive in the forest, where light must penetrate in order to produce second-growth browse, and this, too, suggests the forest ancestry of *Loxodonta*, on which most biologists now agree.

The Wonga-Wongue animals come as close to pure *cyclotis* as any we have seen, not only in morphological characters but in size. But somewhere, Jonah is convinced, there must exist a population with no trace of hybridization, to maintain the genetic characters identified with the forest race. He supposed that such elephants might be found in south Gabon, south Congo, or southwest Zaire.

▼▼▼

Throughout our visit to Gabon, we had to return repeatedly to Libreville, not only because aviation gasoline was unobtainable anywhere else but because special clearances were necessary for light plane travel to what were termed "inhospitable regions." And it was at Libreville airport, on a dead, fetid morning, that we said good-bye to Richard Barnes, whose elephant expertise as well as taut logistical preparations and good company had made an important contribution to our journey.

Richard himself had no regrets about our parting, since he doesn't much care for light plane travel over long stretches of equatorial forest. "I'm awfully glad," he said to me with uncustomary fervor, "that I do not have to get back into that airplane." Had he known what awaited us over the next two days, he would have fallen to his bony knees in simple gratitude.

▼▼▼

Heading southeast from Libreville to Kinshasa, in Zaire, on the first leg of our zigzag return across the continent, we cross the great Ogooué at Lambarene, where Dr. Alfred Schweitzer had his clinic, and continued southeast up the N'Gounié River. Two hundred miles out, the plane leaves the forest and crosses a broad country of marshlands and dwindling strands of trees. Here the forest ends. South Gabon, which we had envisioned as a last redoubt of the "pure" forest elephant, turns out to be a deforested land without visible life, only scarce and solitary huts with brown faded smudges of ancient gardens showing through pale weary greens. "Man-made," says Jonah of this wasteland, and when I wonder aloud about the fate of the men who made it, he says, not altogether seriously, "America."

According to our obsolete colonial air charts, the wandering red road that we are following runs all the way from Lambaréné to Brazzaville, capital of the Congo Republic, which lies across the Congo—now the Zaire River—from Kinshasa. (Like C.A.R. and Chad, Gabon and Congo were formerly a single administrative unit of French Equatorial Africa.) But not far beyond the Congo border the road diminishes into smaller tracks that scatter out among hill villages. These modern villages must differ little from those of former days, and they appear to be continuing the destruction of the land seen farther north, since the land around them is eroded, and their garden patches are miles distant across a worn-out earth.

The colonial road shown on the chart is gone entirely. We follow a southeastern course, picking up a landmark at the Niari River. Having no clearance for a landing in Congo, we must slip in and refill our wing tanks at a mission airstrip north of Dolisie, in open mining country, then take off speedily, following the new paved road toward Brazzaville.

Unaccountably this road swings off to the north, so once again we travel by dead reckoning, tending south across high barren country. The Zaire River cannot be very far, and in fact we cross a river soon thereafter, a swift narrow torrent through a gorge—too small, we agree, to be the great broad Congo with its famous steamers, largest river in all Africa. We forge on, southeast across a vast lonesome plateau. The empty land goes on and on and on, no end in sight, and no great river; more mystifying still, our maps show no roadless area of this extent in southern Congo. We stare at our watches and compass in disbelief. At midafternoon we see a small mission settlement with an airstrip; like it or not, we must land to refuel and find out where we are.

If the peasants who come rushing to the plane cannot read our map, they at least make it clear that they are citizens not of the Congo Republic but of Zaire. When I tell Jonah we are in Zaire, his jaw actually drops—one of the few times in my life that I have witnessed this comic phenomenon, though neither of us are in any mood to laugh. In fact, we are stunned by the realization that that narrow torrent in the gorge, so very different from our expectations, had been the mighty Congo after all.

When I ask for the general direction of Kinshasa, the people point at all points of the compass, and when I protest, one of them reproves me. "How are we to know? We are just here!" Feeling ashamed, I apologize and ask if they will lead me to the missionary. While Jonah refuels the plane, I set off quickly for the house of a kind Italian, Father Nicolo, who puts his finger on the map at a point more than a hundred miles southeast of our destination.

The Zairois, at first friendly and polite, are now comparing their suspicions. They begin to agitate and grow excited, for this place is just east of the Angola border, with its Cuban mercenaries (and its guerrilla war, largely financed, it is said, by the ivory from one hundred thousand slaughtered elephants). As it turns out, the people here are as paranoid about mercenaries as the peasants we met earlier in Haut-Zaïre. On my way back to the airstrip, they tug at my elbow, saying that it is too late in the day to reach Kinshasa. When I shake my head, they insist with increasing hostility that the people need to satisfy themselves that we are not spies; we must stay here until this "brusque" visit is investigated by the proper authorities. The spokesmen, more and more excited, start to shout, drawing attention to their own high sense of civic duty, and I realize with a pang of dread that unless we move fast, our history at Dibwa may repeat itself. I alert Jonah, who has refueled quickly. "We can just make it," he says, by which he means, There's just enough light to get us to Kinshasa, assuming we make no more mistakes. We have to chance it anyway, especially since, this very evening, we have an important meeting in Kinshasa that is the whole purpose of this leg of our journey.

We shoulder our way through the Africans and get into the plane and spin the prop to drive the shouters back. Father Nicolo stays well apart, wishing no trouble. Fortunately, in this mission settlement, there are no firearms. Jonah taxis to the far end of the strip as the spokesmen pursue us, and one tall screeching man in a red shirt holds his ground as the airplane comes at him, waving his arms wildly to flag us down, running aside only at the last minute.

Having done his best to stop us, he is philosophical, no longer angry, and grins and waves with all the rest as we roar past.

The blue-and-silver plane crosses the upper Wamba River, then the Kwango, and returns north over the stark emptiness of the great plateau. As in so much of this country, the darkening villages appear abandoned, their starving inhabitants whirled away as if by wind into the human sink of Kinshasa. We watch the sun move down behind the clouds off to the west. Because the mission station was not on our map, and the missionary rather vague about locations, our heading can only be approximate. Over the great hollow of the river basin, there is mist, and with the last light failing fast, we are not sure if we are up or down the river from Kinshasa. Just as it appears that oncoming night may force us to make an emergency landing in a field, we see the broad expanse of Stanley Pool, then a city tower. As dusk comes, we are making our way in to the international airport called N'djili.

I am limp with strain and exhilaration and relief, and so is Jonah, to judge from the fact that he approaches the airport from the wrong direction and is on the runway when the man in the tower, peering through the descending dusk in the opposite direction, is still instructing him on his angle of approach. Jonah is embarrassed, but not very. He knows as I know that we are lucky to be here at all, that but for clear weather and good visibility, this day could have ended very badly. That we failed to recognize the river is my fault as much as his. Neither of us knew—and his chart failed to show it—that the great wide Congo, below Stanley Pool, narrows to a torrent that plunges down a canyon toward the sea.

Anyway, this is no longer the man who analyzed for days the reasons for the forced landing at Dibwa. Perhaps because light-plane flying in poorly charted jungle countries is so difficult, accounting for "mistakes" seems beside the point, and Jonah can now smile at our mishaps. "We must be the only travelers," he sighs later, "who ever missed both the Nile and the Congo on the same journey."

All is smoothed over at N'djili by M. Mankoto Mbele, the director of Zaire's national parks, whose staff sees us rapidly through customs and escorts us through Kinshasa's streets to our hotel. Later he meets us for a pleasant dinner at the house of Patrick Towers-Picton, a local representative of the European Economic Community who is interested in wildlife, proposed parks, and elephant projects. Jonah speaks persuasively on the importance of forest conservation in Zaire and of the possibility of creating an international forest park in the Sangha River region of C.A.R., Congo Republic, and Cameroon. We return to the hotel at 1 A.M., knowing we must rise at dawn to resume our journey.

▼▼▼

Last night, our host referred to the wilderness between Kinshasa and Kisangani, our next destination, as "Zaire's Bermuda Triangle," because of the number of unlucky aircraft that have disappeared into that forest without a trace. As it turns out, special clearance is needed to fly a light plane into Zaire's immense forest interior. Also, we have not counted on the Kinshasa bureaucracy, which, even more than in Libreville and Bangui, is noisy and rude and inefficient on a heroic scale, so that even the simplest transaction requires at least ten times longer than is necessary. Questions are shouted and our answers scratched down on scraps of paper—snatched up, perhaps, from the floor or wastebasket—that may as well be instantly returned there, so certain does it seem that the information scrawled thereon will never be read again. The demanded passport or other document is waved about, picked up and dropped, or fanned in open incredulity and contempt for the lies and obfuscations it contains, when in fact the only thing amiss may be the bureaucrat's inability to read it.

The show is not intended for the traveler, who knows better, but for the swarm of lesser personages behind each desk—the relatives, the fetchers of soft drinks—who are desperately trying to justify their own niches in this system, and vie with each other in agreeing with the boss. Thus each must grab at and bang down the offending paper, expressing his professional dissatisfaction in the strongest terms, until finally everyone is shouting his own interpretation of the regulations. All this is conducted over the indecipherable static of the airport squawk boxes, which are invariably turned up to highest volume, and which, in conjunction with the senseless human din, make any significant communication out of the question.

Then suddenly the smell of money changing hands is in the air, and disputes collapse like froth in a boiled pot: the time has come to pay taxes and fees. However, the traveler's monies are rarely in the required currency, and no one behind the desk quite knows how to count, and anyway there is no change, and no one knows where change might be obtained. There are hints that the traveler might do well to forget the change, since gifts are in order for these worthy public servants who have cleared up the confusion that these mendacious documents have brought down upon them. To perceive such gifts as "bribes" is to fail to realize that they serve as salaries for these government workers who, in the corrupt anarchy of Zaire, may subsist unpaid for month after month, with no more prospect of a decent life than they had under Belgian rule.

Once customs is through with us, civil aviation refuses to clear our flight; the thousand miles over the forests to Kisangani is too dangerous for a single-engine plane. Eventually Jonah prevails, but it is past 11 A.M., after four hours at the airport, when the last official has satisfied himself that our documents and flight plan are in order. By this time, a large storm front to the north has appeared on the tower computers, but we are not notified of this until we have flown north for a half hour. We are warned to bear west of our course for the next hundred miles, after which we might locate a break in the front, and cross the river to Basankusu. Once again, we are fated to travel late, and will race the last light to Kisangani. In order not to waste time and precious fuel Jonah holds the plane as close as possible to the great storm front, a swirling mass of ugly grays with columns of rain and sudden lightning.

Our course is approximately northeast, but in the next hour and a half the storm forces us remorselessly to the northwest, over the burned and ruined plateaus of the Congo Republic. The storm shows no sign of diminishing, the airplane cannot find a way through. Trying to cut closer to gain time, the plane is caught by an immense wind and plunges drastically. The earth jumps up, causing the cargo to bang the cabin roof, as something breaks. The plane lurches and jolts as it veers away to westward, and a moment later the fuselage is struck by one of the black swifts that hurtle along the dark wall of the storm. The hard ping is like the ring of a hurled stone.

> Suddenly all hell breaks loose; hurricane-force winds slam us up and down with terrifying violence; green forest races up toward us; and fuel barrels and gear fly loose in the rear of the cockpit. I grimly try to regain control of the plane while Peter grabs for the baggage. Twenty agonizing seconds later, the winds subside enough for me to veer northwest. Finally, after we're battered by two more screaming gusts, I turn south, defeated, for Kinshasa . . .

The storm is dangerous, we can see no end to it, and besides, we have used up too much fuel. We race the gray mass back toward the south, but it moves in over the river as the plane banks eastward below Brazzaville. Forced to low altitude by poor visibility, beating its way back up the river, the plane seems blocked by wild wind over the boiling rapids where the Zaire narrows into its gorge below Stanley Pool. Incredibly that gorge carries more volume than any river on earth except the Amazon, and so fierce is the torrent (we are later told) that no one has ever set foot on this forested island that looms through the blowing rain beneath the wing. Once across the rapids, the plane fights for headway among the small skyscrapers of Kinshasa.

> By flying under the low scudding cloud base, over white-foamed rapids, between city skyscrapers where wind blasts hurl us up to the clouds one moment and almost down to the street the next, we reach N'dola Airport at the city's edge . . .*

Jonah requests clearance to land at the airfield called N'dola, which is much closer to the city than N'djili, but a medley of voices less calm than his own is haranguing him with irrelevant questions and issuing conflicting instructions, not only in two languages but from both towers. The plane is now in the black heart of the storm, with lashing rain and thick sinking clouds that keep it down among the buildings and a violent wind that tosses it from one building toward another with sickening jumps and drops and lurches. I pray that my partner is more confident than I that his airplane won't fly apart under such a beating.

I steal a look at him, with some idea that I might as well know the worst, and am relieved though not surprised by what I see. Jonah's face is grim and tense, just as my own must be, but there is no panic, only a twitch of exasperation at the instructions on the radio. When one of his tormen-

*David Western, *Discover*, October 1986.

tors orders him to proceed into N'djili and land toward the south—that is downwind—he answers tersely that he is proceeding to N'dola, after which he breaks off communication. In the tumult, he is holding the plane on its bounding course with sheer physical strength, and he has to concentrate on the approach. N'dola looms in the blurred windshield, and, maintaining his speed, he beats his way in very low over the sprawl of tin-roofed dwellings, lurching and tipping all the way onto the rainswept concrete.

For a few minutes in the lashing rain, we sit in the plane in silence. We have lost a day, and will therefore miss tomorrow's contact at Mambasa, in the Ituri Forest, where people must make a five-hour round trip to fetch us. Also, we have wasted many gallons of expensive fuel. But, for the moment, none of this matters, so grateful are we to be on the ground. I am mightily impressed by the pilot's cool and skilled performance under stress, and saying so, I embarrass Dr. Western by reaching out to shake his hand.

"I didn't care much for that experience," I say, a note of hysteria in my laugh, and Jonah shakes his head. The front, he says, was hundreds of miles long, far longer than any storm front he has ever encountered in East Africa, and the storm jolt that struck us over the Congo Republic he estimated at eighty miles an hour, the most severe he had ever experienced. Jonah had been told that such storms were not uncommon in the Congo Basin, especially in the rainy season, which has now begun, and we still have the whole of Africa ahead of us. Back there over the Congo Republic this afternoon, he says, he could have made an emergency landing on the burned plain, but such a storm would be very dangerous if it forced us off course over the forest, with no maps we could trust and no place to come down.

Silenced by these thoughts, we refuel the plane and complete most of the paperwork for tomorrow. By the time

we return to the city through the raining streets, bitterly
disappointed to be back, our relief has given way to intense
depression. For the first and last time on the trip, we feel
utterly disheartened, and we do not hide it. There have
been bad patches before now—the descent of the Ivindo
River into mist and mountains was one of the worst, so far
as Jonah is concerned—but after two long days of stressful
flying, racing the darkness, rarely certain where we were,
after that scary approach into Kinshasa, and with the prospect of more bad storms to come, I feel tense and worried,
dreading the days ahead.

Though he will not say so, Jonah is worried, too. After
so many weeks spent with this man, day after day, meal after
meal, under strain in the air and frustration in these cities,
I know him a bit better than he imagines. He does not lose
his head, rarely shows anger, and remains commendably
sensible and decisive, but under stress, his voice goes a
notch tighter, and he reverts to a rather stiff, officious manner, using my first name a lot, as if he were speaking to a
child.

At supper Jonah is somber and withdrawn; he has done
all the flying, borne all the responsibility, and he looks
exhausted. Yesterday he was already suggesting that he
should return home earlier than planned, that we should
cut our stay in the Ituri Forest from ten days to five, that
perhaps we should eliminate it entirely, although from the
start we have regarded the Ituri as the main reward of a
long, arduous journey.

In the depths of our gloom, we discuss our drastic
choices, such as skirting the tropical rainy-season storms by
backtracking northward to Bangui before returning eastward, or even, if storms trap us in Kinshasa, storing the
aircraft here until the rains are past, and flying home—he
east, I west—by commercial carrier. Either choice would
eliminate the visit to the Ituri, and neither is an acceptable

defeat; we both know even as we speak that we will get up at dawn tomorrow morning and try again.

▼▼▼

Next morning we are at the airport at six-thirty. The plane is fueled, our flight plan is approved, the miasmal depression of the night before has vanished with the rain. There are even patches of blue sky, and with any sort of luck, I think, we shall escape Kinshasa, getting at least as far as Mbandaka, four hundred miles to the northeast on the Zaire River. But whereas at N'djili our main delays were caused by wholehearted incompetence, at N'dola we are subjected to a merciless fleecing by every official who can lay his hands on us, each one discovering something wrong with embarkation tax, flight plan, even dates on vaccination cards, at least until some hard cash is forked over. The negotiation of so much graft takes time, as we are waved into office after office, and increasingly we are aware that once again the day is starting to get away from us, that even if good weather holds it is nearly a thousand miles to Kisangani. Eventually we make a show of temper, shouting threats to expose such greed to our friend, the minister Mankoto. We bluff our way back to the airplane, but it is well past 9 A.M. when we take off.

Early clouds over the swamps east of the river gradually burn away during the morning. The plane cuts northeast across the Zaire's great wide bends, traversing the plateaus of the Congo, then a vast swamp of raffia palms east of the river. The map shows few roads in this great central region of Zaire, and anyway we have learned not to depend upon these roads, since so many deteriorate and disappear. For navigation we must count upon the rivers. On our left, where the great flood sprawls out over the land in an archipelago of river islands, is the mouth of the Sangha River, which we last saw at Bayanga. Farther on is

the broad delta of the great Ubangi, which has come south
from Bangui. Then, once again, we are over the Zaire,
enjoying the steamers that push barges of cargo between
river towns.

The clouds are vanishing, the day is beautiful, and
passing the airstrip at Mbandaka (formerly Coquilhatville)
I feel a great burst of exhilaration; we have made our escape
from Poubelleville, even if we should meet a storm in the
next half hour. I look over at Jonah, and he grins; he is
happy, too. Already we feel sure our luck has changed, that
the long day we had anticipated as the hardest of our journey will turn out to be the easiest and most enjoyable.

Twenty minutes north of Mbandaka, we turn due eastward from the brown Zaire up the Lulonga, a quiet and
serene black river whose water is so clear that sandbars are
visible deep under the surface off the downstream end of
river islets. Soon the water is a transparent tannin color,
clear as red amber, and to my elated eye intensely beautiful.
Along the river are lone pirogues and tiny villages, none of
them more than a few huts under the shade trees on the
bank. "This is Stanley's Africa," Jonah says, delighted.
"Hasn't changed at all." At last we are flying over forest
that could shelter elephants, and we discuss the one critical
discovery we have made in the past few days: most if not all
of the tropical forest of south Gabon, south Congo, and
western Zaire, which we had thought must be the heartland
of the forest elephant, and which is still included as viable
habitat in charts and estimates of elephant population, has
long since been destroyed or degraded. It is barren land
where no elephant could exist.

The very wide hybridization zone extending deep into
the Congo Basin, in which elephants of pronounced bush
characters may be met with south of the equator and
beyond, establishes beyond question that very dissimilar
elephants live in the forest, and that widespread reports of
a dwarf elephant have a basis in fact. The large hybrid form

with its distinctive bush characters is the "big elephant" with which a much smaller animal is everywhere compared. The so-called *assala* is the forest elephant, *L.a. cyclotis*, which is very small by comparison to the bush race when not heavily endowed with the bush genes. Pygmy elephants—not everywhere distinguished from the *assala*—are not a distinct species or race but simply juvenile *cyclotis*, mostly young males, that separate early from the cow herds and may sometimes form small herds of their own. The two pygmies of outsize tusks and aggressive temperament at Dzanga Pan provided the first evidence, and the herd of little *assala* at Wonga-Wongue confirmed it.

Elephant authorities Iain Douglas-Hamilton and Cynthia Moss, who would separately inspect Jonah's photographs after our return, were fascinated by the discovery of the vast hybridization zone, which has never before been defined; until now, most observers had assumed that those "bush elephants" seen in the forest were wanderers or refugees from the dangerous open country to the north. Furthermore, both Moss and Douglas-Hamilton were fully persuaded by Jonah's explanation of the pygmy-elephant mystery provided by his photographs, which clearly show bush hybrids, forest elephants, and pygmies, all in the same picture. Of that five- or six-year-old that brandished big tusks at a hybrid male more than twice its size, then interacted in a filial manner with its mother, Moss remarked, "Without those tusks, I'd think that was a baby elephant. The tusks make it look sub-adult, at least fifteen years of age." Douglas-Hamilton agreed that on the basis of its tusks it might easily be called an adult "pygmy elephant."

In resolving one enigma, we appear to have stumbled upon another: where is the "pure" forest elephant, with its small head, low round ears, and vertical tusks? We cannot be sure that such elephants don't persist in this vast trackless forest below, but I wonder aloud if in our time the pure *cyclotis* might have disappeared due to a mingling of the bush and forest races caused by the disruptive impact of mankind, not only in two centuries of ivory slaughter but in the accelerating destruction of the forest ever since. Jonah shrugs. Closer to the forest edge, he says, my theory might be sound, but it could not account for the hybrids much farther south. He speculates that the immense contraction of the forest caused by natural drying in recent millennia would account for the fact that the hybridization zone has spread so widely. Only two thousand years ago, conditions were so dry that woodland-savanna elephants were widespread throughout what is now rain forest, with the forest race confined to a few patches. Since this is only about thirty elephant generations, the bush genes are still apparent, perhaps throughout the forest populations.

At Basankusu, we land at the mission airstrip and refuel the wing tanks as people come out on foot and bicycle to greet us; this time we have a clearance paper, and nobody tries to detain us when we depart. Once in the air and headed east, we eat rolls scavenged from the hotel breakfast table, much amused by the realization that this is our first lunch in three days, not because we had no food along but because on both the previous days, the tense flight conditions and suspense had killed our appetite.

The broad flat wilderness of central Zaire is the bottom of the shallow Congo Basin. From here in the center of the continent the green monotone of forest spreads in a great circle to the far horizons. There is only the Lulonga, growing smaller, then its tributary, the Lopori, with scarce and diminishing hut clusters along the bank. Miles from the river, miles and miles and miles from the nearest voice, is the tiny scar of a crude slash-and-burn clearing, but the human being there stays out of sight. Who is this solitary *Homo sapiens*, so content to live so far off by himself, in a closed universe of hut and garden? No doubt he is down there staring up at his own small patch of sky, for not so many aircraft can have passed this way; we are many miles off to the north of the air routes of Zaire. Perhaps there are forest elephants down there, but we do not know.

Some three hundred miles east of its confluence with the Zaire, the Lulonga-Lopori makes a great bend toward the south, and here we forge straight on over the rain forest, sixty miles or so, to complete the crossing of the great north bend and return to the Zaire River. In a sun-filled, windless afternoon, enjoying the peaceful sweep of the upper river, we continue upstream 150 miles to Kisangani, where the Tshopo and the Lualaba come together below Stanley Falls as the Zaire River, the great Congo.

If Kinshasa is one of the saddest cities in all Africa, Kisangani (formerly Stanleyville) is among the loveliest, despite the testimony of its bullet-scarred façades and the bleak aspect of the Place des Martyres; this main square commemorates the victims of the execution that took place here in the violent civil wars of the early sixties, when Kisangani was the headquarters of the rebel government. The happy spirit of the place, in its pretty location on the river, is reflected in the harmony and order of even the humblest wattle-and-daub hut in the clean-swept yards, the absence of litter, the neat bundles of charcoal and vegetable produce set out unguarded by the wayside, and, most important, in the unfrowning demeanor of the people seen on the evening road in from the airport. Along the riverfront, in fire light of setting sun, large pirogues tend the gaunt fish weirs, and a fish eagle crosses the broad, slow expanse of the silver current that carries the weight of the Central Highlands rains toward the sea.

▼▼▼

Flying east from Kisangani, the Cessna follows the Bunia road, a rough red section of the trans-African track that winds across Africa from the Gulf of Guinea to the Kenya coast. This forest region still shows the effects of the anarchic period that followed Zaire's independence in 1960,

when many people, villages, and gardens were destroyed by
the successive waves of soldiers, rebels, and white South
African and Rhodesian mercenaries that swept in and out
of Kisangani. In the quarter-century since, with the region
depopulated and communications broken down, the colonial airstrips and many of the side roads still indicated on
the charts are little more than shadows in the trees, having
been subsumed by the surrounding forest. Excepting the
rivers, the trans-African itself, barely maintained, is the only
landmark, a welcome thread of human presence in this dark
green sea.

On all sides, to the shrouded green horizons, lies the
unbroken Ituri Forest, in the region perceived by Henry
Morton Stanley as the very heart of "darkest Africa." The
Ituri extends north to the savannas and east to the foothills
of the Central Highlands, with contiguous regions of wild
forest to the south and west. In the nineteenth century, the
region was a famous source of ivory, which was carried back
to the coast at Zanzibar by the slave caravans of Tippu Tib,
and by all accounts was a great redoubt of elephants
throughout the decades of the Congo Free State and the
Belgian Congo. Even today the Ituri remains largely intact,
since it lies on the rim of the Congo Basin, above the waterfalls of smaller and less navigable rivers. In Western's opinion, any estimates we make of the Ituri's present population
of forest elephants may be used as a fair gauge for the rest
of Zaire's forests. In so much wilderness, in the absence of
good information, it is tempting to imagine large companies of elephants passing unseen beneath these silent canopies, but past estimates are probably much too high.

▼▼▼

In the 1920s, the colonial authorities moved the scattered
Bantu villages onto the new road, where the people could
be more easily taxed, conscripted for labor, and otherwise
administered. This concentration, and the road itself, at-

tracted ambitious new immigrants—the shopkeepers, hotel owners, gold panners, truck drivers, and the like. The newcomers who make up what anthropologists refer to as "the road culture," with its dependence on the big cargo trucks that comprise most of the scarce vehicles on the trans-African. On the fringes of the road culture live twenty thousand to forty thousand Mbuti (no one quite knows), the largest and most culturally intact of the Pygmy groups that are scattered here and there across the rain forest, from the Central Highlands west into Cameroon; the Pygmies are one of the most ancient of African peoples, and among the continent's last groups of hunter-gatherers.

At the Epulu River, Dr. Western buzzed the camp of American biologists John and Terese Hart, and a number of people ran outside to wave. With the help of the Mbuti, the Harts—John is an okapi biologist and Terese is a forest ecologist—have begun the first serious study of the elusive forest relative of the giraffe called the okapi, which is found only in this region of Zaire.

Due to our difficulties in western Zaire, we are already a day late, and at the airstrip at Mambasa, about forty miles east of Epulu, the missionaries tell us in reproving tones that the Harts had made the five-hour round trip yesterday for nothing, that we must go to the center of town and hitch a ride on one of the trading trucks that also serve as buses in this area. And so, at noon, we find ourselves set down in the shade of a big mango, with plenty of time to observe the village life of these Babila Bantu. The soft-voiced courtesy of village people is the other side of the insecure loud rudeness in the towns, and we have hardly arrived when two little boys are sent out with wood chairs for the visitors; our benefactor never appears.

From across the way drifts the smell of cooking fires. Pale maize in sheaves is drying on the thatch of rectangular small huts of daub-and-wattle. To the sound of chickens, and yellow weavers in the palms, two young women with upright hair in sprigs, using hardwood pestles and an old wood mortar, pound bitter manioc into white flour with alternating thumps, thrusting out colorful *kanga*-clad behinds on every stroke. Nearby, the men chop new bamboo for a hut with a bamboo frame, lashing the cross-pieces to the uprights with green palm fronds. The panga chop and pestle thump fall into rhythmic counterpoint of bursts of laughter, hoots, and noonday squalling. The cheerful faces belie the depredations of both Simba rebels and government soldiery, some twenty years ago, when most of the priests and missionaries of this region fled or were massacred, and the starving people went into hiding in the bush. The last Simba war chief, with his Mbuti guide, was captured in the forest in 1970, and both were shot here in Mambasa's street.

Along the road trundle big bicycles with heavy cargoes; on their head the women tote big shallow bowls of aluminum or tin filled with food or washing. Umbrellas, popular all year round as shelter from cascading rains and equatorial sun, set off a bright new *kikwembe*, the all-purpose wraparound cloth used as a garment throughout eastern Africa.

A red truck does not stop for us. Two hours pass. High sun and soaring cumulus, bright clothes spread to dry on the fresh grass.

From the well, in single file, comes a line of little girls, each with a container on her head. "*Nyayo Polo,*" they sing in wistful harmony as the child bringing up the rear chants in hard counterpart, "*Nyayo Polo!*" The tallest girl, who leads, is Polo. Follow Polo!

In early afternoon, a trucker agrees to carry us westward to Epulu. He is a strong man, bare to the waist, and he wears a towel prizefighter-style around his neck. When Jonah inquires in Swahili how long it will take to reach Epulu, he answers shortly, "It takes time." He is intent on a flirtatious young woman passenger, but his interest is not romantic. *"Citoyenne,"* he insists in a low voice, hard hand extended, and she flounces a little in contempt before she comes up with the fare. Most of these traders on the road, and the shopkeepers, too, are of the Nande, an energetic Sudanic tribe of the foothills to the east who moved down into this depopulated region after the Simba Rebellion to prey upon the mission-softened natives.

I climb onto the cargo and arrange myself to enjoy the journey, much as I did twenty-five years ago, traveling south through Sudan. My *compagnons de voyage* are a noisy band of local people, and the cargo consists of oil drums, shovels, sacks of maize flour and manioc, plantains, a wood peanut huller, and a tethered cockerel, bill gaped wide in fear and thirst. The truck jolts forward to a roadblock set up by the Zairois soldiery for the main purpose of extracting some sort of livelihood from all who pass.

Jolting and trundling through potholed hill country, the truck comes up behind a funeral procession. The driver nudges into the procession, which is led by a chanting semi-naked shaman in a long-tailed fur cap, waving a long fur strip to the beat of drums, and dancing in a continuous slow circle in front of a coffin draped in new blue *kikwembes*. When the crowd will not part for it, the truck takes its place in the procession, grinding along for fifteen minutes in low gear. The mourners turn off on a path into the forest as the sky behind us darkens, with first gusts of a wind that will bring rain.

A man steps from the forest, holding a dead guenon by the tail; the passengers shout and bargain with him, but nobody buys his monkey meat. When the rain comes, a tarp is lashed across the frame over cargo and passengers, and we lurch on, along the deeply rutted road. The truck stops again when a Land-Rover headed eastward turns around; John Hart and a friend, Rick Peterson, have come to meet us. The truck passengers help unload our gear, which includes provisions for the Harts, and we continue westward on this rain-filled main road across Africa that is all but impassable in the rainy season.

Outside the village of Epulu, two small figures carrying spears trot along ahead of us. They jump sideways into the roadside grass and smile and wave hard as we pass. John Hart, an ebullient redhead, thirty-five years old, yells out to them in greeting, and I see that they aren't boys at all but short-legged little men of the Mbuti, called Bambuti by the Bantu cultivators.

Until recently it was supposed that the Mbuti were driven south from the savannas by the expansion of those Bantu peoples who followed the rivers into the forests, probably as a consequence of population pressure or because of prolonged drought; today it is thought by the Harts and others that the two peoples arrived together. The Bantu probably brought agriculture here about four thousand years ago, perhaps in a dry period when this region was not forest but savanna woodland; very likely the Ituri was uninhabited before that time. But unlike the Mbuti, the so-called forest Bantu have never become acclimated to the forest. They maintain their clearings and their bare swept village yards as a defense not only against snakes but against the overwhelming trees, with their darkness and malevolent night spirits. (Even a sophisticated Zairois writer dreads the forest: "Anyone venturesome enough to try to blaze a trail through it would soon beat a hasty retreat. Everyone who knows it well—hunters, medicine men—never strays more than a short distance beyond the clearings . . . Whatever the legends may say, hunting expeditions and incantations of witchcraft never take place very far from settled areas . . . Even to its most intimate acquaintances, the proud forest reveals itself only through a few clearings scattered along its periphery."*

*S. Diallo, *Zaire Today* (Paris: Editions j.a., 1977).

We stop at Bosco's Okapi Sport Hotel and Bar for some cold beer, then head downriver to the Hart camp, where we are met by Terese Hart—called Terry—John's sister Nina, the young Hart daughters, Sarah and Rebekah, and a crowd of friendly and enthusiastic Pygmies. Glad to be in the Ituri at last, we sit down happily to a warm supper of plantains, rice, and manioc greens cooked with bits of fish from the Epulu River. In this dry season, collared pratincoles fly like terns along the river and African cormorants sit like sentinels on the dark rocks.

▼▼▼

The camp is preparing to set off for five days in the forest to the north, where the Harts hope to find a promising location for okapi study. With Rick Peterson, a young anthropology student born in Zaire and raised by missionary parents in Equateur Province to the west, Nina Hart and seven-year-old Sarah will start out a day early, in order to cut Sarah's long trek in half. Because I am still a little lame and because I am anxious to get into the forest, and because Rick Peterson, who is fluent in the Zairian lingua franca called Lingala, can translate for me with the Mbuti, I shall accompany the advance party. Led by a young Mbuti hunter named Atoka, we will join a large group of his tribesmen at their hunting camp on the Lelo River, meeting Jonah Western and the Harts at the Ekare River camp the following day.

Before it slips away into the forest, our path traverses slash-and-burn farm plots dominated by lone trees. By the path is an old calabash wrapped in rotten netting under a shelter of banana leaves, beside which hang a hippo tooth, a piece of wood with a crucifix scratched on it, and a strange wrinkled black fruit. I wonder what the local missionaries would make of this Christianized *dawa*, or medicine, concocted to keep thieves out of the garden; the netting will

▼▼

carry the corpse of the transgressor who does not take warning, says Atoka.

Like the other Mbuti men, Atoka carries little besides the hunting net draped in hanks across his shoulders. With quick small steps, his wife, Masumba, humps along beneath a cargo basket braced by a bark tumpline, an infant riding on her shoulders. The other diminutive women are similarly equipped, for the head cargoes borne with such elegance by the village women are not practicable here on forest paths. Once in the trees, away from judgmental Bantu eyes, the women go bare-breasted; a few wear only a small loin string in order to move more freely in the humid heat.

The path, though ancient and well worn, is narrow and overgrown, and the people keep in touch with one another with loud whoops and hootings, which also serve to push elephants and buffalo and leopards from their path. So close to Epulu, there is little sign of elephant or other creatures, and the whooping is mostly an expression of sheer exuberance and joy at the return into the forest.

At a slow, clear stream, Atoka fashions a fresh green-leaf cup, and we drink gratefully. A monkey hurtles through the branches. There are three species of colobus here, six guenon species, two mangabeys, the chimpanzee, and the olive baboon, but so close to the road they are all heavily hunted. We will see more tomorrow, Atoka says. Soon we come across the first footprint of an elephant, which he believes passed about three weeks ago, to judge from dried mud scraped on a sapling. "This is our soap," he says of the gritty river clay. Farther on, he finds the first hoofprint of okapi, though this print, too, is more than a week old.

In his lyrical and elegiac book *The Forest People* (which is dedicated to Atoka's father, Kenge), the anthropologist Colin Turnbull, who worked here at Epulu in the fifties, perceived the Mbuti as hunter-gatherers who could survive entirely on forest products and whose independent culture was threatened by the demands of the agricultural Bantu, "a rather shifty lazy lot who survived the ravages of Tippu Tib's slave-traders by treachery and deceit." But John Hart, who did a master's thesis on Mbuti hunting and economy based on research done in the Ituri from 1973 to 1975, no longer believes that the Mbuti survived on hunting and gathering in the forest, since for most of the year primary forest cannot supply them with sufficient calories. (He points out that during the sixties, when waves of invading soldiery stripped Bantu gardens, many Mbuti also starved to death.) What he found was a complex symbiotic situation of "cultural reciprocity," in which the Mbuti were in close economic and cultural relation with the forest Bantu. The government encourages them to put in gardens, but as Turnbull remarks of any Mbuti project undertaken outside the forest, it rarely amounts to more than "a lot of noise and big ideas." Terry Hart says, "They realize the value of a garden, and they have the strength and enthusiasm to chop down trees, but they very rarely follow through. They work hard in the Bantu gardens, slashing and burning and at harvest time, but rarely keep up the few gardens of their own."

Both Harts believe that the Mbuti have always led a nomadic rural life in community with the agricultural peoples, who provide them with iron tools, tobacco, and vegetables in exchange for day labor in the fields, hunted meat and honey, mushrooms, forest medicines, thatching, and firewood. The Mbuti are also depended on for sacred songs and dances, propitiary sacrifices, and ceremonies at funerals, marriages, and other rites of passage, being thought of as closer than the Bantu to the old ancestral roots and still in touch with forest spirits that the Bantu—but not the Mbuti—fear. The Mbuti, in turn, depend upon the Bantu to organize their own weddings and funerals, and regulate quarrels. Their relations are mainly amiable, even though the Bantu dismiss the Mbuti as inferiors—undisciplined

▼▼

and undependable wild flighty creatures, woefully lacking
in social or political structure. (Unlike the traditional villagers, the new "road culture" Bantu have few dealings with
the Mbuti, whom they disdain as "barbarians" and "wild
animals.") Among themselves, the irreverent Mbuti use
similar terms for the superstitious Bantu, at whom they
have a tendency to laugh.

"The Mbuti like money like everybody else," John Hart
says, "but when they want to go back to the forest, no
amount of money can stop them. That's what I like about
them—that devil-may-care quality, so rarely seen among
the Bantu. They are happy to sell you their good spear even
though they may need it the next day. But if they are capri-
cious, they are also free; they swoop in and out like birds,
they never worry about tomorrow. That lack of forethought
and dependability can make dealing with them pretty exasperating, but they make up for it in many other ways. Without them, in fact, it would be impossible to work here in the
forest."

The Harts are both bright, cheerful people with prag-
matic determination to make things work, despite the logistical frustrations of operating in Zaire. John came here
originally with the encouragement of Colin Turnbull, and
Terry as a Peace Corps volunteer. After they married, in
1977, she became a student of forest ecology with emphasis
on botany, and John turned to wildlife biology; both received their Ph.D.s last year. They communicate with the
Mbuti in ki-ngwana, a breezy version of Swahili used in
Haut-Zaïre (and not always comprehensible to Jonah Western, who speaks the classical Swahili of the Tanzania coast),
and they share a sincere affection for Africans in general
and the Mbuti people in particular. In return, they have
won the approval of the Mbuti, who help them gladly whenever helping suits them.

▼▼▼

In his years in the Ituri Forest in the mid-seventies and again in the early eighties, John Hart had only a few glimpses of the okapi, about whose natural history almost nothing is known, and Jonah and I have no serious hopes of seeing one. The animal is wary and elusive, despite its large size and boldly patterned legs and high striped haunches—a very odd creature altogether, with its long hyenoid head and a long pink giraffe tongue it uses to pluck leaves at the stem rather than browse them. Probably the one okapi we shall see is the young captive female at the government's Okapi Station at Epulu, where holding pens for zoo-bound animals were set up originally back in the twenties by an eccentric Harvard man named Patrick Putnam— the original settlement here was called "Camp Putnam"—and are now being refitted for a capture project by the Miami Zoo.

What the Harts hope to do after finding a good location is to capture a few okapi in leaf-covered pit traps, fit them with radio collars, then release and follow them, in the hope that eventually they will become tolerant of human proximity if not human company and reveal some of their habits in the wild.

Understandably the Harts are eager to get their study under way before the Ituri is overrun by local gold panners and ivory poachers, and by the inevitable European interests to which Zaire's compliant president has already granted huge timber leases in the forests to the west. At the moment, John says, there are still very few guns in this remote region, and the disruption caused by gold panners may be more serious than the occasional incursion by armed poachers, though the increasing scarcity of local elephants would tend to belie this. What they would like to see—and intend to promote—is a national park in the Epulu region. The Maiko Park in the Maniema Forest to the south is supposed to shelter the okapi and the elusive Congo peacock, but it exists mostly on paper and has no funds for antipoaching measures, nor even much evidence that the two creatures it is set up to protect are there.

The Lelo camp of sixteen or seventeen leaf huts is set in a rough circle in a forest glade near the Lelo River. The round or oval bun-shaped huts, which are made in a few hours, are higher and more open than the huts of the Babinga Pygmies that we saw west of the Ubangi, which were oven-shaped and closed except for the tubular entrance on one side. No fresh leaves have been added since the last hunting trip, two months before, but one woman weaves big round arrowroot leaves into a new latticework of saplings stuck into the ground, then bent and lashed together over her head, deftly locking each leaf by pinning it with its own stem. Leaves of another arrowroot are used for plates and wrapping food packets, and both species are gathered into the women's baskets as the people move along the forest paths, together with wild fruits and tubers, medicines, and the lianas used for netting twine and basket weaving.

In midafternoon, the hunters have not yet returned. There are only naked infants and old women, puppies, a few chickens, a soft murmuring in the fire smoke and sun shafts. Every little while the oldest woman calls out in a deep resonant voice *"UAO-ba-hey!"* She is summoning the hunters home. "This is the forest," Atoka explains. "We must be together." And soon small men appear out of the trees, two here, three there, nets folded like great hoods on their heads. Some carry the spears once used for killing elephants, others have tiny two-foot bows with poisoned arrows, used for birds and monkeys. Each man comes to us quietly, extending a shy hand; some make a little bow. Soon there are a dozen men in camp, and more will come.

"Tata akumi, nzala esili," sing the women. The father has come, hunger has ended.

The hunting has been poor, just two blue duiker, pretty little blue-gray forest antelope with big dark eyes gone glassy in death. The duikers are dressed, singed on the fire, cut up and cooked in bent-rimmed blackened pots. Besides metal blades and cheap Chinese flashlights with dead batteries, the pots are the only road-culture implements in camp. The women scrape manioc and forest tubers, including a wild yam. *Etaba*, they call it, "the potato of our Ancestors," known long before the true potato (and manioc, plantains, and maize) were brought to Africa from the New World during the centuries of the great slave trade. Rick Peterson asks if the people ever planted this "potato" (I had noticed taro planted outside the clearing) and Atoka shakes his head. "*Ye moko aloni yanga,*" he answers in Lingala. *Ye*—"He Himself," meaning the Forest— grew it. The Mbuti speak pidgin Swahili and Lingala, but among themselves they use ki-Mbira, the tongue of the Bambira people east of Epulu. "Ki-Mbuti and ki-Mbira are the same," they say, unaware that their own language was lost long ago.

Each household cooks separately, over a separate fire; some fires have a rack built over them, for drying meat. All are in easy speaking distance of one another, and the older hunters sit with their wives by the opening of their huts, close as two birds. The men fashion chairs of four stout sticks bound in a bundle with vine thongs, then spread in a four-legged seat platform. The younger men gather in the center of the glade, laughing and talking as the children and small hunting dogs wander through. The dogs glean a meager living from the human leavings, and are struck almost every time they come in reach.

The sun is falling now, only the treetops all around are still in sunlight, and the fire smoke that drifts toward the blue sky. The noisy camp, well fed, fills with well-being. This is the Mbutis' world; no Bantu come here.

Men and women alike, in their spare moments, work at the manufacture of the nets that are the foundation of the hunting life. (Hunting with nets is not confined to the

Mbuti, nor do all Pygmy groups resort to it; it is practiced by a Bantu group in Equateur Province, says Rick Peterson, but not by the Babinga Pygmies who were our trackers in Central African Republic.) The inner bark of a euphorbia liana is stripped off in lengths, dried in the fire smoke, then rolled hard on the thigh, after which it is spliced to greater lengths and rolled again into a hard green twine, gathered in hanks. "One can climb into the trees with it," the people say admiringly, though in fact even large duikers break through the nets. The twine is manufactured by both sexes, and the hunters weave it into mesh, then string it with shiny amber seeds from another euphorbia favored by duikers, the better to attract them.

This is the first return to Lelo and the first hunt in two months; therefore offerings and propitiation must be made to the Mangese ya Pori—the Ancients of the Forest, the Ancestors, or "Those Who Were Here Before Us"—to ensure the success of the hunt. At dark, the hunters erect an altar table of fresh saplings in the forest, laying their hunting nets before the altar on the forest floor. An elder, Asumani, chants the names of the Ancestors, tossing cooked rice furnished by the white people in the four directions; after each name, the hunters, seventeen or more, grunt in deep soft voices, "Nyama!" which in both Swahili and Lingala means wild animal, or meat. Chanting the names of Ancestors and spirits will summon up the beneficence of the forest.

Asumani has given us his hut; he and his old wife will sleep beside the fire. We protest that there is no need, that we are happy to sleep outside, but Atoka tells us that to refuse him would be rude.

Though the night is clear, there is thunder from the north; rain comes and goes. Cheerfully the people blame the rain on the thoughtless children who slapped the water while playing in the river. Tomorrow, they say, we shall all go to better hunting grounds on the Ekare River. Exhilarated, the men hoot and whoop, bursting out loudly and spontaneously throughout the evening; often they make a loud hollow report by cupping one hand and smiting an air pocket made by holding the elbow to the chest. Rain, embers, stars. A man gets up and dances joyfully from fire to fire, to make the people laugh, and women are singing brief, wistful songs that seem to echo the haunting birdcalls from the forest.

▼▼▼

Before daybreak arises a great shift and murmur, some loud spitting. Infants are restless, somebody whoops, another person takes advantage of the quiet to vent a grievance, the whole camp is laughing at some shouted joke. Laughter is constant; at one fire or another it springs up and ripples around the circle of leaf huts. Soon the women, tending the plantains laid into the embers, are splicing into twine the shredded bark dried at the fire overnight, while the hunters mend and weave new mesh into their nets before folding them neatly for the journey.

We start off early, led by the elder Omudi, a tiny man who looks surprised and worried at the same time; Omudi wears his net in two drapes over his shoulders and a loop in front, like a churchman's cowl. Vines have overgrown the path, which is very old, the people say; perhaps it was made by elephants, since it was here even before the Ancestors. Omudi opens up the path with little neat clips of his panga, making low tunnels through the undergrowth at just the right head height for a man scarcely more than four feet tall. In other places the understory is open, revealing the trunks of the great trees that forge upward toward the glints of sky above. By comparison to the lowland forests in Gabon and C.A.R., this part of the Ituri Forest seems smaller, drier, more like an immense woodland than tropical jungle. The dominant plants, besides the euphorbias, are the leguminous *Caesalpiniaceae* and the milky-sapped

sapotes, which include the gutta percha rubber trees sought
by the Belgians.

Within the hour the others overtake us, for the Mbuti
have few possessions and travel light. All but the youngest
are self-propelled, running to keep up with the quick pace,
and most will lug something, if only a leaf packet of food.
The men carry their nets and weapons, and the women bear
embers wrapped in heavy leaves and food-filled fire-black-
ened pots, mortars and pestles, and leg-trussed chickens on
broad basket tops.

Everyone goes barefoot but two lepers; these men
wear old European street shoes not because they are
ashamed of their diseased feet but because their soles hurt.
In recent years, the traditional bark-cloth aprons of the
hunters have been replaced by hand-me-down boys' shirts
and shorts from the bales of old clothes sent by church
groups to the Third World, and bought from the depots by
Zairois entrepreneurs who resell them at a great profit to
the Pygmies. A hunter known as Avion wears the black
remnant of an Apple Computer T-shirt; another has a kid's
gray sweatshirt that reads PITTSBURGH STEELERS.

The Mbuti delight in Sarah Hart, a fair-haired child of
seven in lemon T-shirt and sky blue pack who flits along the
path like a forest butterfly. Where we cross a log over a
stream, the Mbuti women, wading the ford above, call out
to her "Salah! Salah!" and she runs off to catch up with
them. Sarah, who returned here with her parents a few
weeks ago, is not at home yet, and I wonder how long it will
be before she realizes that her own kind are nowhere to be
seen, that she is alone in the dark forest with little folk
whose tongue she cannot speak. Soon I hear her voice
raised in apprehension, and I come upon her around a
corner of the path, mouth wide, eyes round, not far from
tears. "I was a little scared," she says. I bend to give her a
reassuring hug, and she puts her arms around my neck.
Later I come upon another little girl, this one leaf brown,

scarcely three. She has run her small nude body to a stand-still and now waits, thumb in mouth, beside the leafy trail, calm in the knowledge that she is safe here in the forest, that someone will be along who will gather her up.

In an overgrown camp by the Bougpa spring, an hour north of Lelo, are big marijuana plants ready for harvest. A hunter walks over, plucks some sticky leaves and smiles, murmuring *"bangi."* Soon women appear, fires are started, the old huts swept out with leaf brooms, the dooryard weeds chopped down to the red earth. From somewhere comes an immense pipe, a hollowed plantain stem longer than the reclining men, who tamp the resinous leaves and inflorescence into the clay bowl. Embers are laid upon the top, and the pipe moves slowly around the circle.

One of the Bougpa huts has been demolished by an elephant, and nearby there is fresh elephant sign, perhaps seven or eight prints and a few droppings. I am inspecting the first one when a hunter overtakes me. *"Tembo,"* I say, and he says, *"Bongo."* Excited, I peer all about for tracks of the beautiful big forest antelope, and the hunter laughs. Both words mean elephant. "Ki-Swahili *tembo,*" he explains, "ki-Mbuti *bongo*" (pronounced *bawn-go*). When he says ki-Mbuti, he means ki-Mbira, though the Pygmies speak this Bantu tongue in the singsong Mbuti way.

Soon the hunters decide that Ekare is too far, it will be too late to make a hunt after arriving, we must hunt here at Bougpa and continue on to Ekare tomorrow. When I suggest that our own small party proceed to Ekare, from where the Harts hope to begin a reconnaissance tomorrow, Omudi says no, the people must stay together. Quickly, without discord, everyone rises to go. Ekare is not far after all, the people say, it has good hunting, the men can make a quick hunt there this afternoon.

Even when nearing the Ekare region, the hunters maintain a continual hooting and shouting, slipping along in swift single file on the shadowed path. "Come on! Let's go!

It's a long way to the camp! There we can rest!"—these are the sort of things that they are calling. Sometimes they imitate birds and animals—chimpanzees, hornbills, duikers. They say that this din does not scare away the animals, not even elephants, which only withdraw from the smoke of human fires. Like all else, fire comes from the great forest, to cook the forest food and provide warmth, and to warn the leopard.

The Ekare camp, in a glade on the ridge above the river, is hidden from the sky by the high canopy. There has been rain here. The huts are rotten but soon they are swept out, and transparent fire smoke drifts on the sunlit air. Everything is done swiftly and easily, yet these easygoing people are never idle even when sitting by the fire but are always working something with their hands.

In early afternoon, the Harts and Western arrive from Epulu with a new group of Mbuti led by Kenge. The people call Jonah Piloto and they call me Mangese, meaning Venerable One, as in Mangese ya Pori, the Ancients of the Forest. Though not yet sixty, I am an elder by African standards. I feel honored by my title and approximately as pleased as I was when a withered old Bandaka woman came out of her hut as we left Epulu, pointing at me and crying out, "Take care of him, for he is old like me!"

In the five-hour walk north from Epulu, Jonah reports, all they have seen are a few monkeys, high in the canopy. As an East African ecologist, Jonah is accustomed to large numbers of large mammals, readily studied; in the forest, as we have learned throughout this journey, large mammals are uncommon and elusive, and difficult to observe even when found. "I'm glad to have come to Central Africa, glad to have seen the rain forest," he says, "because it's one of the most neglected biomes, and one of the most important. But I could never work in forest. So much time is necessary to gather so little information!"

Jonah is particularly disheartened by the relative scarcity of elephant sign in an undamaged habitat where poaching has apparently been minimal: "We must assume, contrary to our hopes, that in large regions of the Congo Basin there are scarcely any." The elephant's decline must be partly attributable to hunting, but John Hart says there are few guns in the villages. As for the Mbuti, they take what they need in the way of food and medicines but affect the forest life scarcely at all.

More and more it seems apparent that unbroken rain forest is inhospitable habitat for large mammals. Except along the watercourses, or in clearings made by the fall of a giant tree, the available food is mostly in the canopy, far out of reach of okapi and gorilla as well as elephant. In the absence of elephants, which modify the forest by creating and perpetuating second growth, other animals are bound to be scarce as well. Jonah concludes that, while high human impact will impoverish the forest, moderate impact in the form of shifting cultivation—that is, slash and burn—creates a good deal of secondary forest that is accessible to animals, and that a patchwork of primary and secondary forest is the optimum condition for prosperity as well as diversity in animal populations. ("Low human population is essential if this is to work," John Hart observes. "Higher populations assure impoverished forest no matter which farming technique is used.")

Increasingly Jonah is fascinated by the impact of man on the environment, which in his view is not always destructive to its wildlife and can, in fact, be very beneficial. In the sixties, he says, European and American biologists turned to the African savannas as the last great natural bastion of primeval life, unchanged since the Pleistocene; they held to the traditional view that this stability, providing time for evolution, was a condition for speciation and diversity, which accounted for the great variety of savanna life. Jonah concludes that, on the contrary, the savanna is a patchwork of different habitats, and is always changing, having been modified for thousands of years not only by fires and elephants but by man. John Hart has learned that a layer of charcoal two thousand years old underlies much of this region—good evidence of a dry savanna period, and of fires set by human hunters. (In South America, there is evidence of fires twenty to thirty thousand years old, and comparable evidence may yet turn up in Africa. Dr. Jan Reitsma, the botanist who accompanied us to Wonga-Wongue, in Gabon, had pointed out that, structurally, tropical rain forests in South America and Africa are very similar, but that while undisturbed forest in South America is still plentiful, Africa has scarcely any. Not only man but the large herbivores have modified African forests, and the greatest modifier is the elephant.

In Dr. Western's view, man has always had a profound impact on savanna systems, ever since he burned off the first grassland to improve hunting. "Remember that savanna woodland between Garamba and Bangassou? Hundreds of miles of what looked like wonderful wildlife habitat, without any sign of human impact—where were the animals? I very much doubt if the complete absence of wildlife was entirely attributable to overhunting. When man and his fires disappeared, the wildlife declined, too. One can't say that man's activities are 'good' for wildlife, but neither are they always bad, and this is particularly apparent in the forest."

Tree burning restores minerals to the old soils for a few years, but it destroys the specialized fungi known as mycorrhizae that are critical to forest growth. Where large populations of primitive agriculturalists burn down the forests, as in the derived savannas seen in Gabon and western Zaire (and also throughout West Africa), the destruction must lead to flood, erosion, and degraded land on which only a few pest species can survive. (This is a necessary consequence, not of intense settlement but of poor land use; large populations have lived off certain Asian lands for thousands of years.)

But where humans are few, and the burning moderate, gorillas as well as elephants are drawn to second growth; abandoned clearings, which the elephants maintain, sustain many other birds and animals. Similarly, disruption and change through fires, floods, and landslides, the silting of deltas, the meanderings of rivers, even big trees crashing down and creating clearings—all these produce a patchwork of habitats that increases diversity of life, since it prevents dominance by a few species. This is why life in the open light of river margins, with thick growth accessible from the ground, is so much richer than in primary forests between rivers, which are almost empty.

The following day, while Rick and I go hunting with the Mbuti, Jonah accompanies the Harts on a reconnaissance of the Itoro River to the north, where elephant sign is more abundant and a good deal fresher, not only in secondary forest but along the drainage lines. But even here, "as far from humanity and habitat destruction as one could get," poachers had left their slash marks in the undergrowth, and Kenge told him that the elephants were far less numerous than they were ten years ago. Even so, he does not feel that enough elephants remain here to create habitat that would support a larger population. If the Ituri may be taken as a rough gauge of elephant numbers in wilderness regions of Zaire, then, as in Gabon and C.A.R., that number cannot significantly exceed one animal every two square kilometers, in a rain forest already more reduced in size than we had anticipated. If anything, Douglas-Hamilton's rough estimates of forest elephant numbers—the most conservative in general circulation, and the ones we expected to corroborate—are much too high.

▼▼▼

The Mbuti were once famous elephant hunters, popularly supposed to run under an elephant and drive spears into it from beneath. "They had to work close, using jabbing spears, but I doubt if they did that very often," John Hart says. "They're the ultimate opportunists; they would bring it down any way they could." Elephant hunting died out in the early seventies, with the decline of the elephant itself, and the only Mbuti who go after them today are those who serve poachers as gun bearers and trackers. ("We hunt neither elephant nor okapi," Kenge says, trying not to laugh, "because that is against the law." However, an okapi slowed down by the nets would almost certainly be killed and eaten. "Very good, too," says Terry Hart, with a charming smile.)

The hunters return in late afternoon with four blue duiker, not enough to feed our growing camp. There are twenty-six huts at Ekare, most of them occupied; there must be sixty people here in all. Sibani the Leper, one of several Pygmies more yellow in skin color than brown, can no longer tend his net due to sore feet, but he has a big bright yellow-green-and-black monitor lizard that he shot with his bow and arrow. With glee, he describes the fury of the finish: "I jumped right into the water with my pants on!" At supper I accept his offer of fresh lizard meat, only to be told, once I had started, that I could not have antelope as well, since mixing the two might jinx tomorrow's hunt.

Toward dark, Omudi makes a lengthy speech about how the people have come back to Ekare thanks to John Hart. "We're here in the forest to be happy!" he cries. "No anger! We're here to be happy! Anybody who has a bad spirit, keep it in town!" And the people seem happy, even those who had wished to linger at the Bougpa camp.

Slowly, as the evening passes, the men begin to sing, keeping time with fire-hardened sticks and an old plastic oil container as a drum. The simple harmonies, rising and falling away like strong quiet fire, are intensified by cho-

ruses and clapping and the counterpoint of solo voices, in
an effect intensely subtle and sophisticated, despite the rep-
etition of the simple lyrics. "Let us all sing this song"—or,
better, put ourselves into this song, be one with this song.
Or "I didn't eat; other people ate." Or "The food we put
out for the Ancestors got eaten by the dogs." For often
there is humorous intent, especially in the love songs: "If
you can't climb the buo tree [a tall, straight-trunked relative
of the elms without lower limbs], forget my daughter."
There are also hunting songs, and honey songs and dances,
especially in August, when the brachystegia trees come into
blossom and honey becomes the most sought-after item of
diet. "Go out with your lover and spend the day beneath the
honey tree" is a song of explicit and joyful sexuality, with
vivid gestures of a honeyed arm thrusting in and out of the
hive.

All songs are implicitly sacred. "The forest gives us this
song," the people say, meaning, "The forest *is* this song."

Another night, a man named Gabi dances slowly with
a bow, tapping the bowstring with a stick, using his mouth
at one end of the string to achieve resonance. Later he
dances as Dekoude the Trickster, a masked green figure
bound head to toe in leaves who gets people lost in the
deep forest. Soon the girls and women rise to dance, in an
intricate pattern in and out of a half hoop of stiff liana that
one of their number, seated on the ground, raises and low-
ers on the waves of music. Before each culminating leap,
each woman holds her hand out over the ground and sings,
"Before I am given another child, this one must be as tall
as this!" Each time this is said, the women laugh loudly at
the men.

The best dancer and best singer in the camp is Atoka's
sister Musilanji, who is lighthearted and bursting with life.
According to John, she is much in demand among the
truckers and other Bantu in the villages, and, not being
possessed of a grudging character that might permit her to

say no, she has contracted syphilis along the way. As a strong and beautiful solo voice in both the women's group and men's, Musilanji sings with all her heart, and later, after everyone has crawled into their huts, she laughs with the same all-out spirit at the dirty jokes of old Sibani, laughing until she rolls upon the ground, gasping for breath, laughing until she hurts and squeals for mercy, her passionate abandon so infectious that, stretched out in our leaf hut across the circle, unable to understand a single word, I laugh hard, too.

▼▼▼

Before daybreak, the cries of forest animals awake the camp, and the din intensifies, with staccato arm claps, as the men make ready to set off on the hunt. Over the breakfast fire, Kenge says, "It is all joy, it is making the *mangese* of the forest happy," and his sister-in-law Asha nods agreement. Kenge, a handsome, serious man, now gives a speech, reminding the hunters that they must no longer kill okapi or elephant, that any outsider found in the forest with a snare must be arrested, that nets are all right because the People come and go and do not harm the forest life.

There is something chastened about Kenge, who is no longer the lighthearted young hunter to whom Colin Turnbull's book was dedicated a quarter century ago. He is now an elder, and he takes himself seriously, and is taken seriously, for everyone knows that his picture appeared in a book. In camp, though he laughs at us with all the others, he sits in a chair with his arms folded, talking mostly to Asha, who cooks for the whites, and keeping himself subtly aloof, as if, at ease in neither world, he was fated to mediate between the groups. "Kenge knows he is somebody," says John Hart sympathetically, "but he doesn't quite know who."

Atoka is all nerved up for the hunt. With great finesse and delicacy, and sounds to match, he mimes the approach, the rush at the net, the finish of the big yellow-backed duiker he intends to kill. His arms and pointed fingers dart in imitation of the antelope's quick legs and sharp hooves, he claps his arm with a loud hollow report to alert the others that his duiker has been netted, he squats, he leaps, grabbing one leg of the animal and twisting it over on its back, screeching in triumph even as he demonstrates how the others will come running with their spears.

Dodging driver ants, Rick Peterson and I cross the Ekare on a dead tree and follow the path into the forest, where we come upon a small unattended fire that one of the hunters had gone out earlier to prepare. Here Atoka drops his net and summons the Ancestors to witness this offering of precious fire to the forest and the purification of the hunters in its smoke; if the forest is contented, all will go well in the hunt. One by one the hunters come, squat down, let the smoke bathe them. Tambo holds a leaf over the smoke, then rubs his chest with it. The men smoke *bangi*, "to give them strength and get them ready," says Atoka. We rise and go.

Moving off the path into the forest, the hunters are quiet and keep signals to a minimum; in the thick cover, each man seems to know just where to go. Already some are stringing out their nets, unwinding the long coils from their shoulders as they run deftly through the understory, then returning along the line to raise the net and hang it firmly on shrub branches and saplings, taking pains to see that the bottom edge is firm against the earth. Atoka's net, overlapping others at each end, is three to four feet high, seventy-five yards long, and by no means the longest. With twelve hunters, the entire set will be a half kilometer around, enclosing about twenty acres in a semicircle.

Atoka's net overlaps that of Asumani, who nods as we go by. "*Merci*" is a word he has learned to say, and he tries it out quietly in greeting. Already the women are appearing, following around outside the nets to the narrow entrance.

A signal comes, they enter and fan out, whooping and call-ing, each one headed for her husband's sector.

We wait just inside the net, on a log that overlooks a forest gorge. It is Atoka's turn for a poor spot, close to one end; he does not expect much. We listen to a great blue turaco, green pigeons, an unknown cuckoo; a scrub robin flits briefly into view, cocking its head in the thrush manner. Off in the distance, a great tree topples of its own accord—a crack of thunder and an avalanche of matter as a hundred and fifty feet of timber, dragging down vines and lianas, snapping limbs and saplings, tears a long slash in the can-opy and thumps the waiting earth. A wave of silence fol-lows, like a forest echo.

The silence is broken by a loud arm clap, for game has been seen near the nets. From the shouts that follow, Atoka learns that a big red duiker, *nge*, has pierced Gabi's net.

Quickly we rise and make another set, not far away. This time an *nge* is entangled. There comes a wild yell from the west, two nets away, and we follow Atoka on a dead run through the trees toward the strange sheeplike bleats of this forest antelope that the hunters imitate so skillfully. The men there ahead of us at Mayai's net have seized the legs of what turns out to be a Peter's red duiker, a species I have never seen. The mesh is freed roughly from its long head and neck as it flops and thrashes, staring up at us with strange blue-filmed night eyes. Without ceremony, Asumani hacks its throat, and at the rush of blood, everyone laughs. Though the forest has given them this food, the hunters are no more reverent toward it than they are to their camp dogs; this irreverence, rare among traditional peoples, seems curious in the light of the earlier propitia-tion of the forest. "*Ekoki*," they say to us, and "*malamu*." Both words mean "good."

Returning to fetch Atoka's net, we pass the deaf man, Poos-Poos, who has the narrow shoulders of a woman and often wears his *kikwembe* tied around his neck, the way a

Pygmy woman wears it near the road. Poos-Poos is griev-
ing. A *seke*—a white-bellied duiker—approached his net,
then ran away. But later, when the men have gathered after
an unsuccessful set, Poos-Poos cheers everyone with a very
comic imitation of his drunken self leaving the truck-stop
bar, trying to find his way back to the forest, putting twigs
in his eyes, butting his head into the tree trunks. The hunters laugh, and laugh still harder when they see that Rick and
I are laughing, too. They feel protective about Poos-Poos,
who cannot articulate, and often emits weird hoots, shrill
cackles; Mayai accounts for him by tapping his ear and then
his temple, to indicate why Poos-Poos is incomplete, and
when he does this, Poos-Poos, his soft brown eyes wide and
round as a lemur's, smiles an enchanted smile, as if blessing
us all.

Yet Poos-Poos, able in every chore, has his own net and
spear and travels as an equal with the hunters except in
rainstorms, when he loses his bearings and has to be led by
the hand. He is very kind and popular with the small children, and he is alert, as he has to be, to keep up with the
rest in an existence so dependent on good hearing. Poos-
Poos is chronically in a high state of tension, and his strange
face, slightly askew, is scarred by grievous marks of concentration, pinching his forehead, that are lacking in his lighthearted companions. Perhaps he is not retarded as I had
imagined, but on the contrary, atremble with trapped intelligence, wild with frustration.

▼▼▼

Slipping through the forest, the hunters see bees moving
back and forth, and the hunt is suspended while they search
without success for the hive. We cross a pretty tributary
brook known as Ekare's Daughter. An elephant has crossed
ahead of us, and okapi sign is everywhere. Then the set is
made, we wait again, watching a bird party of leafloves and
greenbuls that glean the understory foliage, in shafts of

sun. Another *nge* and also a blue duiker, *mboloko*, are taken, to great whoops of triumph that drown out the hoots and yelling of the beaters.

In the next set, a blue duiker escapes, nothing is caught. Rain comes. The Mbuti seek out a big tree with heavy lianas, which thicken the canopy above with their own leaves, providing shelter. With his hands idle, Atoka is restless. "This is the work of the Forest," he says. "We hunt, we wait, we get up and go again." So far today he has caught nothing, but he knows that in the partition of the antelopes his family will be given meat. "The first thing we learn is *kosalisa*—to take care of others. We Mbuti do no one any harm. If I sleep hungry, you sleep hungry; if I get something from the forest, you will have it, too."

In the next surround, a heavy animal wheels and crashes away through the thickets just in front of us, and a woman who has seen the creature comes running down the line of nets shouting, "*Moimbo!*" This is the yellow-back, largest of all duikers, up to a hundred and forty pounds. But the rarely caught *moimbo* slips past the line of nets and flees; only a blue duiker is caught. Another blue duiker, on the final hunt, comes to Atoka but pierces his net in an explosive jump at the last second. Atoka does not complain or appear disheartened, and on the way home he remains behind to gather up wood for the fires. This evening we will eat antelope with the others.

The following day three animals are caught. One is a *moimbo* and another is a water chevrotain, not an antelope at all but a relation of the primitive tusked deer of Asia. The *moimbo* was speared by old Pita, and Atoka, with wild snorts and cries, acts out each second of its final moments, to show how the big yellow-back, pierced between the ribs, twisted frantically on Pita's spear, heart pumping.

Even dressed out and cut in pieces, the *moimbo* was too big to fit in Pita's old wife's basket, and Tambo's young wife, asked to help carry the meat, threw a tantrum in the forest, relieving the tensions that build up in an Mbuti camp. She worked herself into a frenzy, screeching and rolling on the ground to ensure attention, hurling wild insults at the people in general and her husband in particular. Gentle Tambo, one of the few unexuberant Mbuti, tries to ignore her like everybody else, but after a half hour, when her drama threatened to disrupt the hunt, he felt obliged to come and beat her. Returning to camp, she started in again, accounting for her behavior with a tearful and aggrieved oration that the people heard out with intense discomfort, after which she took shelter in another hut, among one of the households which, while not rejected, seem subtly excluded from the group that leads the hunting and the singing. (The small family in the hut beside my own, I notice, rarely join in the jokes and banter, which for all I know may be at their expense.) A long, tense silence was broken by some ribald observation that collapsed the whole circle of huts in grateful laughter, after which camp life proceeded in the same gay and offhand way as it had before.

▼▼▼

On the first of February we left Ekare, walking straight south to Epulu, about fifteen kilometers away. At the Bougpa spring, black colobus monkeys were making their deep rolling racket; near Lelo two big red colobus, long tails hanging like question marks, sprang into the bare limbs of a high tree to watch us pass. Kenge, who helps Terry Hart with her botanical collections, identified various fruits and medicines along the way, including an orange shelf fungus used by the Mbuti to cure diarrhea. He pointed out odd termite nests like huge gray mushrooms in the tree roots, and the orange paste spat out by fruit bats, and a place where the forest hid the People from the successive waves of soldiers, rebels, and mercenaries who pillaged and murdered in this region in the first years after independence.

On the night of our return there was an *elima*, or girl's initiation ceremony, and the sound of drums and chanting came from the Mbuti camp along the road east of Epulu. Later we heard shouting from the Babila village that could only mean trouble, and next morning the local *gendarme* turned up in his crisp green beret and green uniform with red shoulder tabs and made a complaint to Terry Hart, who was talking with me on a terrace overlooking the river. Kenge had got drunk and stirred up trouble, and his family had led in a drunken brawl that had ended with the destruction of a Bantu house, and Atoka and the spirited Asha had been jailed, the *gendarme* said. He suggested that their American friends pay for the damages, having brought them back out of the forest where they belonged. The Harts were mistaken in treating the Pygmies like real people, he continued; they should simply be given food and a few rags to wear. As for Atoka, he should be "tortured," said this new African, by which he meant—to judge from prior episodes—beaten bloody with clubs, since there was no other way for him to repay his debts. It turned out that the victim had provoked Atoka by denouncing the Mbuti as "*nyama*," or "wild animals," an opinion in which the *gendarme* fully concurred. The Pygmies had to be treated like the animals they were, he assured Terese Hart, who winced but said nothing. We stared away over the striking rocks that emerge in the dry season from the Epulu River, which winds southwest to the Ituri, the Nepoko, the Aruwimi, and a final confluence with the great Congo west of Kisangani.

▼▼▼

In Mambasa at daybreak, old Father Louis, who was away in Italy on leave when the Simba rebels killed the other Catholic missionaries at this station, is already up and about, and says good-bye. He has red cheeks and a saintly smile. "I must go to the church," he explains vaguely, waving both hands. From the evangelist mission, we pick up mail to be posted in Nairobi, and at 6:30 A.M. leave the mission strip and fly southeast along the overgrown red road toward Beni, where the huge forest ends at last in a populous agricultural region of small hills. The hills open out over the valley of the Semliki, and from here we can see for a brief time the Ruwenzori peaks, in equatorial snows seventeen thousand feet high, named by Ptolemy the Mountains of the Moon.

Where the Semliki River winds down through Zaire's Virunga Park into Lake Edward, the silver-and-blue plane passes through the Central Highlands. A soft bed of clouds lies on the land between the Virungas and Ruwenzori, but everywhere else the clouds have burned away. Coming out of the dark forest and mountains into the sun of the savanna, the silver plane bursts free into the open air.

In fresh morning light, the plane drifts out across Lake Edward, forty miles wide, with a lone fishing boat far out on the broad shine, and halfway across Jonah turns to look at me. "We are leaving Zaire," he says with a big grin, as relieved as I am to be back in East Africa. (Not long after our return to Nairobi, Kes Smith notified Jonah from Garamba that the Zairian authorities had come hunting for us twice, intending to arrest us on our return journey.)

Until the most recent despot in Uganda restored the old colonial names to lakes and parks in the hope of reassuring frightened tourists, Lake Edward was Lake Idi Amin Dada. (Lake Albert, farther north, is at present Lake Mobutu Sese Seko, though this, too, must pass.) The far shore is the southern part of Ruwenzori National Park, in southwest Uganda, and here we see herds of hippo at the water's edge. The destruction of Uganda's wildlife under Idi Amin was continued by the unpaid and lawless Tanzanian soldiery who helped depose him, but when the Tanzanians left at last, in 1980, an attempt was made to control any further slaughter, and the animals have started to come back. In the past weeks, the latest tyrant had been deposed by the latest reformer, Yoweri Museveni, in whom the desperate Ugandans have great hope, but Uganda was still in a state of anarchy, and we would not land here to refuel.

Like most of the Ugandan landscape that is not under marsh or open water, the land beyond the national park has been cleared of its last trees, and because this soil, the product of volcanoes, is richer than the ancient, leached-out soils beneath the rain forest, it can support a dense agricultural population. (However, it is the rural population in this region of Uganda that more than any other in the world is beset by AIDS.) Farther south, toward the border with Rwanda, the soil pales out into savanna, and the farmers are replaced by a semipastoral people with large herds of cattle. Their Masai-type oven huts and large corrals are enclosed by thornbush to discourage lions.

The savanna land flows on into Rwanda, and Jonah, more and more content, remarks, "It's nice to have the freedom to fly and know that you can land anywhere if you have to." I have the same sense of well-being, understanding why he was reluctant to say such things over the forests. To acknowledge the strain would not have helped and might have harmed us.

The plane crosses the soft hills and lakes of Rwanda's Akagera National Park, where a group of young elephants released in 1974 have increased to more than forty. The twenty-sixth and largest of this group was killed after it charged and killed Adrien Deschryver's friend, the photographer Lee Lyon. Jonah descends to a low altitude, and we fly for fun for the first time in weeks; though we see no elephant, we enjoy the hippo and buffalo, eland, topi, and impala, and also a few sitatunga in the papyrus swamps and lakes that stretch away east of the park into Tanzania.

An hour beyond the Tanzania border, boat sails rise

from the fishing villages in the archipelago of islands in the southern end of Lake Victoria. White pelicans glide along the shores, and a flock of avocets slides beneath the plane over the silver shimmer of the open water. The inland sea stretches away one hundred and fifty miles into Speke Gulf and the mouth of the Mbalageti River, in the Serengeti Park, where we can put down almost anywhere to refuel. "From Lake Victoria," Jonah says, "it will be wildlife country all the way into Nairobi."

Over Speke Gulf, Jonah reflects a little on our journey. He feels it was "tough but fantastic," and I agree. In regard to the forest elephant, he has no doubt that both natural densities and the extent of forest habitat are less than the most pessimistic estimates. "We just don't have the reservoir of forest elephants that we were counting on," he says, "which puts even more pressure on the bush elephant to sustain an ivory trade. The bush elephant is already in serious trouble, and because of its role in creating habitat, its disappearance will be followed by a substantial collapse of all of the large mammal fauna, which has already happened in West Africa." These are the findings he will document for presentation to world wildlife authorities to lend weight to conservation arguments, including a campaign to ban the worldwide trade in ivory. Though not good news, it will help end the ivory trade and protect the future of the elephant in Africa.

The Serengeti Plain is a hundred miles across. Flying low over its western reaches, the plane dodges the vultures that attend the endless herds of wildebeest and zebra that scatter away across green grass below. Hyenas in a ditch, a lone male lion. Thousands of wildebeest are streaming across the plain south of the high rock island known as Simba Kopje, near the long road that comes into the park from Ngorongoro and Olduvai Gorge. Nowhere on the Serengeti, in this high tourist season between rains, do we see dust raised by a vehicle, not even one. More ominous

still, on a hundred-mile west-east traverse of the whole
park, not one elephant is seen where years ago I saw five
hundred in a single herd. "Poachers," Jonah said. "The
Serengeti elephants are down seventy-five percent. What's
left of them are mostly in the north, toward the Masai
Mara."

In 1961, the Serengeti was my ultimate destination in
East Africa; in the winter of 1969, it was my home. We land
and refuel at Barafu Kopjes, a beautiful garden of huge pale
granite boulders and dry trees, in the clear light, where
years ago I accompanied George Schaller on long walks
across the plain to learn how primitive humans might have
fared in scavenging young, dead, or dying animals. The
wind is strong in the black thorn of the acacia, and a band
of kestrels, migrated from Europe, fill their rufous wings
with sun as they lift from the bare limbs and hold like
heralds against the wind on the fierce blue sky.

Then we are aloft again, on a course northeast toward
the Gol Mountains, in a dry country of giraffes and gazelles.
Olduvai is a pale scar down to the south, in the shadow of
the clouds of the Crater Highlands, and soon the sacred
volcano called Ol Doinyo Lengai rises ahead, and the deep
hollow in the land that is Lake Natron, on the Kenya border. We will fly across Natron and the Athi Plain and be in
Nairobi in an hour.

EPILOGUE

In the course of a forest elephant survey in January and February 1986, I had an opportunity to look into reports of the pygmy elephant. The survey combined 12,000 km of aerial reconnaissance over Zaire, C.A.R., Cameroon, Gabon, Congo Republic, and western Uganda with more detailed ground work at five locations in three countries—C.A.R., Gabon, and Zaire. Peter Matthiessen accompanied me on the entire trip, and Richard Barnes, who is conducting a detailed study of forest elephant for New York Zoological Society, joined us in C.A.R. and Gabon . . . We were fortunate in getting a clear view of about a hundred and twenty elephants in three different locations in C.A.R. and Gabon . . . Our direct observations confirm [that] the pygmy elephant is a juvenile forest elephant . . .

Pygmy elephant reports do not rest solely or even mainly on mistaken age identity of forest elephants. After direct observation of elephants in C.A.R., Gabon, and Zaire, in discussion with field biologists, indigenous forest peoples and hunters, and after reviewing the literature and looking at photos taken of elephants throughout these countries, I

▼▼▼

believe there is a far more compelling reason for the belief in the pygmy elephant: there are genuinely two races of elephant in the forest . . . Yet the bigger form is the regular bush elephant, the smaller one the forest elephant . . .

   The Pygmy peoples are correct about there being a big and small race of elephants in the forest. It is the naturalists who have wrongly deduced that two sympatric races of elephant in the forest must mean that there are two races of forest elephant.

—David Western*

   Forest elephant numbers are very hard to estimate, not only because of the forest canopy but because of the variety of habitats—tall and low forests, disturbed and undisturbed areas, swamps, abandoned gardens—all of which affect elephant numbers. In 1989, after completing his studies in the field, Dr. Richard Barnes concluded that there might be about 400,000 animals in forested regions of West and Central Africa (a more recent estimate is 250,000), and that among all of these countries, Gabon was the most promising because of huge and uninhabited forest areas, large elephant populations (he estimates 74,000—1990) and small numbers of humans, low rate of deforestation, and an absence of those military weapons that have made poaching so devastating elsewhere. Gabon, Barnes feels, might well become the last great refuge of *Loxodonta africana*.

   In 1986, on David Western's recommendation, Wildlife Conservation International (WCI) and the Leakey foundation returned Dr. Richard Carroll to southwest C.A.R., together with botanist Michael Fay. At the end of December 1990, their original idea of a forest wildlife reserve came into being with the creation of Dzanga-Sangha Dense Forest Reserve and the contiguous Dzanga-Ndoki National Park, which together total 1,737 square miles of range of

*"The Pygmy Elephant: A Myth and Mystery," in *Pachyderm* (Newsletter of the African Elephant and Rhino Specialist Group) December 1986.

forest elephants, bongo, gorilla, and other species threatened by the destruction of this habitat. WCI also seeks to
help establish contiguous forest reserves in the northern
Congo Republic and in southeast Cameroon, which has the
highest density of forest elephants—and probably elephants of any kind—now left in Africa. Since an estimated
40 percent of elephants are now in rain forests, and since
the rain forest itself becomes more precious every day, this
reserve is a stirring project that demands support from
conservation groups around the world.

WCI's researches into forest elephant numbers, and
the finding that these numbers were so low, had a direct
effect on the campaigns of recent years to achieve full protection for the whole species, all the more so when it was
realized that, small as it was, the forest population comprised nearly half of Africa's remaining elephants.

In 1970, as described in my book *The Tree Where Man
Was Born* (1972), the problem in East Africa was too many
elephants; since then, 80 percent of East Africa's elephants
have been destroyed. In the legendary elephant park at
Tsavo, in Kenya, they are down from an estimated forty
thousand in the mid-sixties to 5,360 in 1988. In 1977, when
Iain Douglas-Hamilton was completing his studies at
Manyara Park, in Tanzania, there were 453 animals in dis-
crete herds; by 1987, his own air survey could locate but
181, most of them juveniles. With the "big ivory" already
gone, the poaching trade had turned upon the females, and
not a single matriarch was left to provide these frightened
orphan bands with continuity and direction.

In 1980, as recounted in *Sand Rivers* (1981), Tanzania's
remote and vast Selous Game Reserve held an estimated
one hundred ten thousand elephant; that number was
halved by the time of an aerial count made six years later.
In a single decade, the entire continental population was
reduced from 1.3 million (1979) to 625,000, while the price
of ivory doubled to one hundred dollars a pound. This

made it worthwhile to kill juveniles as well as females, with three times the number of animals killed to produce the same quantity of ivory. And all too commonly the officials in the afflicted countries participated in the ivory trade, even though the income from illegal ivory was far less than the income from world tourism, which was now threatened.

The loss of the rhinos was another blow to the tourist industry. In 1970, an estimated 60,000 black rhino remained in Africa; at the time of this writing, there are fewer than 4,000, of which perhaps 500 are in Zimbabwe. A few relict animals in Cameroon and Chad are probably the westernmost in Africa. In Kenya, the surviving black rhinos are being transferred to a fenced sanctuary at Lake Nakuru, and mostly in Nairobi National Park, where the population has increased to more than sixty.

On a Sunday evening in October 1987, Kenya's five captive white rhinos were slaughtered by poachers and their horns hacked off within sight of the warden's house in Meru National Park; the same year, three Kenyan rangers were killed at Shaba Game Reserve in a poachers' ambush. As Jonah Western wrote me from Nairobi, "Elephants are running into deeper trouble than ever. Ivory is up to $160.00 a kilogram. Poaching in Tsavo and Meru is out of control. Armed gangs with AK-47s have taken over. It's war out there." The following May, when paleontologist Richard Leakey was made head of the wildlife department, he ordered his rangers to shoot poachers on sight. Not everyone cared for Leakey's methods, but from the elephant's point of view, they worked. Thirty poachers were killed in the first four months after his appointment, while the elephant death rate shrank from three a day to less than one every three days. Last July he captured world attention by persuading President Daniel arap Moi to burn twelve tons of confiscated ivory, a three-million-dollar pile eighteen feet high.

In October 1988, the United States Congress, under

pressure from strong public sentiment as well as effective lobbying by conservation groups, passed the African Elephant Conservation Act, which stipulates that all ivory imported into the U.S. come from countries that adhere to the 102-nation Convention on International Trade in Endangered Species (CITES) ivory control system; Congress also established the "African Elephant Conservation Fund," to help finance the elephant's cause. Within a few months— May 1989—Tanzania, Kenya, and six other African countries called for an end to the ivory trade worldwide. To avoid a last-minute slaughter by the poachers, the U.S. government immediately declared a ban on ivory imports, a move endorsed a few days later by the European Economic Community (EEC).

Only the countries of southern Africa, more distant from organized poaching, have enjoyed an increase in elephant population; Zimbabwe (where the people own the elephants, and villages share in safari fees and tourist income) must actually cull about one thousand animals each year. Similarly, Botswana and South Africa, which also make profit from a sustained yield of ivory, resist the ban, and so do Zambia, Namibia, and Malawi; these countries feel, not without justice, that they are being penalized for mismanagement and corruption farther north. Though sympathetic, Dr. David Western, addressing the world conference of CITES convened in Lausanne, Switzerland, in October 1989, withdrew his support of controlled sales in these southern countries in favor of a total ban. "The demand for ivory internationally is so overwhelming that the option of sustainability is declining," Western said. The CITES conference duly adopted the position of world conservation groups that a partial ban would almost certainly be ineffective. For the first time, CITES placed the elephant on the endangered list, which automatically put a halt to the legal trade. This worldwide ban—not incumbent on the southern countries though destroying their markets—be-

came effective as of January 18, 1990. Within the year, the
ivory market had collapsed, and though sporadic poaching
still continues, it is much diminished almost everywhere.

Today (1990) Dr. Douglas-Hamilton estimates the
African elephant population at 609,0000—a remnant of the
millions of elephants that once wandered the whole continent. By comparison to the black rhino and mountain gorilla, this appears sufficient, but it is a far less healthy
population than it seems. For these are not stable family
groups with matriarch leaders but makeshift, neurotic
bands of scared young animals that will not reproduce in an
efficient way for years to come.

> Of all African animals, the elephant is the most difficult
> for man to live with; yet its passing—if this must come—
> seems the most tragic of all. I can watch elephants (and
> elephants alone) for hours at a time, for sooner or later the
> elephant will do something very strange such as mow grass
> with its toenails or draw the tusks from the rotted carcass of
> another elephant and carry them off into the bush. There is
> mystery behind that masked gray visage, an ancient life
> force, delicate and mighty, awesome and enchanted, com-
> manding the silence ordinarily reserved for mountain peaks,
> great fires, and the sea.*

I wrote that twenty years ago, and have seen nothing
since to change my mind. Indeed, elephant mysteries are
still being discovered. It has now been learned that this
animal can transmit low-frequency alarms and other ele-
phantine messages across miles of wilderness, and increasingly it is credited with the apprehension of death that we
had heretofore reserved to our own species. Except fire and
man, these great animals have more impact on habitat than
any force in Africa, and the prosperity of many other crea-

---

*Peter Matthiessen, *The Tree Where Man Was Born*, (New York: Viking Press,
1972).

tures may depend on them. This is as true in the forest as on the savanna. The very survival of the bongo, okapi, and lowland gorilla, which browse on the new growth in elephant-made gaps in the canopy, may depend upon the survival of the forest elephant.

—January 1991

PETER MATTHIESSEN was born in New York City in 1927 and had already begun his writing career by the time he was graduated from Yale University in 1950. The following year, he was a founder of *The Paris Review*. Besides *Killing Mister Watson* (1990), he has also published five other novels, including *At Play in the Fields of the Lord*, which was nominated for the National Book Award, and *Far Tortuga*, as well as the collection *On the River Styx and Other Stories*. Mr. Matthiessen's parallel career as a naturalist and explorer has resulted in numerous and widely acclaimed books of nonfiction, among them *The Tree Where Man Was Born*, which was nominated for the National Book Award, and *The Snow Leopard*, which won it. His other works of nonfiction include *The Cloud Forest* and *Under the Mountain Wall* (which together received an Award of Merit from the National Institute of Arts and Letters), *The Wind Birds, Blue Meridian, Sal Si Puedes, Sand Rivers, In the Spirit of Crazy Horse, Indian Country, Nine-Headed Dragon River,* and *Men's Lives*.

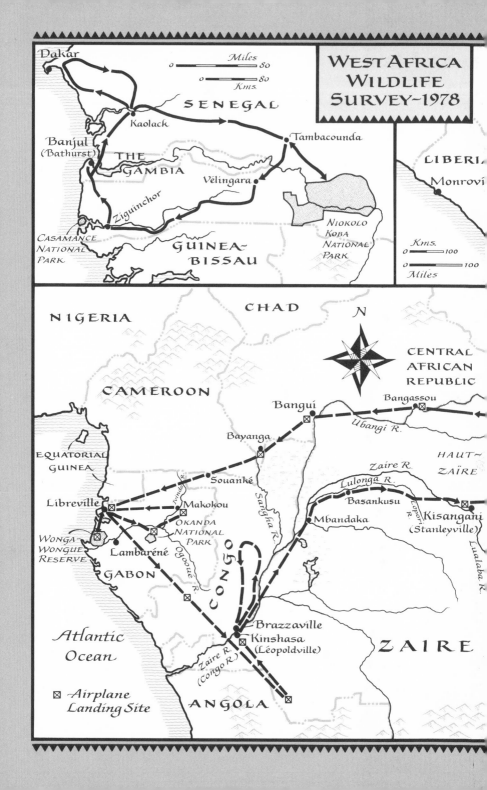

WEST AFRICA
WILDLIFE
SURVEY~1978

Dakar

Miles
0 ———————— 80
Kms.
0 ———————— 80

SENEGAL

Kaolack

Tambacounda

Banjul
(Bathurst)

THE
GAMBIA

Vélingara

Ziguinchor

CASAMANCE
NATIONAL
PARK

GUINEA-
BISSAU

NIOKOLO
KOBA
NATIONAL
PARK

LIBERIA

Monrovi

Kms.
0 ———————— 100
0 ———————— 100
Miles

NIGERIA

CHAD

N

CENTRAL
AFRICAN
REPUBLIC

CAMEROON

Bangui

Bangassou

Ubangi R.

Bayanga

EQUATORIAL
GUINEA

Souanké

Zaïre R.

HAUT~
ZAÏRE

Libreville

Makokou

Lulonga R.

Basankusu

Kisangani
(Stanleyville)

OKANDA
NATIONAL
PARK

Mbandaka

WONGA-
WONGUE
RESERVE

Lambaréné

GABON

CONGO

Brazzaville

Kinshasa
(Léopoldville)

ZAIRE

Atlantic
Ocean

Zaïre R.
(Congo R.)

⊠ Airplane
Landing Site

ANGOLA